PICTURE SHOWS

Also by Andrew Yule

HOLLYWOOD A GO-GO

FAST FADE:
David Puttnam, Columbia Pictures and the Battle for Hollywood

THE BEST WAY TO WALK

THE BEST WAY TO LAUGH

LOSING THE LIGHT:
Terry Gilliam and the Munchausen Saga

LIFE ON THE WIRE:
The Life and Art of Al Pacino

PICTURE SHOWS

THE LIFE AND FILMS OF
PETER BOGDANOVICH

ANDREW YULE

LIMELIGHT EDITIONS

New York

Library of Congress Cataloging-in-Publication Data
Yule, Andrew.
Picture shows: the life and films of Peter Bogdanovich / Andrew Yule.
p. cm.
Filmography: p.
Includes index.
ISBN 0-87910-153-9
1. Bogdanovich, Peter, 1939– . 2. Motion picture producers and directors—United States—Biography. I. Title.
PN1998.3.B64Y8   1991   91-33290   CIP
791.43′0233′092—dc20
[B]

Dedicated to the memory of
Lady Annie Henrietta Yule (no relation),
patron of British National Pictures and
Anglo-American Distribution

ACKNOWLEDGEMENTS

Grateful thanks are extended to the following interviewees (and to the others who preferred to remain anonymous), whose kind cooperation helped to make this book possible. In Los Angeles: Peter Bogdanovich, Anna Thea Bogdanovich, Neil Canton, James David Hinton, David Scott Milton, Polly Platt, John Ritter, Cybill Shepherd and Billy Wilder; in Wichita Falls and Archer City on the *Texasville* location shoot: Eden Ashley, Peter Bogdanovich, Antonia Bogdanovich, Louise (L.B.) Bogdanovich, Timothy Bottoms, Eileen Brennan, Jeff Bridges, Loyd Catlett, Iris Chester, Rick Fields, Steve Foley, Phedon Papamichael, Annie Potts, Al Ruban, Barry Spikings, Nicholas Von Sternberg and Bonnie Weeks; in New York: Dan Talbot; and in London: Alexander Walker.

Wherever dialogue is quoted, this represents the recollection of at least one person present when the conversation took place.

A special "thank you" to all the critics and their journals mentioned in the book, and to my secretary Hattie Forrest.

PREFACE

"Peter, Peter Pumpkin Eater
Had a wife and couldn't keep her.
He put her in a Pumpkin shell
And there he kept her very well."

Of all my visits to Peter Bogdanovich's Bel Air home in May and June 1989, the most extraordinary came toward the end of the sojourn in Los Angeles. The day began with a visit to the Universal studio in the San Fernando Valley, where Bogdanovich's first wife, Polly Platt, was temporarily headquartered. This was the woman Bogdanovich had deserted for his leading lady, Cybill Shepherd, while he directed his breakthrough movie, *The Last Picture Show.*

Platt talked with remarkable candor about her first meeting with Bogdanovich, how they had lived together before their marriage, their early adventures after their move from New York to Hollywood in search of movie fame, and the birth of their two daughters, Antonia and Alexandra.

A delightful, attractive blonde, Platt had clambered from the wreckage of their relationship and her abandonment and made an exceptional career and life for herself. She had worked with Barbra Streisand

on the production design of *A Star Is Born*, scripted and co-produced
Louis Malle's *Pretty Baby*, been nominated for an Oscar for her design
work on *Terms of Endearment*, produced the sleeper hit, *Say Anything*, and
jointly executive-produced Danny De Vito's smash, *War of the Roses*.
Most of this, she revealed, had occurred during, and in spite of, a
monumental struggle against an alcohol addiction that had developed
after the marital breakup.

Bogdanovich's apparently unstoppable rise had continued after *The
Last Picture Show* with *What's Up, Doc?* and *Paper Moon*, then had ground
to a halt as he tried to turn Cybill, his live-in lover, into a star in such
ill-fated vehicles as *Daisy Miller* and *At Long Last Love*, leaving both their
careers temporarily grounded. Only when Bogdanovich was forbidden
by David Begelman at Columbia to feature Cybill in yet another flop,
Nickelodeon, was she allowed to break free and play a part in Martin
Scorsese's *Taxi Driver*. By the close of the seventies, however, and the
end of their seven-year affair, both their careers were ice cold. Cybill's
amazing comeback in the mid-eighties with NBC's smash hit, *Moonlighting*, neatly coincided with Bogdanovich's own return to a major studio
and commercial success with Universal's *Mask*.

I left Platt's offices at noon, first arranging to meet her again for
brunch that Sunday at the Registry Hotel in Universal City, then drove
westward along the Valley to keep my lunchtime date with Cybill in her
Encino home. I had ample time to reflect on the chronological ground
I was covering, and the fact that, remarkably, the passage of time and
all it had brought had failed to dim Platt's obvious affection and regard
for Bogdanovich.

The visit with Shepherd was another delight. Big star? Not a bit of
it. She emerged without a scrap of makeup, positively glowing with
health. "Hi, honey," she greeted me, teasingly eyeing me up and down.
"I'm going to have a bowlful of melon. Would you like some?" She
smiled, then added, with a giggle, "You look as if you could use it!" All
afternoon she talked of the affair she and Bogdanovich had begun
during the fateful winter of 1970 in Wichita Falls, Texas, and of the
years of "going steady in public" that had followed, with all the attendant press attention—the good, the bad and the hurtful.

While Bogdanovich was abroad shooting in Singapore, Shepherd
took the opportunity to escape from the pumpkin shell Bogdanovich

built around each of his women. "I lived with Peter for seven years," she told me, "and he was obviously not the person I was meant to marry. For seven years I said, 'This is so complicated. I can't deal with it. Just let it go.' Then one morning I woke up and realized it wasn't really complicated at all . . . !"

After their split in 1978 Bogdanovich began to frequent Hugh Hefner's Playboy mansion, where he met the next woman in his life, the young and lovely Dorothy Stratten, then being groomed as a future Playmate. With Dorothy, Bogdanovich scaled the delicious peaks of giddy physical passion and deep, romantic love, recapturing an ecstasy he had thought lost forever. As the hideous details of her murder in 1980 at the hands of her jealous husband echoed round the globe, Bogdanovich's charmed existence changed overnight from Fairyland to Hell. When he came within a hairsbreadth of being institutionalized, Platt and Shepherd rallied round, together with Stratten's family and his daughters, to rescue him from the brink.

In 1989 Shepherd was set to to entrust the relaunch of her screen career to Bogdanovich, reuniting with the rest of the cast in Larry McMurtry's sequel, *Texasville*, almost two decades after *The Last Picture Show* had propelled them to stardom—Peter and Cybill, as well as Jeff Bridges, Cloris Leachman, Eileen Brennan, Timothy Bottoms and Randy Quaid. As with Platt, Shepherd's loyalty and affection for her ex-lover, two failed marriages later, were being demonstrated in the most dramatic manner imaginable.

All too soon I had to leave Shepherd for my final meeting of the day with Bogdanovich himself in the Bel Air mansion where his creditors had permitted him to continue living since his declared bankruptcy in 1985. I drove across Mulholland Drive after my climb from the Valley, then decided to park the car for a while before descending the Hollywood hills. The perpetual midafternoon haze that hung over the vista below seemed particularly dense and oppressive. Bogdanovich had conquered these same Hollywood hills with his early successes and had known and had loved a series of extraordinary women. And how many lives, I asked myself, had been in such close contact with not one, but *three* murders? There was the horrific incident Platt had described after she and Bogdanovich had filmed *The Wild Angels* for Roger Corman in the late sixties, the stabbing of their close friend Sal Mineo in the midseventies; finally Stratten's brutal killing. Wasn't Bogdanovich's life already remarkable enough, even without these astonishing peaks and valleys?

His place was still uncertain in cinema history, despite the almost mythic effect *The Last Picture Show* had produced on the American psyche. His avowed adulation of the likes of John Ford and Orson Welles had backfired on him with a vengeance, as had his star-making efforts with Shepherd. Absence from the limelight had caused Bogdanovich to regard himself as a maverick, independent filmmaker in the mold of John Cassavetes. The difference was that Cassavetes had always chosen independence; Bogdanovich had had it thrust upon him. Contemporaries like Scorsese and Coppola had largely overtaken him, despite their own indulgences and occasional falls from grace. Bogdanovich yet remained, according to many cineasts, one of America's foremost directors. Even his return to the mainstream, however, with Universal's *Mask*, had brought about a fight of unparalleled bitterness with the studio. *Texasville*—hopefully—was about to balance the books and reestablish him.

My first encounter with the man, several weeks earlier, had taken place after an introduction by a mutual acquaintance, Jake Eberts, *Texasville*'s executive producer. Bogdanovich had studied the notes I had made on his life and career and agreed to a daily series of interviews, first to clear up any inaccuracies, and then to expand on and illuminate the bare facts, often with invaluable hindsight. His demeanor was initially grave and his entrance like something out of Poe's "Fall Of The House Of Usher." "I suppose," he said as he seated himself opposite me, staring owlishly, "that there's nothing I can say to persuade you against writing this book?"

"Absolutely nothing," I replied. His earnestness disappeared and he broke into the amiable, lopsided grin that was soon to become as familiar as his outfit. "OK," he said with a shrug, "let's go."

After the stifling heat of the Valley, and my meetings with Platt and Shepherd, there was a refreshing breeze on Mulholland that made me linger. I knew, as did Bogdanovich, that our session that day was going to be unusually difficult, for we were covering the period of his time with Dorothy, her murder and its aftermath.

The lopsided grin was back, but fainter than usual by the end of our meeting. "That was rough," he told me, "really rough." So it was—but highly informative, for I felt as if I had spent a couple of hours in Stratten's company—or at least the Stratten that Bogdanovich still conjures up with such animation and warmth.

As I was about to leave a tall blonde girl rushed past me and greeted Bogdanovich with a hug before the two of them wandered off together. I would be formally introduced to Louise, Stratten's sister and Bogdanovich's new bride, several months later in Texas. Stratten had never made it into the safety of the pumpkin shell, whereas Louise had grown up inside its protective walls.

A life encompassed in a day, I reflected, as I drove home to nearby Benedict Canyon. Platt, Shepherd, Stratten—and Louise, all of the women who formed such a crucial part of the Bogdanovich saga. Genius? Egomaniac? Someone for whom Krafft-Ebing would need to redraft his *Psychopathia Sexualis?* Yet, if the loyalty of women meant anything, a man to be reckoned with nonetheless. There was clearly much more to Bogdanovich than met the eye.

What were the early influences that had charted the course of his life? What were the demons that drove and continue to drive him? "Of course talk to Polly, Cybill and Louise," friends had advised me, "but check out his parents first. They're the key to understanding Peter."

That suggestion began a fascinating and revealing odyssey through the quirky, complex riddle that is Peter Bogdanovich.

CHAPTER 1

Born in 1899, Borislav Bogdanovich was a member of the Viennese aristocracy and a Serbian of the Greek Orthodox faith, whose father's early death in 1910 left his family ill-prepared for the ravages of the First World War. Since his mother was far too young and inexperienced to cope on her own with the upbringing of a large family and the governing of their finances, their inherited fortune was soon lamentably depleted. The youngest of five children, Borislav was forced to stand by and watch as his world of privilege crumbled.

With the return of peace his brothers and sisters sought and found professional positions. Borislav was a brilliant piano player, frustratingly unable to carry his ability to the concert hall because of an innate shyness: even in his final tests at the Belgrade Conservatoire, his professors had to be persuaded to sit in another room while he played. Circumstances forced him to swallow both his pride and his shyness to earn a modest living as a music teacher. Unfortunately, the handsome youngster had a predilection for gambling that swallowed his wages, together with what little family money remained. To succeed as a painter was a long-term goal, a dream the young man kept alive. In the aristocracy, however, one did not paint for a living, one painted to create.

Thirteen-year old Herma Robinson was the daughter of a wealthy importer in Belgrade, whose household Borislav visited in 1929 when he was hired to give Herma piano lessons. While far from beautiful, she had a boldness about her deep-set features and an already burgeoning voluptuousness that was not unappealing. Her family was Jewish, but in his desperate struggle to survive as an artist, the ingrained bigotry with which Borislav had been raised was swept aside. Although young Herma was struck by the tall, dark and dashing 30-year-old Borislav, her father, Henry Robinson, was not. A deep and terrible animosity was born. In the eyes of Robinson, an orthodox Jew, Borislav—the penniless piano teacher and struggling artist—was an unfit suitor for his daughter. There was a possible element of jealousy at work, for Herma's father had given up his architectural studies to become a businessman and may have resented Borislav's ability, however tenuous, to cling to his art.

Following Herma's defiance of her family's wishes and her marriage to Borislav in 1934, an uneasy truce was established with the Robinsons. After setting up their home in an old mill house in Zagreb, their first child, Anthony—the very image of Borislav—was born two years later. The proud parents nicknamed him "Tonka."

By 1938 the lengthening shadows of Naziism threatened Jews everywhere. Desperate to escape to America, Henry Robinson pleaded with Borislav to help him and his family escape with their fortune intact. If Borislav would go to Paris and arrange exit visas for the Robinsons', his father-in law promised he would never know poverty again; as soon as they were all settled in the New World, Borislav and Herma would receive a substantial sum of money. Borislav agreed and left for Paris, first instructing young Herma to take care of baby Tonka. He was particularly worried about a staircase in the old house that led to a balcony overlooking the old paddle wheel. Yes, it was boarded up, but there was a weakness there. "Make sure Tonka goes nowhere near it," Borislav warned her.

His wife's answer was to carefully build a wall of books to prevent Tonka from crawling up the stairs. The first few days of Borislav's absence were spent uneventfully, with Herma busying herself about the house. By midweek she had begun to prepare a cauldron of split-pea soup.

As she stirred the thick, boiling mixture, suitably fortified by the local vegetables that made it into a stock pot that would last several days,

Herma heard little Tonka begin to cry. She found him just outside the kitchen, where he had been trying in vain to pull down the wall of books that confronted him in his efforts to get to the staircase. Thinking how proud Borislav would be, Herma carefully replaced the few books that Tonka had managed to dislodge and carried the child into the kitchen, setting him down on a chair to change his nappies. As she straightened up, her head touched the handle of the stockpot, spinning the cauldron off the stove and emptying the boiling liquid over her baby son. Although Tonka only screamed for a few seconds it seemed like eternity. Then he fell silent.

Later the events of the next few hours were recalled only sketchily by Herma. "I'm having a nightmare," she told herself over and over again. "But nightmares end, even the worst of them, so I'm bound to wake up soon. TONKA!" There was the endless, rickety journey over country roads to Belgrade in a neighbor's car, the baby mute and swaddled in sheets that barely covered the ghastly blistering. It was the stentorious tone of the resident doctor at Belgrade Hospital which made Herma realize that this was one nightmare from which she would never awake. "Your son," he told her, "has severe burns extending to three-quarters of his body area. He is in deep shock. We are doing our best, but I do not think we can save him. He may never come out of his coma." After three days little Tonka succumbed.

With Borislav's arrival the nightmare escalated. As he listened incredulously to her tearful, halting explanation, he looked at Herma with such naked accusation and loathing that she prayed to die. The funeral brought meaningless words of comfort, pity and solace, then there was the return home to the empty cot and the deeper emptiness inside that nothing again could ever fill.

A family friend relayed the news of Herma's pregnancy a few months later. "The whole thing's just too horrible," he told neighbors. "Borislav, coming from a rabidly anti-Semitic background, marries Herma, a Jewess, for her money. She accidentally kills his son while he's away from home obtaining exit visas for her family, then he makes her pregnant again. Dear God, can you imagine what a *hate-fuck* that must have been?"

Borislav had done his work in Paris well and soon the Bogdanoviches and the Robinsons embarked for their new lives, although ostensibly they were only visiting New York for the World's Fair. Herma was seven months pregnant when her second son, Peter, was born prematurely on July 30, 1939, only days after they docked in New York City. Just as Tonka had resembled Borislav, Peter would go on to develop his mother's features.

Once the family had settled down in Kingston, New York, where Henry Robinson's brother had a trucking business, they successfully pleaded their case that they be allowed to remain because of the outbreak of war in Europe. Borislav loathed living with his in-laws and being stranded in a foreign land. He was unable to speak a word of English and without even two pennies to rub together, he moved quickly to settle his business with Herma's father. "A bargain is a bargain," was his opening thrust. "You promised to settle half your fortune on Herma to get us started here."

Disapproval, religious intolerance and professional jealousy was a heady cocktail from which Borislav's father-in-law seemed to have drunk deeply. "I didn't mean *all at once,*" he countered. "Look, Borislav, we're no longer in the old country. New rules apply. What I have in mind now is an arrangement whereby Herma will come to work for me once I get my import agency established. Security is more important than a lump sum. If my daughter works for me, there'll always be food on your table. How many people can say that?"

Tonka's death, the dreadful sea voyage, what he saw as the hideous squalor in which he and Herma and baby Peter were trying to live in Kingston—perhaps, in truth, the real reason he had married a Jewess from a wealthy family in the first place—suddenly boiled over. "We had a bargain," Borislav yelled. "Your daughter killed my child while I was away obtaining exit visas. Now you dare to renege on your promise . . ."

"You expect me to give you a lump sum you can gamble away?" Robinson retorted contemptuously. "You must think me some kind of idiot. We all regret the death of little Tonka. But now Herma has given you Peter instead. Count your blessings, Borislav. You want a little money to live on? Fine, that's a different matter. You're a painter, yes? Then *earn* the money. Go paint 'Robinson & Company' on my brother's trucks!"

That Borislav and Herma went on to reach some kind of renewed rapport, at least enough to enable them to live together, says much for the stoicism and resilience of human nature. While Borislav's betrayal at the hands of Henry Robinson was something which had to be suffered, and could occasionally be broached, Tonka's death was never discussed between them. Herma's reaction to the tragedy was to seal off her emotions. In the eyes of her son she closed herself in completely, although he had no idea of the underlying reason. Until he was 23 years old he never even knew he had a brother. "Be careful, be careful," was the Bogdanoviches' constant entreaty to their son. Young Peter would suffer not a single physical injury in his entire childhood.

Borislav desperately missed his homeland and found it hardest of all to resign himself to the likelihood that he would never see his family again. As foreigners, he and Herma were viewed with suspicion in America. English had to be learned from comic books and the radio. Giving piano lessons in order to earn his living he regarded as out of the question, a thing of the past. Had they not landed him in this mess in the first place? Unfortunately, however, Borislav's style of painting, with its complicated and colorful Byzantine roots, was not widely appreciated in America. His feeling of being high and dry in a foreign land was unleavened by any sign of the compensation that even a modicum of success would have brought.

Gradually even his painting was neglected as the forties wore on, and Borislav increasingly spent his time in silent contemplation of the apartment walls, sunk deep in a stygian depression.

By the late forties Borislav's sanity had begun to unravel. His mother's death in 1948 formed the climax to a decade of despair. Ten-year-old Peter visited his father in hospital, but had no idea what a "nervous breakdown" meant, let alone what "shock treatment" entailed.

CHAPTER 2

Although the recognition he would receive in his lifetime was still far away, Borislav was too well versed in the vicissitudes of other artists through the ages to indulge in despair for too long. Gradually, he made a recovery, sustained in part by a new-found revival of confidence in himself.

After a short stay in Kingston, Bogdanovich and Herma found a place on West 67th Street in New York, an apartment house populated in the main by artists, next to the Hotel Des Artistes, near Central Park. Peter was left behind with his grandparents for a spell in Kingston while his parents settled in Manhattan and looked for work. It took a long time for the scars from his "abandonment" in Kingston to begin to properly heal.

When they were able to send for him he found Borislav and Herma sleeping in the living room, which doubled by day as the studio. The whole family ate in the kitchen, while Peter occupied the only other room across the hall. When a sister, Anna Thea, was born in 1952 a move was made to a larger apartment on Riverside Drive, on the fifteenth floor overlooking the Hudson River.

Growing up in a European household, where his parents had taught themselves English by reading the funny papers, had a profound effect on the young Bogdanovich. Apart from the fact that he knew how to

speak Serbo-Croatian before he learned English, he absorbed European sensibilities from his parents. Some of these, like respect for tradition and pride in his cultural heritage, would stand him in good stead
in the future. Others, like a certain reserve and arrogance, usually had
the opposite effect.

Friends saw aspects of his upbringing as constituting at the very least
a case of benign neglect. He denies this, although he had a lonely
childhood, being left largely to his own devices when he got home in the
afternoons from school. "It's true that my father never said, 'You must
do this, do that, think this way,' " he concedes, "but I was very good
at doing things on my own, constructively using my time. When I was
a kid he used to take me to galleries and museums all the time. He
prided himself that he could take me with him into a museum at the age
of five and have me recognize painters' work. My father's forgetfulness,
like being unable to remember the names of my teachers or the classes
I was taking, was all part of an act he put on, being amusingly absent-
minded. But I was never in any doubt that my father loved me."

A friend from those days looks back on Herma and her role in the
family unit. "She was well read, an original thinker who believed in
man and superman, but they all had a difficult time living without
money. They were always in hock to some money lender, at one point
for up to $25,000. Herma in particular was incredibly courageous. She
was indomitable, she never gave up."

Whatever else Bogdanovich may have questioned about his childhood, lack of money seems not to have troubled him. "Sure, we were
poor," he admits, "but we were never *acting* poor. My parents sent me
to private schools and a very good boy's summer camp simply by
borrowing money all the time. I grew up thinking that everybody had
more money than we had and it took a long time to realize there were
people who had even less than us. I didn't have a dress shirt, just a
short-sleeved shirt and I couldn't afford too many haircuts. I don't think
it bothered me at the time, but later on I had feelings of insecurity and
being a bit of an outsider."

Herma was her son's first director and dialogue coach, helping him
with his accent when he landed the lead role in *Finian's Rainbow* in sixth
grade. Bogdanovich recalls one argument his parents had in front of
him. He had been given a small portable typewriter as a thirteenth
birthday present and proceeded to compose a play which he proudly

read to his parents. "When my mother said it was derivative of some movie I got very upset and ripped it up. My father took my side. "You must never criticize the young," he told my mother. She never did again, in that way. Basically my mother and father always encouraged me tremendously." To Anna her big brother was the archetypal hero, able to make his parents laugh and forget their money problems.

Bogdanovich regarded the family's shortage of money as a fact of life that was no reflection whatsoever on his father. Borislav was an *artist*. "He could walk down the street and everyone would turn and look at him," he still says proudly, "because he looked like someone very important. He always wore a hat and gloves and a cane, and the clothes he bought in Prague in the early twenties, and always looked like a European gentleman. He taught me to wash my hands when I came in from outside and hang up my clothes. He had this aristocratic bearing in every single thing he did. Inside the house, when he was painting, things were different. He wore a hat with the top cut off and a pair of pants I think were held together with paint."

The first movie that Bogdanovich remembers watching is *Dumbo*. As a child he would live inside the movies he saw, acting out the parts all week long. He was a great mimic, his schoolmates considering his Jerry Lewis impression in particular a knockout. Combined with a pleasant singing voice, there was clearly a latent all-around performer in there, just desperate to burst out. Bogdanovich adopted a breezily pragmatic way to obtain free books—he became a book critic! For tickets to movies, he became a movie critic. Soon he was contributing a column to his high school magazine on books, movies—and the theatre.

He left high school at sixteen years of age without a diploma, because of a failed algebra exam. At the graduation ceremony he was still duly summoned and solemnly presented with a bulky, face-saving envelope, just like the graduates. On opening it later, he found it contained a blank chunk of cardboard.

As his ambition began to focus on becoming an actor and director in the theater, he took a friend's advice and enrolled in an acting class at Stella Adler's Theater Studio. This involved the small matter of lying about his age; although he was only sixteen, he solemnly assured the redoubtable Ms. Adler he was all of eighteen year old. Since he was tall for his age the ploy worked, and the youngster was soon appearing alongside visiting actors such as Signe Hasso, Edward Everett Horton, Richard Arlen and Sylvia Sydney.

At the same time, he enrolled at New York's Columbia University for a general studies course, and to keep himself on screening lists began contributing reviews to *Ivy*, a magazine circulated to all Ivy League colleges. During these years he acted in summer stock for four seasons, two of them with Shakespeare festivals, most notably, in 1956, the American Shakespeare Festival Theatre, in Stratford, Connecticut. Two other aspirants at the ASFT that year were Geraldine Fitzgerald's sixteen-year old son, Michael Lindsay Hogg, and a 22-year old actor/ writer, David Scott Milton.

"Peter could be very, very funny," Milton recollects, "with his mimicking of Cary Grant, Jerry Lewis, Marlon Brando and others. Then there was the serious side of him; he was always reading things like Albert Camus. I pronounced the author's name wrong at first, and here was this sixteen-year old correcting me! He was always ready to goof off. There was a tremendous problem with the costumes in the production of *King John* we were both in; they hadn't been built for mere men to wear and weighed a ton each. Under the lights everyone started dropping like flies and there was a rush to rip out the padding and make the costumes workable. All of us young actors came on stage as soldier extras wearing these tremendous costumes with visors. You could just see our eyes. On opening night I looked around and nearly burst out laughing on the stage. Peter had turned his visor round, so that there were these 50 soldiers with their faces covered—and one bare face, Peter's grinning."

The event that gave Bogdanovich the notion he would one day want to look beyond acting and directing in the theater was his first viewing of Orson Welles's *Citizen Kane*. The film made a deep impression and prompted him to attend film history classes at Columbia University. "They all had the dream of being great film directors," lecturer Cecile Starr remembers, "but Bogdanovich and another student, Brian De Palma, seemed to hold on to the dream, while the rest were too easily seduced by reality. The last time I saw Peter was in a Shakespeare play outdoors in Central Park in 1958. Halfway through the first act I recognized the tall, expressive, yet somehow awkward figure that even in a crowd of 30 or 40 people was unmistakably Bogdanovich. Just before school had ended, he told me he was hanging around Joseph Papp's theater for the experience of doing whatever had to be done. And there he was on stage carrying a spear."

Bogdanovich was intrigued when he heard that Adolphus Mekas, the brother of documentary filmmaker Jonas Mekas, had written a script, *Hallelujah the Hills,* specifically with him in mind as the lead actor. However, when he heard more about it, he decided it was not for him. "It meant taking my clothes off and appearing bareass," he recalls, still indignant at the very thought. "I told them to forget it."

He embarked on a tour of *Othello,* did summer stock in Massachusetts and briefly worked in television. In 1958 he directed a scene from Clifford Odets's *The Big Knife* during an acting class at Stella Adler's that involved five actors. Ms. Adler made her entrance while the scene was in progress and stood up when it was over. "Brilliant, darlings," she said, "but you've been directed. Who directed you?" Informed that Bogdanovich was responsible, she turned to her by-now bespectacled protege. "Brilliant, my boy," she declared.

Inspired by this triumph, Bogdanovich typed a single-spaced two-page letter to Odets in Hollywood asking permission to stage *The Big Knife* off Broadway. A few weeks later he was awakened by Herma, who handed him Odets's reply delivered in an envelope embossed with the legend, "20th Century-Fox Studios." "Dear Peter Bogdanovich," the first line ran, "You have my permission to do the production."

When Bogdanovich walked down the street that morning, he was several feet above the pavement, his world forever transformed. It still took him nine sobering months to raise the $15,000 he needed to stage the play, which he directed and coproduced off Broadway in the 1959/60 season to good reviews and a two-month run. When the lead actor, Carroll O'Connor had to leave two weeks before the run ended, Bogdanovich the performer decided it would be easier just to play the part himself rather than recast. A year or so later, when he met Odets in Hollywood, he asked him why he had taken a chance and entrusted his play to an unknown kid. Odets looked at him through dense clouds of cigarette smoke and shrugged. "I took a drop in the ocean," he replied.

After *The Big Knife* closed, early in 1960, Bogdanovich looked round for something else to do. Although he had by now seen a great many movies, most of them were current pictures. He had learned from his father that if he wanted to become an artist of any kind it was necessary to know not only his craft but its history as well. Bogdanovich's Cecile Starr class had given him a start; now he decided that he must see all the key older movies. He visited Dan Talbot who was just starting up the New Yorker Repertory Cinema, conveniently situated two blocks from the Bogdanovich home on 89th Street and Broadway. "I've heard of you," Talbot told him, "and I've read some of your reviews. I remember something you wrote about *Intolerance*. I *hated* it!"

Undaunted, Bogdanovich's proposition was that he compose the program notes for Talbot's movies in return for permanent free admission. When this was accepted, a friendship sprung up between the two men that still endures. Talbot initially paid Bogdanovich $15 a week for his services, then $25 as he became deeper entrenched. Soon Bogdanovich was suggesting programs he particularly wanted to see, then coaxing Talbot into charging five cents a copy for his mimeographed program notes—proceeds to P. Bogdanovich.

It was Talbot who insisted that Bogdanovich be aware of the French New Wave, movies like Jean-Luc Godard's *Breathless*. "It didn't take the first time he saw it," says Talbot, smiling, "but I managed to persuade him to go back and see it again. He got it that time." In his own quiet and authoritative way, Talbot exerted considerable influence on his young friend, for the New Wave was peopled by young ex-*Cahiers du cinéma* critics-turned-directors like Godard, Francois Truffaut and Eric Rohmer. It was a precedent unknown in the U.S. and a phenomenon that provided an interesting career signpost.

Bogdanovich's other influences on movie matters in those early days were Andrew Sarris, the *Village Voice* columnist, and Eugene Archer, the second-string critic of the *New York Times*, both of whom were avid disciples of the *Cahiers* school and its view of the director as the true *auteur* of the movie. "They opened my eyes to films," says Bogdanovich, "getting me to see stuff like Howard Hawks's *Land of the Pharoahs* and John Ford's *Fort Apache*. I'd seen lots of films by both these guys, but I'd never noted their names as the common factor, it had never sunk in. Then I was stupid about certain things, for example I didn't like Hitchcock's *Psycho* at the time, I thought it was brilliant but immoral—something idiotic like that. I remember sitting over coffee one night and they explained to me why *Psycho* was a great film.

"My taste was really formed when I booked all those films at the New Yorker. We had a series called 'The Forgotten Film' and in the first two weeks we had ten Howard Hawks pictures. That was a revelation to me, for I'd always loved Hawks without knowing he was the director. I loved *Rio Bravo* when it came out, then I said, 'Wait a minute, he did *Red River*,' and I put it all together. I'd liked *all* his films, but I hadn't known who he was! Many's the night Andy Sarris, Gene Archer and I—a junior initiate—used to sit around the grey, windowless upstairs office of the New Yorker, listening to Gene expounding on the relative merits of Ford or Hawks, or the superiority of Hitchcock over Antonioni, or Samuel Fuller and Frank Tashlin and their influence on Jean-Luc Godard. Another time the subject would be the genius of the later Welles, the likeability of Tay Garnett and Allan Dwan; why Gary Cooper was better than Paul Muni or why later Rossellini was more personal than early Rossellini. Another night we would hear about the sublime Jean Renoir, Mizoguchi, Max Ophuls and so on."

Although Bogdanovich still harbored theatrical ambitions, movies began to loom ever larger. He wanted to meet the great Hollywood directors and stars, and decided that his journalistic sideline was the perfect vehicle. By the beginning of 1961, when he had saved enough money for a two-week trip to Hollywood, he contacted Robert Silvers, the editor of *Harper's Magazine.* The erudite Silvers was impressed with the extremely confident and self-assured 22-year old and presented him with a letter of introduction. Armed with this passport, and through his own various contacts, he was able to organize interviews with Laurence Harvey, Walt Disney, Alfred Hitchcock, Billy Wilder, Richard Brooks, Angie Dickinson, Mark Robson, William Wyler, Gordon Douglas, Robert Wise, John Sturges and Jack Lemmon.

While in Los Angeles he tried to talk Clifford Odets into letting him do another of his plays, but although pleased with the way *The Big Knife* had turned out, the playright demurred. Instead, he got him an invitation to meet Cary Grant.

On Bogdanovich's return to New York, he took a call from David Balding, an entrepreneur who had gathered enough money to do a season of summer theatre. Bogdanovich accepted the job of artistic director of the project, which involved selecting the plays he wanted to direct himself and helping pick others. Also hired by Balding to be a director was Michael Lindsay Hogg.

Another call came from Richard Griffiths, Curator of Film at the Museum of Modern Art. Having read and been impressed by Bogdanovich's notes for Orson Welles's *Othello* at the New Yorker, he asked him if he would consider doing a 25,000-word monograph on Welles on the occasion of their forthcoming retrospective on the director—for a fee of $125. On the same day the offer was made, a young woman entered Bogdanovich's life. Polly Platt was petite, blonde, pretty—and already a widow at nineteen years of age.

CHAPTER 3

Polly Platt was born in 1941 in Houston, Texas, to Colonel and Mrs. John C. Platt. She traveled all over the world with her parents, gaining most of her primary education in France and Germany. After junior high school she enrolled at Boston's Milton Academy and graduated from there to go on to the drama department at Carnegie Tech in Pittsburgh, where she majored in scenic design. She left college in 1960, married and with her husband Philip moved to Tucson, Arizona. They and some close friends from Carnegie Tech shared what seemed like a fairly modest ambition: to bring "good theater" to the Southwest, and to this end, they opened a theater in an old Salvation Army building, with Anouilh's *Thieves' Carnival* their first production. Disaster struck soon afterwards when Philip was killed in an automobile accident.

Platt returned to New York after the funeral and stayed with a school friend in Greenwich Village while she tried to reassemble the fragments of her life. After working on an off-Broadway production, she was put in touch with David Balding and hired as a costume designer for his forthcoming summer theater season. He asked her to meet with Bogdanovich, his artistic director. *"Who?"* she asked. "Bogdanovich," Balding repeated. Try as she might, she had difficulty remembering the name.

Platt made her way to the New Yorker cinema, where Dan Talbot was in the middle of running his Forgotten Film series. When she asked for "Peter MacDonavich" at the ticket counter, she was told there was no one there by that name. Undeterred, she tracked her quarry down in Talbot's upstairs office. During what Bogdanovich regarded as "the interview," he asked her about her experience. "Well," she told him, "I designed the production of *Women of the Tomb* that's playing right now off Broadway."

"Did you?" came the reply. "Oh, I never go to the theater."

"Who *is* this arrogant young punk?" Platt thought to herself. "Look," she pointed out, "this isn't an interview, David Balding's already given me the job."

"He has?" Bogdanovich replied, completely unruffled. "Then why don't we go out and get some coffee?"

As he swiftly swung the conversation round to Orson Welles and the monograph assignment he had just been given, Platt got the distinct impression that if she had failed to recognize Welles's name she would have been out on the street immediately. But, aside from wanting to hold on to her job, she had another reason for hanging in. She found the tall, pale young man with the slightly lopsided grin and intense, owl-like eyes extremely attractive. Unknown to Platt, the position of designer was not the only one vacant. Having just been dropped by his high school sweetheart, Bogdanovich had "decided" that whoever got the costume design job would be his girlfriend for the season as well. This was one interview Bogdanovich definitely *was* conducting.

David Scott Milton reentered Bogdanovich's life as he and Platt began summer stock at Phoenicia, New York, staging plays by authors as diverse as Tennessee Williams and Agatha Christie. "Both Peter and Michael Lindsay Hogg were eyeing Polly," says Milton. "Michael really fell in love with her, but Polly never knew that although she dated him for a while before she and Peter got together. Michael called me one day to say that he was heartbroken she had chosen Peter over him." The deciding factor had undoubtedly been Bogdanovich's habit of serenading his girlfriends with love songs of the day, the performer in him once more well to the fore.

Borislav answered the door on Platt's first visit to the Bogdanoviches' 90th Street and Riverside Drive apartment. She found herself confronted with a tall, imposing, haunting figure, wearing pajamas that were covered in paint and a hat perched on his head from which the top had been cut. "For ventilation," he explained as he saw his visitor's puzzled expression. Platt felt as if she had inadvertently strayed on to an incredible Marx Brothers set: " 'Boro' had painted his way through every room; there were canvasses floor to ceiling."

Herma had stopped working for her father by this time and was making frames for Borislav's paintings, evidenced by the lumber-filled halls and the large band saw she kept just outside the kitchen. She gilded the frames herself with 24-carat gold leaf, an art she had perfected since her husband's sale of a few paintings to a local five-and-dime store tycoon. Platt thought Herma was one of the most striking characters she had ever met, a large-boned woman with enormous breasts and boldly-carved European features. Her long hair was worn in a bun, with fly-away pieces loosely trailing behind. As she got to know both parents she realized that each in their own way was a match for the other.

"Boro would start painting a group of peaches and oranges which nobody would be allowed near, even when they were green, moldy and shriveled up. They would only be thrown out when he said so, not before. Herma? She just went about her business, *very* European. They never talked *together* about what was going on; even at the beginning I sensed this yawning gulf between them. Herma talked a lot about Shaw's *Man and Superman*. Borislav would fall asleep while she was talking about Mozart or Tolstoy, whom she adored. Everyone would fall asleep for that matter, except me. I was fascinated. Herma was very sexy and voluptuous, all woman—and an incredibly powerful, energetic woman. What was strange to me was that few people really liked her. I think people were jealous of her enormous intellect. I loved her. She was aggressive and protective of Peter." [Platt was aware that to many of the Bogdanoviches' neighbors and acquaintances Herma was regarded as nothing less than her son's super-protective Raging Lioness at the gates of Peter.] "We came to blows occasionally over her selfishness with her son. She told me she approved of me because Peter had already been involved with the daughter of a wealthy family and she thought it would be a bad relationship for him. I could see why Peter *had* to be someone special. Herma liked me because she knew we had something in common—we both adored Peter. Borislav? He never really loved him the way he should have."

For his part Bogdanovich was never entirely sure whether or not his mother really approved of Polly. "If my son or daughter marries someone I do not like," she had once told him, "I will smile and be nice to them. They will never know I don't like them, because I do not want to lose my son or daughter."

What speaks volumes for the way both parents felt about Platt is the way they soon treated her as one of the family. Herma unburdened herself for the first time in almost a quarter of a century, but only after she and Platt had had a discussion about what it felt like to be suicidal. She fought back the tears as she revealed the story of Tonka, the brother Bogdanovich still knew nothing about. Later she tried to tell her son as well, but she became so choked up that Platt, who found it heartrending to see such a powerful woman breaking down, had to finish the story. Platt thought Borislav had come to love Herma, but realized she might be looking at their relationship "through rose-colored glasses." He was an old-fashioned European man who expected his woman to wait on him hand and foot, but he still showed his wife respect.

Platt believes Borislav married Herma for three reasons. "He told me he knew she was a virgin, and that she would be a good mother to his children. But he admitted, quite straightforwardly, that he'd never really loved her back then, and I thought that money was the main reason for the marriage, since he'd been penniless."

When Bogdanovich's high school sweetheart reappeared on the scene, he decided he had passed the point of no return and stuck with Platt. Still he bridled at the thought of being tied down. "Do I really want to do this?" he asked himself as he and Platt went apartment-hunting. Whether he did or not, the couple soon moved into a place of their own, three blocks away from his parents.

Bogdanovich saw his life at this time as just floating along on a river, without his ever actively making a decision. He was trying to make things happen on a professional but not on a personal level. As one of his friends put it, half jokingly though wholly in earnest: "You sure know a lot about Tennessee Williams, Peter, but not an awful lot about life." Bogdanovich wondered what he meant at the time but came to agree with his friend in later years.

While other couples might have been discussing moon and June, Bogdanovich would fret to Platt about whether his name would fit on playbills or on the screen. For a while he was determined to shorten it to "Bogdane," until Borislav's derisive reaction jolted him out of the notion. Platt was content to listen to his schemes and to act in an advisory capacity, for she was without what she saw as his male obsession with fame, a phenomenon she observed with a mixture of awe and chagrin—until his obsession gradually became hers.

Platt's influence was everywhere, as a designer, editor and all-around organizer. "Peter wanted to be famous and I wanted it for him," she says of those early days. "I thought if he didn't get what he wanted, he wouldn't be happy. The two of us were totally committed to his success, like little Communists to the cause." In 1962 they committed themselves to another cause—marriage.

With aspiring actor George Morfogen drafted as best man, the ceremony was held at City Hall—with much hilarity. One minute the judge was chatting with them quite informally, the next he walked behind a podium, drew himself up to his full height (Platt thought he looked like a praying mantis) and assumed what he obviously considered a suitable air of *gravitas*. The judicial words were then intoned in a sonorous, theatrical voice. The threesome almost broke up halfway through the ceremony, then laughed all the way home in the subway.

Bogdanovich drew together all his Hollywood notes and composed a single piece, but his 70-page memoir was rejected by *Harper's*—even after Robert Silvers' suggestions for cuts were followed—and then by *The Atlantic Monthly*. Bogdanovich kept the material on ice for the right occasion, which he figured would surely arrive, and at Platt's suggestion rewrote the piece, which she then helped him edit.

Having decided that he must see absolutely all of Howard Hawks's films, Bogdanovich figured out how to arrange this and advance himself at the same time. With Paramount about to release Hawks's *Hatari*, he called their publicity head, Saul Cooper, with a proposition: if Bogdanovich could persuade the Museum of Modern Art to assign him to write a monograph on Hawks's career and do a retrospective of his movies to tie in with the opening of *Hatari*, would Paramount foot the bill? When Cooper agreed, Bogdanovich called Richard Griffith at the Museum. "If I can get Paramount to foot the bill, would you be interested in doing a retrospective of Hawks to coincide with the opening of *Hatari* and assign me to do the monograph?"

Griffith's agreement secured, Bogdanovich saw all of Hawks's movies in the six-month retrospective that MOMA staged—and was paid for it. Paramount flew him and Platt to Hollywood to interview Hawks. The scam was repeated a year later, this time with Universal on the receiving end, prior to the opening of Hitchcock's *The Birds*.

From 1962 onwards Bogdanovich wrote a series of articles for *Esquire,* the contract originating from a chance meeting with Harold Hayes, the magazine's managing director, at a dinner before the preview of *Hatari.* Platt found herself sitting next to Hayes and held forth on her movie views. Hayes was impressed, despite having his taste light-heartedly trashed over a dozen times. Platt introduced her husband, and a week later Bogdanovich phoned Hayes. "I'm the fellow whose wife insulted you all through dinner last week," he said by way of introduction. Told of the article Bogdanovich had originally written for *Harper's,* Hayes asked to see it. Ten days later he called Bogdanovich. "We're going to buy that piece," he told him, "and we want you to go to Hollywood and do another for us right away, a profile of Jerry Lewis."

Courtesy of Hayes, Bogdanovich at 23 was thus established as a profile writer, a position that gave him further chances to call on and interview those legends of the American cinema he idolized. *Esquire* also paid Platt's way on these trips, enabling her always to be with him during the interviews and available for observation and notetaking. Apart from seizing the opportunity to brush up on his Jerry Lewis imitation, Bogdanovich also called on Frank Capra, Leo McCarey, Allan Dwan and, again, Howard Hawks.

The Jerry Lewis profile revealed the comedian at his most swollen-headed and brattish, lord of all he surveyed on the Paramount lot. "They say to me, I'm an egomaniac; what do I wanna do four things for?" he rhetorically demanded. "Why do I have to direct, produce and write too? D'ya think it's so easy? D'ya think it's such a pleasure? For each cap I wear, it's eight hours work. So I'm doing four things, that's 32 hours a day—there ain't that many. Why do I do it? 'Cos I'd rather work that way than work with incompetents. I'm getting the best people I know for the job." Bogdanovich somehow managed to squeeze an admiring article out of the undoubtedly complex Lewis, which, many felt, was fine for a profile, but hardly made him an ideal role model.

In Arizona's Monument Valley to meet John Ford on location for *Cheyenne Autumn,* Bogdanovich and Platt struck up a friendship with actor Sal Mineo. Although he and Bogdanovich were both the same age, Mineo had grown up faster, his education gained on the streets of the Bronx. Running with street gangs at the age of eight, he was expelled from school at nine and had executed a heist of school gym equipment at ten. Dancing classes ("Call me a sissy and you're dead!") had led to his stage debut in *The Rose Tattoo,* then an appearance as one of Yul Brynner's little princes in *The King and I.* His dark, Italianate baby face and soft brown eyes made him a natural for Hollywood, where he made his debut at fifteen, appropriately enough in Universal's Brink's robbery—Tony Curtis epic, *Six Bridges to Cross.* A year later he was at Warners playing Plato opposite James Dean in *Rebel Without a Cause,* for which he received his first Academy Award nomination. He appeared with Dean again in *Giant.* Cheerfully and unashamedly bisexual, the precocious Mineo was quoted after Dean's death as saying, "We never became lovers, but we could have—like that," and later, "I got a girl in every port—and a couple of guys too."

By the time Mineo was nineteen he was able to buy his parents a house that just a few years earlier would have been beyond their wildest imagining. The magnificent $200,000, 20-room mansion in Mamaroneck, Westchester County, had originally been built for Mary Pickford. It fronted on the Long Island Sound and D.W. Griffith had shot *Birth of a Nation* on its grounds.

The genre of the largely indifferent movies that followed *Giant* earned Mineo the nickname "The Switchblade Kid," but then another Oscar nomination came his way, this time for Otto Preminger's *Exodus.* Nevertheless, by the sixties the Hollywood establishment—and moviegoers, it seemed—had come to regard Mineo as an anachronism, the fate of so many who peak early and come to symbolize an era. "Where you start is pretty much how you wind up," Mineo pointed out. "I mean, you get typed in the first thing that clicks, then they don't give you no more fuckin' chances. Hollywood don't flex its muscle brain."

When Bogdanovich and Platt returned to New York, their friendship with Mineo continued and he introduced them to his parents, Salvatore Sr. and Josephine, his elder brothers Michael and Victor, his younger sister Sarina—and to Jill Haworth, the young actress he had fallen for during the filming of *Exodus.*

Bogdanovich had never met someone his own age as instantly disarming as Mineo, or a character who took himself less seriously. For a while they hung out together, taking buses and taxis everywhere and riding the subway after Mineo's driver's license was suspended following three speeding offenses in eighteen months. The actor introduced Bogdanovich and Platt to Beatles records, which they played together late into the night as they talked of their hopes for the future. Mineo knew that his acting career had slipped, but was cheerful and optimistic about his prospects as a director. Unfortunately, Harold Hayes' attitude at *Esquire* cruelly reflected Hollywood's when Bogdanovich did a Mineo profile. After at first agreeing reluctantly to back the assignment, Hayes scrapped Bogdanovich's eventual article. "I just couldn't stand the idea of having Sal Mineo in the magazine," Hayes admitted.

Long before Sal Mineo's tragic death, his constant search for vehicles in which he might demolish Hollywood's preconceptions would yield Bogdanovich a hefty dividend.

The reactions of his ex-colleagues to Bogdanovich's success varied. Dan Talbot was glad to see him getting on and continued to encourage him. Andrew Sarris, having in the spring of 1963 brought out an entire issue of the magazine *Film Culture* devoted to American film directors, was building up resentment. He believed that Bogdanovich had absorbed many of his opinions and was regurgitating them as if they had been freshly minted. One day when Platt innocently remarked how well Bogdanovich's career seemed to be going, Sarris suddenly confessed that he "hated Peter" for lifting all his insights without a word of credit. He saw Bogdanovich as the "Howdy Doody" of the Hitchcock/Hawksians. Having long labored in his apartment on critical appreciations of these and other artists, Sarris then had to stand by and watch as Bogdanovich flew off to Hollywood, all expenses paid, with a tape recorder and a list of questions culled from Sarris's ideas.

He knew Platt would tell Bogdanovich of his outburst. "And I *wanted* him to know how I felt," Sarris has acknowledged, "but I didn't want to confront Peter directly. What good would it do? I envied his chutzpah. I only wish *I* had more of it . . . Peter's description of himself as a junior initiate is as good a way of describing a punk kid rip-off artist as any. His ridiculous attempt to evoke an atmosphere of camaraderie in the backroom of Dan Talbot's New Yorker Theater is about as far from the truth as any whopper ever dreamed up by Baron Munchausen. Peter was regarded by Gene Archer and me as the Sammy Glick of *auteurists*. In fact, people around New York reacted to Peter's glib brashness in his early days as much as people in Hollywood reacted to it in his later days. You cannot speak to Peter for more than fifteen minutes without feeling the chilling breeze of self-adulation."

In 1963 Bogdanovich acquired the rights to stage *Once in a Lifetime,* the Moss Hart and George S. Kaufman play he had successfully put on at Phoenicia. This time he planned an off-Broadway production for the 1963–64 season; for it he would need $30,000.

After he and Platt raised all the money themselves, they had a violent row one night when Bogdanovich suddenly challenged Platt's assumption that her brother could stay with them for a few days. He woke up the next morning hemorrhaging from a duodenal ulcer and was rushed to a hospital. But the play had to go on, since a nonrefundable deposit had already been paid to the theatre.

Once in a Lifetime opened—and closed—on Platt's birthday, killed stone dead by withering reviews. "One of Mr. Bogdanovich's troubles," a critic wrote, "is that he does not trust his authors. He seems to believe that the audience will not get a comic point unless it is whacked over the head with it."

Bogdanovich had failed to conquer Broadway, or even its lower reaches. Movie director Frank Tashlin, who had met the couple during their Hollywood stay for the Jerry Lewis interview and for whom Platt had translated *Cahiers du cinéma* articles, was in New York at the time and arranged to see them. "Look, Peter," he told him, "you're depressed about *Once in a Lifetime.* So you have to decide what you want to do in life."

Bogdanovich looked at him lugubriously. "I want to make pictures," he blurted out.

"Then what are you doing here?" Tashlin asked. "If that's what you really want, come to the West Coast where they're made! Move to Los Angeles, it's the only way. You have friends there—and I'll help all I can."

Three months later the couple took Tashlin at his word and, in a 1951 convertible they had purchased for $150 from Bogdanovich's *Esquire* earnings, they left New York for California.

CHAPTER 4

Bogdanovich had brought himself to the attention of the movie world both as a knowledgeable reviewer and as an able compiler of retrospectives and monographs. Harold Hayes maintained that "Talkies," Bogdanovich's first article published in *Esquire*, in August 1962, was as good as anything the magazine had ever run on the subject of film.

He continued writing articles for *Esquire* from the little house he and Platt found on Saticoy Street in Los Angeles. Together they survived a couple of lean years in Hollywood before the breaks arrived. (Furniture for their home was provided by the local Salvation Army; "lean" as in writing articles for *TV Guide* to survive.) "We were invited everywhere," Platt recalls, "to John Ford's, Howard Hawks's—we were always eating out, which was important to me because we had only so much money and I didn't have to shop for those nights. Now I can see why people found us so charming. If I met young people now who knew as much about my career as we did then about theirs, it would be overwhelming. We were completely fascinated by the directors; we asked them questions and they told us their stories."

Sal Mineo was the first to offer Bogdanovich a job in Los Angeles—writing a script for William Maxwell's *The Folded Leaf*, although the project fell through when Mineo failed to secure rights to the novel. Platt and Bogdanovich fooled around for a while on a home-movie thriller that Mineo intended to direct and that was to star Bogdanovich and Mineo's live-in singing discovery, Bobby Sherman. But no film ever materialized from this either. "We kept breaking up too much," Bogdanovich explains with a smile.

Before long Mineo was recklessly spouting stories of other pastimes. "It's really fantastic," he enthused after being allowed to attend a Hell's Angels get-together. "They have their own laws, their own code. I saw an initiation. It's pretty rough. They have rituals—for courage. They lash you to see how much you can take. They have a sexual rite—you do it in front of the group."

Although she and Bogdanovich went on to write a script, *Marco and His Brothers*, with Mineo in mind, Platt has always been more guarded in her views of the actor than her ex-husband. "I can't say I ever felt any love for Sal," she admits. "I didn't like him or dislike him. I remember his kindnesses, but he frightened me; I thought he was scary . . . a bit weird. He had two huge paintings in his apartment, about 4′ × 4′, one of which was just a woman's breast with a finger touching the nipple, the other just above the pubic area. And we were both so naive, we had no idea what was going on. We met him for dinner one night, then drove him to a seedy motel on Hollywood Boulevard, the type with rooms over the entrance. We just left him there, he was obviously meeting someone to get laid, but we never even thought about it at the time."

In late 1965, while Bogdanovich and Platt were attending a screening of *Bay of Angels*, a mutual acquaintance introduced them to Roger Corman. He knew of Bogdanovich's work and called him a few days later. "You're a writer. Wouldn't you like to write for pictures?"

"Sure, I'd love to," Bogdanovich replied.

"You see," Corman explained, "I'm looking for something along the lines of *Lawrence of Arabia*, or *Bridge on the River Kwai—but cheap.*"

Bogdanovich swallowed, his mind boggling, before stammering out the reply, "Oh, well. *That* doesn't sound too difficult."

He and Platt were soon at work on a World War II story, *The Criminals*, which remains unfilmed. But Corman called Bogdanovich again early in 1966. "I'm starting a picture called *The Wild Angels*," he explained. "Would you like to work on it?"

"Sure," Bogdanovich replied. "What do you want me to do?"

"Oh, I don't know," said Corman. "Just be around!"

Bogdanovich had to pinch himself to make sure he wasn't dreaming. Instead of the long slog which might have been expected before anything came of *The Criminals,* here he was being propelled straight into the making of a movie—in whatever capacity.

Corman's estimate of the shooting time for *The Wild Angels* was six weeks, and he was prepared to pay Bogdanovich and Platt $125 a week, rising to $150 during shooting. In any case, filming of *The Wild Angels* would develop into an odyssey that stretched out to 22 weeks.

When the script finally arrived, just ten days before the start of shooting, the Bogdanoviches were dismayed. It seemed to them the most facile drivel, containing instructions like "Shoot from horse's point of view, then cut to frog's point of view as the motor cycles go by." Bogdanovich stormed into Corman's office and flung the script down in front of the startled producer. "Roger, this is a Disney picture," he told him.

Corman nodded agreement. "I know, I know. What am I going to do? I don't have the time to rewrite it."

One pregnant pause later, during which time Bogdanovich says he felt the earth move under his feet, he suggested to Corman that he and Platt undertake the rewrite. When Corman gratefully agreed, the couple were on their way and between the two of them proceeded to rewrite three quarters of the material. Their second task was to scout locations for the picture, which took them all over Southern California in a car furnished by Corman.

When George Chakiris quit the lead role in *The Wild Angels,* Peter Fonda was auditioned. He arrived wearing aviator glasses and looking every inch the part. With the glasses off, however, he appeared less suitable; Bogdanovich made a mental note to have him wear shades throughout almost the entire movie.

As shooting rapidly began to fall behind schedule, Corman threw out several sequences and fretted over the remaining scenes. "I can't do all of this," he muttered. "I'll have to get the second unit to do it."

"Roger, there *is* no second unit," Bogdanovich pointed out.

"I know, I *know.*"

Bogdanovich saw his chance: "Listen, I'd love to do it."

With the go-ahead from Corman, Bogdanovich went on to form a second unit, with Platt as both unit production manager and Nancy Sinatra's double, and to shoot backgrounds for the main titles—the sequences of Fonda riding through Los Angeles, the mountain chase, and a scene that was prompted by one of the real Hell's Angels commenting to Corman: "Hey, man, you don't show how we dig our bikes."

"Let's show him *screwing* it" was Bogdanovich's literal suggestion— which was followed. When it came time to add music to the scene, Bogdanovich was asked for advice. He shrugged. "Why don't you put in the sound of a couple of cats screwing?" he joked. Again his suggestion was accepted. And when union problems arose at American International, Bogdanovich helped cut some of the footage, after being shown how to work a Movieola and moving the device into his living room.

The members of Hell's Angels Corman had hired as "technical advisers" felt only contempt for their producer, who to them epitomized the square establishment. Since Bogdanovich was forever at Corman's side, and self-important to boot, they hated him, too. Thus, when Corman, needing more extras, instructed Bogdanovich to join in the final rumble, the outcome was all too predictable: Bogdanovich found himself set upon by the vengeful gang.

In 22 weeks Bogdanovich and Platt received a paid course, courtesy of Corman, in almost every aspect of movie making—scouting locations, scripting, directing, acting, cutting, sound work—as well as fetching laundry and being beaten up. Unfortunately, there was a by-product of his unpopularity even more serious than the fight with the Angels.

The feeling of resentment toward Bogdanovich among the second-unit crew gradually became one of almost tangible hostility. They too saw him as Corman's favorite, and their grudge was twofold: not only were they asked to follow the instructions of this "nobody," but he displayed what to them seemed incredible arrogance. Relations were especially strained with the young, handsome camera assistant from South America.

After the last day of shooting, Bogdanovich and Platt repaired to a restaurant for a quiet celebratory dinner. As they were eating, the cameraman came storming in, stopped at their table and loudly began to demand the keys to the car the couple had used during the shoot. "You'll get the keys when I've finished my dinner," Bogdanovich informed him with a glare. Platt sat there petrified as the Latino stared at her husband, hatred burning in his eyes.

The stifling heat in the crowded restaurant—it was 105 degrees outside—seemed to Platt to intensify as the cameraman began shouting obscenities at Bogdanovich before being grabbed from behind by two waiters and shoved outside. Platt gazed at her husband, still determinedly cutting up his lamb chop.

"Peter," she said, "maybe you should let him have the keys. . . ."

"He'll—get—the—keys—when—I'm—good—and—ready," he spat out, staccato style.

"Look, give *me* the keys. I'll hand them over and that'll be an end to it."

"Fine, go ahead if you want to," Bogdanovich replied, sliding the keys across the table.

Platt left the restaurant, looked around the parking lot and saw the Latino standing with his back to her, savagely kicking the tires of their car. As she approached he turned, and then as she held out her hand with the keys, he drew back his right arm and swung a punch that landed on her jaw. She fell to her knees, skinning them on the gravel, and passed out cold.

Afterwards she heard that Bogdanovich had come charging out and a scuffle had taken place. Although the Palm Springs police suggested that Platt file charges, she declined to do so. In her misery, with a badly swollen jaw and a broken tooth, all she wanted was to put the incident behind her. But, with Bogdanovich showing deep and constant concern, she could not stop crying for several days.

A year later she was out walking her newborn daughter, Antonia, in her stroller. "It was like a movie," Platt recalls. "The stroller went over this newspaper and there was a photo of the camera assistant on the front page. He had stabbed his girlfriend to death with two knives, claiming "he saw his mother inside of her." I remembered him talking about the girl and showing me her picture on the set. I just stood there gripping the stroller and shaking. If only I'd done something *more*, if only I'd sworn out that warrant, that girl might still be *alive*. It was an important event in my life that I'll never forget—I knew, of course, that I'd taken that punch for Peter." The incident was the Bogdanoviches' first close encounter with violence and murder.

Early in 1966 Borislav and Herma, now in serious financial difficulties, left the confines of New York and moved with Anna to the open spaces of Arizona, having discovered they could live there far more cheaply—and in a house, not an apartment. Although at first Borislav grumbled endlessly over the move, he gradually became enchanted by the desert surroundings. Then a wonderful event occurred: Walter Bimson, chairman of the board of Valley Bank, the largest banking chain in Arizona, fell in love with Borislav's work and more important, bought several paintings to hang in his banks. After Herma managed to have a small studio built for him, Borislav began to paint more of the Western subjects Bimson loved: landscapes, buffalo herds, Indian portraits. The move to Arizona soon began to assume the aspects of a miracle.

The Wild Angels having proved to be a considerable hit, Corman called on Bogdanovich again, this time with an offer to direct a picture of his own. There were several conditions attached, however. "Boris Karloff made a picture with me called *The Terror*," Corman explained, "and part of the deal is he still owes me a couple of days. Here's what I want you to do: shoot with Boris for those two days, get about 20 minutes of footage, then take about 20 minutes of Karloff's outtakes from *The Terror*, shoot another 40 minutes with some other actors, put it all together and I'll have a new Karloff picture! Oh, there's just one other little thing I want you to do first. I've just bought a Russian picture called *Storm Clouds of Venus*—unbelievably bad film, but I've got a deal with American-International Pictures to buy it providing I put some girls in it. Just shoot for five days and stick some girls in. Then you can shoot the Karloff picture. It'll all be a one package deal."

Bogdanovich and Platt wrote the script for what became *Gill Women of Venus*, knowing it would take them months to sort this out before they could get to the Boris Karloff project. "We shot a week with Mamie Van Doren and seven other girls in the middle of nowhere above Malibu," Platt recalls. "She had her period and wouldn't go in the water. We were out in the Pacific, her husband was there and he said to her, 'There are sharks in that ocean!' She wouldn't go in there at all. What a mess! Everybody got seasick and the boat cost $300 a day. I realized after that the trip had been unnecessary, we could have shot anywhere. An ocean is an ocean." Work on *Gill Women of Venus* continued until October 1966. Only then could they move on to the Karloff project.

Before they started the script, the couple thought of Karloff as the heavy. Then Bogdanovich had an idea for a joke. "We'll make Karloff an actor, then the footage from *The Terror* will be of one of his performances, and we don't have to incorporate it into our story." The only fairly good sequence he could see in *The Terror* was a flood scene that lasted about 20 minutes. His notion was to cut it down to two minutes and open the picture with it, following which "The End" would appear on the screen. There would then be a cut to the inside of a projection room, where the lights would come on to reveal Karloff seated in the front row next to his producer, Roger Corman. Karloff would turn to Corman and say, "Well, Roger, it's really frightful, isn't it?"

Platt's contribution, the thought that modern-day horror was unmotivated killing, came out of long discussions about why the old type of horror picture was no longer frightening. Platt thought it was because of Vietnam and mass murders. Fritz Lang contributed by telling them how he had come to direct his child-murder classic, *M*. But the idea really took root at a breakfast Bogdanovich had with Harold Hayes, who talked of the apparently mindless killings perpetrated in 1966 by Charles Whitman, a student at the University of Texas, who, after murdering his wife and mother, locked himself in the University's library tower and proceeded to shoot at random 44 people, fourteen of them fatally.

Bogdanovich and Platt took their thoughts to veteran director Sam Fuller for further discussion. "Sam was incredibly influential," Platt recalls. "Peter had the idea of a movie within a movie, then Sam got hold of it and added to our ideas. Originally we thought that the boy who played the sniper and the veteran actor played by Boris should never meet. Sam turned this around and suggested we have the old horror actor *tracking* the psychopath."

Roger Corman took one look at the finished script and told Bogdanovich to go ahead and cast it. He would foot the entire $130,000 bill for the picture. Platt thought of the title, *Targets*.

CHAPTER 5

In Hollywood, Bogdanovich introduced David O. Selznick's son Danny, an art critic friend from his New York days, to many of the famous directors he knew. In return, Selznick put Bogdanovich in touch with Orson Welles, long one of his idols. Years earlier, Bogdanovich had mailed to Welles the monograph he had written, addressing it message-in-a-bottle style to "somewhere in Europe." "I read that," Welles told him over the phone, "and I thought it was the truest material ever written about me."

When the two men met for the first time in the Polo Lounge of the Beverly Hills Hotel the next day, Bogdanovich presented Welles with a copy of the book he had just completed on John Ford. Welles looked at it admiringly. "It's a pity," he declared—and although the voice was booming and filled the breakfast room, the tone was almost plaintive— "that you couldn't do a little book like that on me."

"Hey, I'd love to," Bogdanovich replied, falling right into it. Another odyssey had unwittingly begun.

With Bogdanovich aiming in *Targets* for a contrast between Karloff's world and that of the youthful sniper, Platt came into her own with her set design. Karloff's sequences were all shot against warm background colors of brown, gold and yellow, while the sniper's scenes were in cold shades of green, blue and white, exaggerating the starkness of a typical San Fernando Valley home and emphasizing the environment's sterility. At one point Bogdanovich wanted to shoot the film in Los Angeles during the Christmas season in order to make use of such delights as the plastic angels lining Van Nuys Boulevard and other bizarre street decorations.

Instead, the movie was shot in the spring of 1967, in 23 days, with cinematography in the hands of "Leslie" Kovacs. When Bogdanovich first met the Hungarian, he discovered that his real name was "Laszlo." "So why Leslie?" he asked. "Well, I've only shot a few indie movies before this," Kovacs replied, "nothing that I've cared to use my real name on." When *Targets* was finished, he told Bogdanovich he would like to be known as "Laszlo Kovacs" for the first time. Critic Stanley Kauffmann dropped a howler in maintaining that Bogdanovich had named Kovacs after a character in Jean-Luc Godard's *Breathless,* presumably as some sort of ham-fisted homage or in-joke. Even after Bogdanovich wrote to Kauffmann to advise that Laszlo was alive and well and living under his real name in Pasadena, the critic never ate his words.

Boris Karloff enjoyed the rare opportunity of playing an intelligent role. In one scene he was to recite Somerset Maugham's "Death Speaks," the epigraph of *Appointment in Samarra* (Sam Fuller's idea); when Bogdanovich asked if he wanted it written on boards, Karloff answered that he already knew it. With his wife Edie present on the set he did the whole piece perfectly in one take. When it came to the final line in particular, after the merchant has asked Death why he had made a threatening gesture to his manservant that morning in Bagdad, causing him to flee for his life to Samarra, Bogdanovich asked the actor to think about dying and linger on Death's reply: "That was no threatening gesture, it was only a start of surprise. I was astonished to see him in Bagdad, for I had an appointment with him tonight in Samarra."

The hush of admiration was followed by Bogdanovich yelling, "Cut!"—whereupon the entire crew burst into applause.

Karloff thanked his director profusely after viewing the completed picture. "It meant a lot to me," he said. "I consider it one of the very best I've ever done." It was to be his last. He died just one year later.

Sal Mineo agreed to do a walk-on in the movie as a favor, but unfortunately his scene turned out to be superfluous and wound up on the cutting room floor. "I thought you were my friend," he joked to Bogdanovich. *"Some friend!"* The incident was emblematic of the continuing decline in Mineo's fortunes, which saddened both Bogdanovich and Platt. Gone was Mineo's Bentley, in its place a rented black Cadillac convertible. And when the couple moved to a new house, after the completion of *Targets*, Mineo asked if he could have some of the Salvation Army furniture they no longer needed. Platt was glad they were able to repay his generosity to them, even to this small extent, for they had spent a lot of time driving around with Mineo in his Bentley days and the actor had picked up many dinner checks. She felt a distinct pang as he gratefully loaded their old furniture into his Cadillac and left for his new reduced-rental accommodations. Contrarily, Mineo himself was as bright and breezy as ever and showed no signs at all of self-pity.

Bogdanovich and Platt felt that *Targets* would get a more favorable response if released by a major studio rather than by Corman's regular American International outlet. Corman generously allowed them to try this route—as long as he made his usual profit—and they asked Danny Selznick, who had worked as a runner on the shoot, to help. He screened the movie at his father's home in Tower Grove. With Peter Fonda, Jack Nicholson, Dennis Hopper and James Coburn in attendance, the reaction was disappointingly muted; the only member of the group even to talk to Bogdanovich after the screening was Jack Nicholson. But a bonus for Bogdanovich's crew came when almost to a man they were hired by Nicholson, Hopper, Fonda and producer Bert Schneider—whom Bogdanovich had yet to meet—when that team went on to make *Easy Rider*. And for Laszlo Kovacs, *Targets* brought him his long-sought-after union card.

Bogdanovich had discussed *Targets'* music with Sonny Bono, who found him a handful of incredibly bad rock 'n' roll tapes that he had recorded and rejected but that seemed suitable for sound effects on car radios and the like. Bogdanovich felt it made no difference if the music was good or bad, just as long as it was loud, non-anachronistic and dirt cheap. *Easy Rider* adopted the same idea—only with a classier brand of rock 'n' roll, and a proper score as well. The final irony came when Bogdanovich used old records again in *The Last Picture Show* and one critic accused him of copying the technique from *Easy Rider*.

Still looking for a distributor after the Selznick and other let downs,

Bogdanovich arranged a showing of *Targets* for *Variety* and *The Hollywood Reporter*. "Write about it if you like the movie," he suggested. Both journals did and ended their favorable reviews: "No distributor." Robert Evans at Paramount was a great admirer of the movie (Carol Saroceno, a friend of the Bogdanoviches—and Evans's secretary—had urged him to see it), but he had been unable to arouse any enthusiasm for it on his board. Now he sent the trade notices off to Charles Bludhorn at Gulf and Western, the studio's parent company. Evans was promptly authorized to buy *Targets* for $150,000, which meant a profit for Roger Corman of $20,000.

The film was finally released in August 1968, its subject matter having been deemed particularly sensitive following the assassinations earlier that year of Martin Luther King and Robert F. Kennedy. Even when it did open, it was only in a narrow release, although in Harold Hayes's view this had the effect of focusing serious critical attention on it. In the way that these things work, *Targets* was no longer just a movie; it became a rallying cry for the cause of gun control.

The first time Bogdanovich's parents saw their son's fledgling effort, he could tell they both liked it, although their reactions were typically understated. "It was *very* good," Herma told him with a warm smile and a hug. Borislav said even less, but to this day Bogdanovich remembers his reaction. "He just looked at me in a certain way coming out of the theater in Phoenix where we'd arranged a screening for them. He nodded, but in a way that spoke volumes. He was saying that he profoundly understood what the movie was about, that it was a tragic film, that he understood that *I* understood, in fact. Everything was in that look he gave me—praise, pride, pleasure. I didn't really need more." Was the pride Bogdanovich had always taken in his father being generously returned, or is Bogdanovich idealizing Borislav's reaction?

Variety described *Targets* as a good programmer—given its fairly modest budget: "Peter Bogdanovich, former writer about films turned screen writer-producer-director, has made a film about much suspense and implicit violence. . . . Bogdanovich can raise moments of shock, terror, suspense and fear. Feats are all the more remarkable in the face of typical low-budget shortcomings." The movie was well received in Europe and was praised by the likes of Penelope Houston in *Sight and Sound*, although she was quite blunt about what she perceived to be the source of Bogdanovich's inspiration: "Bogdanovich is most powerfully

Hitchcockian in the way he introduces his first killings," she noted. "Hitchcock spelled out the method and Bogdanovich has learned the lesson."

Another old friend of Bogdanovich's from New York, Henry Jaglom, encouraged producer Bert Schneider, one of the few *Easy Rider* participants who hadn't already done so, to see *Targets*. Schneider did, was impressed and called Bogdanovich: "Any time you want to do something," he told him, "let me know."

Supported by small grants from both the California Arts Commission and the American Film Institute, Bogdanovich then turned out a documentary on John Ford. Originally, the AFI had wanted King Vidor to be the subject, but Platt had suggested John Ford instead, since he was so much more interesting to talk to. After Bogdanovich agreed to do the film, Ford proceeded to cause problems of his own, however: "Ford was *impossible,*" he recalls with a chuckle, "he was everything you've ever heard and more. He was scary, terrifying and mean, but could be very funny. He had dark glasses and a patch over one eye and pretended to be deafer than he was, so he'd make you repeat everything ten times till you wished you'd never asked the question in the first place. He liked me though, and I really liked him a lot, together with his daughter and his wife, Mary. She talked a lot like him and said to Polly one day, 'If you want to stay in the movie business never believe anything you hear, unless you see it with your own eyes.' Pretty good advice, I'd say." Ford laconically greeted Bogdanovich's documentary as "a good job on a dull subject."

The dry spell that followed *Targets*, which consisted mainly of turning out unproduced scripts, was at last broken by a call from David Picker at United Artists. Would Bogdanovich care to go to Italy to direct a "Mexican Revolution western" with James Coburn and Rod Steiger that was being produced by Sergio Leone? Bogdanovich knew the westerns Leone had directed and was unimpressed; he felt that Leone was far from being in the tradition of the Hollywood masters whose triumphs Bogdanovich had chronicled. Nonetheless, he agreed to do the film and he and Platt researched the period and developed some ideas they felt could be interesting. Bogdanovich left for Italy a month before Platt, to work with Leone's writer and co-producer, Luciano Vincenzani. When Platt arrived with Antonia, the couple touched base again with Orson Welles while the maestro was shooting part of his independent production *The Other Side of the Wind*, near Rome. They shared some wonderful times with Welles and his long-time friend Oja Palinkas.

Bogdanovich quickly discovered that Leone's notion of taking a producer's back seat was limited. What he really wanted was a surrogate director, someone to press the buttons for him. Each script conference would begin with a rush of Leone's fractured English and much fractured acting, all of it accompanied by dramatic gestures. Bogdanovich's initial efforts to react with enthusiasm soon turned into undisguised exasperation. "Now you will cut here. *Beeg* closeups, two beeg eyes," Leone, who claimed not to speak any English, would suggest through an Italian interpreter.

"I don't like those kinds of closeups," Bogdanovich would protest.

"You don't *like* close-ups?"

"No, I don't."

"What you like, then?"

"Long shots."

Vincenzani was left to translate much of their dialogue. "You're funny," he told Bogdanovich at one point. "Here's a guy who's made his whole career with close-ups—and you tell him you don't like close-ups!"

Leone soon proudly revealed the title of the picture they were about to make. "Ees called *Duck, You Suckers!* That ees something you say in America, no?"

"No," Bogdanovich replied, deadpan, "that is *not* something we say in America, Sergio."

Bogdanovich estimates he quit the project about an hour before he would have been fired anyway and he now regards the whole Italian venture as simply an amusing experience. Platt remembers *Duck, You Suckers!* as one of the most bizarre episodes in their lives. "I arrived in Rome a few weeks after Peter. Sergio was just crazy, he fell asleep in meetings all the time. I wanted Peter to tell David Picker the whole thing was ridiculous. We got something wonderful from the experience, though—I got pregnant with our second daughter, Alexandra Welles, named after Orson, of course. I think the reason she's so beautiful is she was conceived in Italy!"

With Antonia's birth in November 1967—they named her after Herma and Borislav's first son—the Bogdanoviches' marriage had begun to run into difficulties. "Neither of us had any understanding of what it meant to have a child," Platt maintains. "A woman is overwhelmed. I was, Peter wasn't. I became interested only in the child, and that took me out of the running as Peter's pal and companion. He simply couldn't understand why our life didn't go on the way it had before. We couldn't afford babysitters; we used to leave her with Verna Fields, our friend who'd cut *Targets*. I just couldn't handle it, I was always nervous about the child and what she was doing, I couldn't bear to leave her with a stranger. I was taken by surprise how much I loved my baby, I didn't realize it was nature at work, I'd never stopped to think of it before. I realize now I should have taken her with us, but she was a fussy little baby who had colic. All of a sudden I worried about doctors' bills and such.

"Before Antonia, Peter and I used to stay in the house together. We'd sleep late, then I'd do housework in the morning, we'd collaborate in the afternoon and go to the movies at night. After Antonia was born, collaboration became difficult. Our lives changed completely.

"For one thing, I couldn't concentrate when the baby was awake. My resentment with Peter built when he didn't change or adjust. Of course, I expected him to understand everything without my telling him. He insisted on sleeping late and not being disturbed. I realize I should have got Peter up to help me with the child, but I took my lesson from his mother, whom I thought of as a successful wife and mother. But I hated him for it. The only person who saw it happening was George Cukor, who had taken an interest in me long before the baby. He'd offered me a job doing research for a film once. Peter, Antonia and I had lunch in his house and I didn't realize he was watching us during the meal. Afterwards he collared me and said, 'Don't let that child run your life.' It was prophetic, because I did just that. Not smart. I was always tortured by my need to be with Antonia and later, Sashy, *and* my desire to work. My dual passions were children and movies. Every woman suffers from that who has a career. I eventually resented my children after Peter and I split up. I loved them, but I wanted to be free."

Early in 1969 Bogdanovich and Platt attended the rehearsals of a play Sal Mineo was directing, John Herbert's *Fortune and Men's Eyes,* about homosexuality in prison. The play had already been staged in New York, where it had some impact. Long interested in prisoners' rehabilitation, Mineo adapted the play and cast teenagers in roles written for 30-year olds. His actors included young hopefuls like Don Johnson, many years before *Miami Vice* came his way, and Michael Greer. "Welcome to our prison," he told them at the first rehearsal. "I've been in prison myself, as success came too early for me, so I know what it's like." Mineo planned to include considerable nudity and simulated sex in his staging of the play.

Like Bogdanovich before him, Mineo hoped that directing in the theatre might prove a gateway to directing movies. At the same time he was fully aware that directing the play amounted to an admission of his own sexuality. "Once I did *Fortune and Men's Eyes,*" he later told interviewer Boze Hadleigh, "I probably lost half my future chances. But that'll change, it's already changing. I think it's only going to change in a big way in the future, if gay actors and stars and directors come out. That'll show the guys in charge that we're here and we're gonna stick around and not keep playing bury-the-queer-in-the-fairytale roles."

Mineo never lost his talent to amuse Bogdanovich; one minute he'd be yelling in exasperation at his actors, the next he'd turn his back on them and wink broadly at his friend. "I've got something for you," he told Platt one day over coffee, "a book that would make a good movie." The paperback novel he handed her was Larry McMurtry's *The Last Picture Show.*

Bogdanovich was disappointed to discover that the title of the book, which had led him to expect something like a treatise on the history of film, merely alluded to the decline of a small Texas town in the fifties. "What's Sal thinking about?" he asked Platt. "This thing's all about Texans. I don't know anything about these people."

After they both finished the novel there was a rapid change of mind, although initially neither had any idea of how to turn it into a movie. The characters were beautifully drawn, an elegiac air hovered over the proceedings, but nothing much seemed to happen in terms of narrative progression. Was the whole thing too subtle to be filmed, a series of nuances that the camera might find difficult to capture? When they finally decided to submit the project to Bert Schneider for his opinion, it took him just two days to get back to them. "I think it's stunning," he enthused. "Let's make it." It turned out that aspiring producer Steven Friedman had an option on the McMurtry book that he had picked up for $35,000, and that succeeded in earning him coproducer credit on the picture.

All the techniques and ploys the couple had pressed into service in the past on such relative "training exercises" as *The Wild Angels, Gill Women of Venus* and even *Targets* would pale into insignificance alongside what they were to do on *The Last Picture Show*—on both a professional and a personal level.

CHAPTER 6

Eight months of preproduction followed the signing of *The Last Picture Show* deal in January 1970. While Larry McMurtry was working on the script with Bogdanovich and Platt, the threesome drove around Texas scouting locations. In the end they settled on the writer's home town of Archer City, which he had chosen to call Thalia in his book. Bogdanovich was against the name for two reasons: Thalia had already been the setting for Paul Newman's *Hud*, adapted from McMurtry's first novel, *Horseman, Pass By*, and it reminded him, he claimed, of the Thalia art house cinema in New York, where he'd been obliged to sit through what he termed "all those boring foreign movies." He was presumably referring here to a time before Dan Talbot's influence enabled him to sort out the wheat from the chaff. Platt finds this particular statement of her ex-husband's hard to credit: "He *loved* the Thalia," she insists. "So did I." In the end the name of the town was changed to Anarene, after a town in the area which had disappeared in the interest of redevelopment.

Columbia's initial reaction to the suggestion—initiated by Orson Welles, championed by Larry McMurtry and eagerly taken up by Bogdanovich and Platt—that the movie be shot in black and white was that the studio would be unable to sell it. Platt's argument to producer Bert Schneider was that hundreds of films were made in color every year. Was that any guarantee of success? When Schneider, having listened, coaxed Columbia to poll exhibitors, the results surprised the studio: "If it's a good movie, we'll book it regardless. People will come to see it anyway." So the vast majority felt, and so black and white it was.

Bogdanovich and Platt set to work on the fateful casting. Jeff Bridges came along expressing interest in the role of Sonny. "He's not Sonny; he's Duane," Bogdanovich thought as he listened to Bridges' account of how the part should be played. His feeling was that while Duane was basically an unpleasant young man, he should be played as attractively as possible, since he was as much a victim as any of the other characters.

The buzz on Timothy Bottoms, who had just completed Dalton Trumbo's *Johnny Got His Gun,* was considerable. Bogdanovich asked to see him and found that his extraordinary eyes looked as if they carried the sorrow of the ages inside them. Perfect for Sonny, he felt.

Veteran cowboy star Tex Ritter was originally considered for the role of Sam the Lion. Bogdanovich thought Ritter a delightful man, but didn't think he was right for the role. (When Ritter died, his actor son John was pleased to receive a letter of condolence from Bogdanovich, and the two men kept up a correspondence afterward, with Bogdanovich vowing to cast John Ritter himself as soon as the right part was available.) Three months of coaxing were required to persuade Ben Johnson to play Sam the Lion. The actor, who simply didn't want to do it, was eventually persuaded by John Ford's intervention and because he was fond of Bogdanovich and Platt since their meeting on *Cheyenne Autumn.*

Ellen Burstyn auditioned for the parts of Sam the Lion's waitress, Jacy's mother and Coach Popper's wife. As far as Bogdanovich was concerned, she read them all equally well. "You cast it," he says he told her. "Call me tomorrow and tell me which part you've decided on." Not according to Platt. She maintains the decision to cast Ellen as the mother came after seeing Cloris Leachman, who had been recommended by Bob Rafelson. She was considered perfect for the coach's wife, as was Eileen Brennan for the waitress. Clu Culager was cast as Abilene, and Randy Quaid, discovered (by a casting scout) in Houston doing a nightclub comedy routine, was signed to play Lester.

While these had been fairly straightforward casting decisions, with no ramifications outside the confines of the movie, Bogdanovich's choice

for the part of Jacy, the high school tease, would change his life forever—and Platt's as well.

Bogdanovich first glimpsed Cybill Shepherd while shopping at a
supermarket with his wife. There she was, as they stood at the checkout
in the spring of 1970, on the cover of *Glamour* magazine. Although they
were immediately struck by the cornsilk hair, peaches and cream com-
plexion and aquamarine eyes, it was the teasing combination of sensu-
ousness and cool, clean, All-American beauty that captivated them.
"That's Jacy!" they agreed. Bogdanovich pictured her as a butterfly
flitting from flower to flower and wilting them all, ideal for the role of
the teen-queen. This scenario would spill off screen once shooting was
underway, with Bogdanovich among the first to succumb.

A cousin of Cybill's back in her hometown of Memphis, Tennessee,
had entered the then sixteen-year old in the Miss Teenage Memphis
contest, with a first prize of a trip to New York and a chance to enter
the televised Miss Teenage America competition. Winning in Memphis
but failing to make the finals in New York, Cybill returned home in a
flood of tears, fuming, "I lost to a girl who danced the *hula!*" Two years
later, it was back to New York, determined this time to emerge trium-
phant in the Model of the Year contest. This Cybill did, with the
sponsors of the competition guaranteeing to make up the difference
between the $25,000 prize and whatever she earned during her first
modeling year in the Big Apple. It didn't cost them a cent. Cybill had
turned her back on the way-down-south code of pleasing men by being
hospitable, modest, soft and submissive. It was goodbye forever to the
three hours spent getting ready for a date, lakeside holiday barbecues,
cream sauce poured over biscuits, ham smothered in red-eye gravy and
fried okra with greens.

Named after her grandfather and father—Cy-Bill, she had always
been a rebel. "That child—all she likes to do is read and ride horses,"
one relative chided. Her unblemished good looks were marred only
slightly when, at age six, she ran straight into a barbed wire fence while
chasing a male cousin. After several stitches and a little plastic surgery,
she was left with only a minute scar on her lip as a reminder of the
incident. "Cybill and I had our ups and downs growing up," her
four-years-older sister, Terry, admits. "She was a tomboy and loved

sports and books. She had no interest in playing with dolls or helping to make chicken dumplings."

When the family lived in New Orleans in 1958, her father introduced her to Dixieland music. "When other kids were listening to Elvis," Cybill recalls, "I was listening to Frank Sinatra and the big bands like Stan Kenton and Woody Herman. I guess I've always been something of a displaced person."

Back in Memphis, at fifteen she was discovered lowering herself out of her bedroom window to meet her long-haired rock-guitarist boyfriend. Bill Shepherd's response was to nail her window shut. Although she had skipped the Elvis-worship stage that had gripped her friends, a real-life encounter with "The King" would bring about an instant conversion. It began with an invitation to join Presley and his gang one night in Memphis's Crosstown cinema, which the singer often rented in the late evenings to run his favorite movies. "There were about 30 people watching the film," Shepherd recalls, "but people sort of got up and drifted away, and suddenly there he was in the aisle. Then he was sitting next to me, all dressed in white. It was *mythic*, he looked *great*. And he *smelled* great—he really did."

A family dinner at Graceland of chicken-fried steak preceded a trip Cybill made to Las Vegas to follow Presley. "I really liked him. I thought he was very warm. And one of the most beautiful men I've ever seen." As Cybill began to spend more time with the singer, however, his drug dependency quickly came between them. The "Well, it's time to go to sleep now, here's-your-pills lifestyle" was not for her.

Shepherd's move to New York and the $500 a day she eventually earned as a top model freed her financially from her parents—and freed them as well, for they divorced after her departure. Her modeling contract forced her to give up plans she had made to study art in Florence. Instead, she juggled her engagements so she could attend English classes three days a week at New York University.

"Have *ah* got a panty hose for *yew!*" Shepherd purred on her first television appearance, her southern accent very much to the fore. "It's sheer to *here*. The panty is just a little bitty thing, which is why Burlington call it Brief Top." Ads for Coca Cola, Breck, MacLeans, Ultra-Brite and Cover Girl followed in quick succession. Over a two-year period she appeared on the cover of *Glamour* fifteen times, along with *Life*, *Seventeen*, *Vogue*, *Harper's Bazaar* and *Redbook*. Her earnings in 1970 amounted to over $81,000.

The latter part of Shepherd's New York sojourn found her living on Barrow Street in Greenwich Village, following her meeting with an older man, a Manhattan restaurateur, who introduced her to music, theater, abstract expressionism and European literary figures. "I never learned how to make friends," she confided on *The Last Picture Show* set, "but I sure learned early how to fill needs."

Shepherd had received other film offers, all of which she had turned down, before Bogdanovich and *The Last Picture Show* came along. One screen test she had made, for Roger Vadim, had required her to appear nude, an experience she had vowed she would never repeat. Nevertheless, because her agent advised her to consider Bogdanovich's offer despite the single nude scene demanded, she agreed to meet the Bogdanoviches in New York—first Platt, who liked her and passed her along to the director.

At that point in her career, Shepherd claims to have been totally indifferent to anyone in movies. "Every model I knew had taken acting lessons, so I didn't want to do it. . . . And I'd met a number of producers and not been impressed. I was very nervous, though, when I first met Peter. He asked me what I was reading, and I think I said something like *War and Peace* by Dostoievsky, or *Crime and Punishment* by Tolstoy, that sort of thing. He guessed I was nervous."

Already cast, Shepherd tried to call Bogdanovich before leaving for California for further consultations before the movie began shooting. "I've changed my mind," she intended to tell him, "I just can't do the nude scene." If that meant her losing the part, so be it, she had decided. When she failed to get through to him, she caught the plane anyway but made her point when they met in Los Angeles. He finally managed to convince her that the scene would be done with taste and on a closed set.

Cybill describes the transition from commercials to moviemaking as like living in a hall of mirrors. "But I trusted Peter. I believed instinctively that what he told me was right and would work. It was funny, the whole crew seemed to feel the same, although we had only *Targets* to base it on. We just knew that he was confident, that he was right."

"Texans really thought I'd captured their state," Bogdanovich recalls, laughing at the memory. "It was shot in Texas, the writer was from Texas, and almost all the actors, except the leads, were from Texas. Ben Johnson was from Oklahoma, which was close. The cameraman, Bob Surtees, was a little cantankerous on the movie, but he was over 60 at the time and I was a kid. Also, he didn't approve of some of the sex in the picture, he thought it was a bit much. The dogs screwing on the front lawn put him off quite a bit. 'We'd never have shot this stuff over at Metro!' he'd say. Actually, we got in a lot of trouble for that shot. You don't see much of it in the picture because I took most of it out. Nice Texan people were driving by and watching us filming these two dogs, under a lot of lights. 'What the hell's going on?' they would ask. 'This picture company's going too far!' "

Only a few weeks into shooting, Bogdanovich came across an amusement park nametag Cybill had tucked into the side of her dressing room mirror. After "My name is" she had filled in "Cybill Shepherd." Then after "I belong to" she had stenciled "no one." "Not for much longer," Bogdanovich silently vowed.

Platt was the first to see that her husband was attracted to Shepherd. "I'm miserable and deliriously happy at the same time," she confided to someone on the set. "My baby girls are with Peter's parents in Phoenix, and I miss them to the point of pain. Part of the agony is that Peter's no longer my friend or lover or companion. Peter is making a *movie*. He has a terrific nostalgia for his teenage years in the fifties—Holden Caulfield ice-skating at Rockefeller Plaza with wholesome young girls in knee-socks—and somehow he's managed to transfer these feelings about his own adolescence to the totally different experience of the kids on the film. Have you noticed? He's very tender with the young actors. So I end up 'doing' Cybill, her overall appearance as Jacy, to lock into Peter's longing fantasies. In reality, I've created a rival for myself, I guess. Well, anything for art, huh?"

Platt, the designer of the film, was by Bogdanovich's side and gritting her teeth as he held forth to a visiting reporter on the aptness of Cybill's casting. "There are certain actresses who have the quality of threat about them," he declared. "That's why I chose her. Ava Gardner had it, Lana Turner had it and Cybill has it. It's in their eyes and you can't manufacture it."

Even though she knew that Bogdanovich had always wanted "a girl like Cybill," Platt did not feel threatened by the prospect but, rather, strangely sure of herself. "Maybe subconsciously I wanted to be rid of the trapped feeling I had," she rationalizes, "for Peter had become already more and more controlling."

Despite Shepherd's recollection of the confidence the cast and crew had in Bogdanovich, he was again hugely unpopular as an individual. Policies like keeping the technicians segregated in the lunch room and not allowing them even to speak to the cast aggravated the situation. "There was a reason for that," Bogdanovich defends himself. "I thought the action scenes in *Targets* were good, but not the acting—outside of Boris. So in this picture, which wasn't about action, I knew it would stand or fall on the acting performances. So yes, I was very solicitous and protective of the actors. I fired one still-man for talking to Cybill. These were all young actors, they'd never made a picture and I thought they could easily be thrown. The one time Steve Friedman came on the set, he ended up talking to Cybill, telling her she should be more enthusiastic in the role. I called Bert Schneider that night and said if Steve wasn't out of Texas by the morning, I'd kill him. I never saw him again until the Oscars; he was sitting in a green tuxedo in the front row. I thought if we won Best Picture and he went up to collect it, I'd be sick."

Bogdanovich was a tireless task master, insisting on the most complex shots and persevering until he got them exactly right. In one night scene Shepherd had to park her Ford convertible near the dance hall before being greeted by Randy Quaid. After they talked for a while, Jeff Bridges and Timothy Bottoms had to drive into the parking lot in front of them in their Dodge pick-up. Bottoms then had to leave the truck and head for a side entrance of the dance hall, while Bridges was to move forward and embrace Shepherd—just before a pan to Clu Culager as he escorted his date through the front door of the dance hall. All this was to be done without a cut, and against a backdrop of dozens of extras parking their cars, walking toward the dance hall and laughing, talking and arguing. "All that in one fluid take!" a dolly operator groaned. "Hell, Peter, it's not only difficult, it's impossible."

Shepherd ruined the first take when she missed her mark as she parked her car. She stammered out an apology. Eight takes later, when Jeff Bridges accidentally rammed his pick-up into the dance hall entrance, Bogdanovich shook his head: "Oh, well, back to the drawing board," he was heard to murmur philosophically.

"We're as out of luck tonight as a barber in Berkeley," a key grip offered, while an assistant assured a blue-with-cold Platt, "Ain't a horse that can't be rode and a cowboy that can't be throwed." The shot was eventually perfected on the twelfth take. "It wasn't the demands Peter made that got everybody's back up," one crew member confided. "It was the *way* he made them. Sure, he worked as hard as any of us, he worked his buns off, but did he have to be so obnoxious at the same time? He acted like the school geek out to revenge himself on the crew, who might have been the bullies back then. When he and Shepherd paired up we all thought 'Wow! School Geek Gets Girl!' "

Today Shepherd can pinpoint the moment she was won over by the movies—and by Bogdanovich. "Up until *The Last Picture Show* I didn't really know if I wanted to act. Then one day in Archer City, a real grey day with the north wind blowing and the arc lights switched on, I was sitting across the street from where they were shooting an exterior. I watched the crew for a while, then Peter walked across the street, with his hair blowing in the wind, and I just fell in love completely with the movies. I thought it was such fun *I* should be paying *them* to do this.

"I fell passionately in love with Peter three-quarters of the way through shooting. We just had enormous attraction for each other, a chemical attraction. It may surprise you, but Peter made me feel truly beautiful for the first time. And he was the first person other than my oldest, closest friend—Jane Howard, a psychologist—who talked to me as an intellectual or artist, or both. As an *equal*. That was very important to me coming from the South and looking the way I do. I'd spent a lifetime just watching people watch me talk. Peter's approval was the validation I needed. I was really insecure, particularly being considered a beautiful woman, particularly with blonde hair, the whole sort of dumb blonde syndrome."

When Bogdanovich and Shepherd consummated their affair one sultry Friday evening in a Wichita Falls hotel room, there was a certain innocence about it, even if the fall-out was hurtful. "It was inevitable," Shepherd maintains. "It had nothing to do with plotting, or with any foresight on the part of either one of us. It was a profound passion for both of us, and there was simply no choice. We tried to keep it from happening, but there was no question I should be with him. It was a mess, a real bad situation for everybody."

To begin with, Bogdanovich wasn't sure if he was falling in love with Shepherd or with Jacy. "It was the way she said things and flirted reflexively, just like Jacy, that always amused the hell out of me. At the same time I found it incredibly attractive. I'd never sowed my wild oats as a youth, never fooled around, so falling for someone like Cybill was unusual for me. It wasn't premeditated—Cybill was just *overwhelming.*"

When Bogdanovich got back to the Archer City hotel the next morning, Platt knew he had been with Shepherd and moved out of their suite into a room of her own. Only hours later Herma phoned with the shattering news that Borislav had suffered a stroke. Distraught, Bogdanovich flew to Arizona, where he found his father in a deep coma. A few days later, just before Thanksgiving, he died.

With this, following the birth of her second daughter just three months earlier, Platt felt unable to cope emotionally with events. She could not then and still cannot acknowledge the "grand passion" that gripped her husband and his leading lady. "Each of them had designs on the other," she maintains. "I certainly wouldn't lie about the marriage being in trouble, but I thought Peter and I shared something that no one could take away. 'Do you think she'd give you a second look if you weren't a director?' I asked him once. *I* had given him a second look and had complete faith in him. What he did devastated me. 'Peter, it's a *bad script,*' I warned him when he first began to fall for Cybill. He used to say he felt old and she made him feel young, and he'd never been with a girl like that. I understood his desire—I wanted it for him, but I didn't want the consequences, of course. And I couldn't imagine how horrible the future would be.

"You want to know the truth? I really felt when he started his affair with Cybill that half of it was to get her to take her clothes off for that nude sequence! She knew it was there when she took the part, but then she started giving him such a hard time. She blamed it on her boyfriend back in New York, said he didn't want her to do the scene. When Peter's father died, I knew that was the end of my marriage because Borislav, who had thanked me for having his grandchildren, would have told Peter, 'Go ahead, have your affair with this girl, but Polly is your *wife*, these are your *children*. They're *more important.*' He would have shown Peter how to be a good man, I thought."

The affair gradually became known to the cast and crew, with Jeff Bridges among the first to be told. "He'd liked Cybill as well and something had been brewing there," says Bogdanovich. "When Cybill and I got together, he handled it very well. He was very chic about it."

When it was time for the long-anticipated nude sequence to be shot, Bogdanovich and the camera operator were the only two present on the set. If he was reminded of his own reluctance to bare his all in *Hallelujah the Hills* as a boy of eighteen, he pressed ahead anyway.

Even after the scene was completed and the film released, Shepherd never reconciled herself to the experience. "In Memphis," she declared, "they think of women as children, but treat them well. In Hollywood, they think of women as children, but treat them badly. You see nude men on the screen, but you only see their rear ends. What does it do to an actress to take her clothes off and stand in front of a camera? It's degrading. It's not the moral question but a question of power. To take part of your power away, they make you nude."

With shooting finished, Shepherd returned home to Memphis for the Christmas break, while Bogdanovich and Platt in Phoenix tried to cope with their future, with his widowed mother, with Anna and their daughters. Although they managed to put up a united front for Herma's benefit, it was a sad visit. Back in Los Angeles in January, the facade quickly crumbled. Bogdanovich was either on the phone to Shepherd in New York, where she had resumed her modeling career, or he was busy cutting his movie over at BBS Productions until the early hours of the morning.

Shepherd ended the affair she had been having before she met Bogdanovich and moved into her own $400-a-month apartment in a luxury high-rise in Greenwich Village. It was late in January 1971, after Shepherd had flown to Los Angeles to spend a weekend in a hotel with Bogdanovich, that Platt decided she could no longer tolerate the situation. "I was alone with the kids at midnight and I called him—I knew where he was—and told him to come and get his things and leave. He stood in the doorway when he arrived and his eyes were full of grief. 'Just remember,' he told me, '*You* did this to us!' "

CHAPTER 7

Anna Bogdanovich had many interests as a child—mainly centering around people, music and dance—and if put to it, she says she regards composing as her strongest suit and voices raised in song as her greatest delight. Music and sociology eventually became the two passions in her life, her studying for a degree in psychology being purely at her mother's insistence. Herma had seen how cruelly the world of art had dealt with Borislav and was determined that Anna would not suffer the same fate.

Anna loved Platt, who first came into her life when Anna was eight years old. Platt was the sister she never had, and Anna was unable to fathom the couple's breakup. They had been a match to look up to and to emulate, a fun-loving pair who loved animals and plants. Shepherd stood little chance of replacing Platt in Anna's affections. First, she was resented as the cause of the marital split. Then she was given the blame for the detour Anna saw her brother's life taking.

Bogdanovich now treated interviews as confessional opportunities, answering accusations of arrogance with disarming ease. When asked what he'd learned by making *The Last Picture Show*, he replied, "I found I could do it! I'd been acting like I could, but I didn't know if I really could. You live in fear that you can't do it, and that it's not going to be any good. And it never really is any good for me until I see it all put together. Was there a moment of doubt, ever? Several thousand. Right up until the two weeks of prefilming rehearsals, there were times when I wondered if I should make the picture at all. I thought it was going to be boring and dreary. I didn't really know I could make that kind of picture. I wasn't sure I could work with actors or get the kind of performances I wanted. So now, what does it come to? I'm a director. It consumes my life. Directing is everything. Making movies is everything."

Sal Mineo made his stage directing debut with *Fortune and Men's Eyes,* which opened to considerable acclaim in New York and Los Angeles in the 1969–70 season. Exuberant with success, he revealed at that time an almost inevitable element of self-delusion that could well have served later as his epitaph. "They could do one thing," he said of his contemporaries, "and when it went out, they were lost. I was able to change. I learned that from James Dean." Serving to illustrate Mineo's need to dwell on past glories and associations was a full-page photograph of Dean in the *Fortune and Men's Eyes* program and a painfully sincere dedication: "Jimmy—in memory of your friendship and inspiration, I dedicate this production to you. Sal."

Mineo harbored the not unreasonable expectation that he would be entrusted with MGM's movie version of *Fortune and Men's Eyes.* He was crushed when he heard that the assignment had gone elsewhere.

In 1971 Mineo attended a screening of *The Last Picture Show* for Columbia executives in the company's New York headquarters on Fifth Avenue. If Bogdanovich's film career was about to explode, Mineo's remained moribund. He had appeared in only two movies in the past six years, both of them potboilers, and after *Fortune* proved no more than a flicker of life, he was reduced to acting behind a monkey mask in his latest film, *Escape from the Planet of the Apes.* When Boze Hadleigh asked him if his bisexuality had held him back, he demurred: "I doubt it. Everybody's got those rumors following them around, whether they're true or not. Everyone's supposed to be bi, starting way back with Gary Cooper and on through Brando and Clift and Newman—you want me to stop? Besides—what's wrong with being bi?"

Sitting next to Bogdanovich, who was displaying all the symptoms of imminent nervous collapse, Mineo squeezed his hand at several points during the preview. "It's playing great," he assured him. "Is Sal just saying that to please me?" Bogdanovich agonized.

In fact, the subsequent industry buzz proved so favorable that his next project was lined up well before *The Last Picture Show* was released. In an effort to impress him, his new agent, Sue Mengers, called Bogdanovich: "There's a picture over at Warners that Barbra Streisand's doing called *A Glimpse of Tiger*, but the studio's thrown out all the footage and the director and everything else. I think you should do it. But first John Calley and Barbra have to see *Picture Show.*"

Mengers had another message. Steve McQueen wanted to see *The Last Picture Show* as well to decide whether Bogdanovich was a suitable director for McQueen's next opus, *The Getaway*. Arriving for the screening, McQueen barged into the projection room with his entourage. Bogdanovich walked forward, his arm outstretched. "Hello, Mr. McQueen," he began, "I'm—"

McQueen stared at him. "Could you wait outside, kid? We've got to see this picture."

Bogdanovich returned to his office; two hours later McQueen walked in, beaming. "You're a picturemaker, man," he told him. "I'm just an actor, but you're a picturemaker. You only made one mistake, kid."

"What's that?" Bogdanovich asked.

"You cut away from that nude swimming scene too soon. I wanted to see more of that!"

Fortified by McQueen's interest, Sue Mengers called John Calley at Warners. "Bogdanovich is doing the next McQueen picture," she blithely informed him. "I know you want to see *Picture Show*, John, but the thing of it is, we can hardly let the head of Warners see it before Columbia's boss. I've got Bert Schneider to agree to let you watch three or four reels, then you have to get out. Barbra, of course, can see it all."

For Calley a few reels were enough. "It's wonderful," he told Bogdanovich. "I couldn't stand that I had to leave, and Barbra's still sitting there crying." Sure enough, Streisand's eyes were wet when she emerged, and she was very complimentary. She and Bogdanovich talked for almost an hour outside the screening room, then walked downstairs to her waiting limousine and talked for another hour. "I read *A Glimpse of Tiger*," Bogdanovich told her. "It can't make up its mind if it's a drama or a comedy. I'd rather do a comedy with you."

"Why can't we do something like *Last Picture Show?*"

"Well, we can sometime, but right now I want to do a comedy, a farce. This time I want you to be yourself, not someone hiding behind some brassy part. Just be your wacky self." Bogdanovich's impression was that Streisand was insecure about almost everything except singing; she believed that to be a "serious actor" meant really *acting* with a capital "A." He saw her as someone desperately wanting to be won over and reassured. "I want you just to breeze through our movie," he told his new star.

If Streisand failed to get her own way on the drama-comedy question, she had already made up her mind that her costar would be her current boyfriend, Ryan O'Neal. Since, like Bogdanovich, they were both represented by the ubiquitous Mengers, this presented no problem and the general agreement on O'Neal helped considerably to appease Streisand—until she heard Bogdanovich's proposed title. *"What's Up, Doc?* What kind of *title* is that?" she grumbled. "Are we making a *cartoon* or something?" On the verge of 30, and mindful of the fact that her father had died at 35, Streisand was suffering from heightened mortality awareness.

"Perhaps I'll die young like my father," she lamented. "And what will I leave behind? Some record albums, a few lightweight films? That's not enough. I'd like to do some important work."

The McQueen project fell apart when the star refused to accept Bogdanovich's casting suggestion of Cybill Shepherd for the role Ali McGraw went on to play in *The Getaway.* McQueen collared Bogdanovich at a party years later. "If we ever again discuss doing a picture together, it'll be different," he told the director. "You'll have to listen to me more."

"If we ever do that," Bogdanovich coolly replied, "we'll do it exactly as I want, Steve. *That'll* be the difference." For the moment, as so often, Herma's words of wisdom—that he would catch more flies with honey than he ever would with vinegar—were forgotten by her son.

Actor and writer David Scott Milton had lost touch with Bogdanovich since the midsixties in New York. Their reunion came at a dinner party at Barbra Streisand's house while *What's Up, Doc?* was in preproduction. When Milton arrived he found Bogdanovich holding forth in the company of Freddie Fields, Polly Bergen, Sue Mengers and her mother, Ryan O'Neal and Streisand herself. He was talking in a grave and dignified manner and looking every inch the successful Hollywood director. As Milton and his wife Yvonne took in the scene, the thought occurred to him that perhaps Bogdanovich had changed since their last meeting. This was quickly dispelled as Bogdanovich caught sight of them. "Dave!" he cried, his voice going up a full octave. He then strode over to greet them warmly. "What are *you* doing here?"

"Still the same old Peter," Milton realized gratefully. What struck him at this and subsequent encounters with his old buddy was the dichotomy between Bogdanovich's essentially childlike nature and the ambitious, accomplished front he chose to present professionally. "It's Peter's way of dealing with the world," he explains, "this switching of roles to the business pro. But his natural self is much more puckish. And it's a delightful quality."

With two months to go before shooting was to start, Bogdanovich began with a sketchy outline of the story, then worked with writers Robert Benton and David Newman on the first two drafts of the script. At this stage Barbra's character was a stuffy, highbrow and bumbling musicologist who encounters zany, eccentric O'Neal while attending a convention. "It's inspired by Howard Hawks's *Bringing Up Baby*," Bogdanovich announced, providing future ammunition for his critics.

For Platt the call to join the *What's Up, Doc?* team came quite unexpectedly. Would she care to reunite with her husband—on a strictly professional basis—and supervise production design on the new Streisand movie? Although Platt didn't know it at the time, the offer originated with Streisand herself, who had insisted on hiring "whoever designed *Last Picture Show.*"

After the estrangement Platt had already been thrown a lifeline by none other than Orson Welles. Working with him on his still ongoing production of *The Other Side of the Wind* had given her the perspective she needed to help her maneuver through a difficult time. It also gave her a unique opportunity to get a handle on the true relationship between Welles and Bogdanovich. "Orson was clearly jealous of Peter," she maintains. "At best it was a strange mixture. I think Orson wanted Peter to make the same mistakes he had. But was I grateful for the work he gave me! He kept me going flat out—I hardly had time to think about being depressed!"

Platt decided to accept the *What's Up, Doc?* assignment. "I couldn't get in the union," she recalls, "and realized that if I did a Streisand picture, they couldn't keep me out. I was the first woman production designer to get into the Art Directors Guild."

Unofficially, Platt gave the script the once over. "Switch the roles," she suggested to Bogdanovich. "Make Barbra the eccentric, not Ryan." The idea galvanized her husband. "That's a *great* idea!" he told her. "That'll be *my* idea!" (John Calley later claimed it was this notion that turned *What's Up, Doc?* into "a gold picture.") Platt proceeded to move the location of the film from Chicago to San Francisco, which she regarded as a make-believe town. She wanted Streisand to be totally unlike a New York-type, more like someone who had just fallen out of the sky and into the action.

John Calley suggested writer Buck Henry to do a final polish on Streisand's character, and Henry turned out to have more ideas. They sparked Bogdanovich again, and together he and Henry did a brilliant rewrite in three weeks. Bogdanovich was the first to acknowledge that the finished script, in terms of dialogue, was mainly Henry's although certain elements of the Benton/Newman plot remained. Platt's contribution remained unsung.

Howard Hawks called Bogdanovich while he was on a huge Warners soundstage conducting rehearsals with Streisand and O'Neal. "Your script's OK," Hawks told him, "but you made a mistake in saying you stole the idea from *Bringing Up Baby*. I never said who I stole it from! Anyway, you haven't stolen the leopard."

"Howard, I couldn't do that," Bogdanovich replied.

"And you haven't stolen the dinosaur either, but that's OK, the spirit's there. Who's in your picture?"

Although Bogdanovich replied, "Barbra Streisand and Ryan O'-Neal" under his breath, he swears he saw Streisand narrowing her eyes at him, clearly wondering what his phone conversation was all about. There was silence on the line, which Bogdanovich decided to break, this time even more sotto voce. "Howard, I know they're not Katharine Hepburn and Cary Grant—"

"You're damn right they're not!" Hawks agreed.

Later the veteran director was back on the line after viewing some rehearsal shots Bogdanovich had sent over. "They're straining too hard for laughs," he said. "Just tell them to read the lines and play off each other and don't let them be cute."

Bogdanovich managed to get Randy Quaid a small role in *What's Up, Doc?* Although it wasn't much, he felt that Quaid was so good that if he came to Hollywood and found himself an agent, he'd have a career in movies. John Hillerman was another from *The Last Picture Show* who was cast, together with Michael Murphy, Kenneth Mars and M. Emmet Walsh.

Madeline Kahn, invited to make her screen debut as Eunice, O'-Neal's fiancée, was wary of working with Streisand. She had heard that in Streisand films a lot of performances tended to end up as outtakes. "But I soon found out that Peter had control," she said later. "As for Barbra—well, we're both Jewish, we're both from New York and I sing and she sings. I thought we'd have a lot to talk about. But Barbra wasn't having any of that. Ryan was great, very funny and helpful, but Barbra preferred to keep a polite distance."

Even to hardy veterans, with whom Streisand might have been expected to unbend a little—actors like Mabel Albertson, Liam Dunn and Austin Pendelton—Streisand came across as benevolent royalty visiting and tolerating the serfs. Aside from this, she annoyed everyone by constantly turning up late on the set. The other actors were also less than thrilled by the lavish trailer provided to her by Warners, although O'Neal gallantly defended it on the basis of her superstar status.

"I spent a lot of time making Barbra happy, going up to her hotel room and making jokes," Bogdanovich recalls of the location work in San Francisco. "I'd heard all these terrible stories about her, but we had a good time. I'd just kid her, and when she got angry I'd laugh. I wasn't scared of her, she was two years younger than me, and it wasn't as though she were a big star, not to me at any rate. As far as I was concerned, she was a good singer, a good actor who'd done a few pictures, and so had I. At first I gave her line readings, which I do all the time, reading the part through the way I wanted her to. Being an actor myself, I have a tendency to do that. It doesn't come from ego, I just don't know how to direct any other way. Barbra immediately called Sue. 'This guy's giving me line readings!' she complained. A week later, after I'd stopped, she asked me to do it again when she saw me giving it to the other actors. I guess I took it to the limit, though, on that song she did, 'As Time Goes By.' It was the height of impudence for me to give *Barbra Streisand* line readings on a song—but I did it anyway."

Ryan O'Neal could see the source of his costar's problems better than most. "Barbra doesn't work from a confidence base," he points out. "She likes to go into a project thinking it's the worst, and she builds from that. Peter used to scold Barbra because she didn't do what he said. Barbra can do a scene twenty different ways and they all sounded right to me. She'd say, 'Pick one.' But Peter always wanted one she hadn't done. He tried to condense her and pull her back. He made her cut her nails. He wouldn't let her wear makeup, hairpieces or all the things she's used to doing, because all her movies had been purely vehicles for her before."

"Ryan, we're in a piece of shit," Barbra told her costar on several occasions, "I mean, we're really in trouble." Bogdanovich had to put his foot down on several occasions when Streisand tried to take over directing the movie. "I know from funny," she declared at one point, "and this ain't funny."

Ryan O'Neal went to see Cary Grant before shooting started to get advice on his performance. "Wear silk underwear," Grant told him. "Say, 'Where's my drink?' Be comfortable." Buck Henry will testify that Bogdanovich *fed* O'Neal his character on *What's Up, Doc?*, line readings and all. "Ryan was unsure about comedy," Bogdanovich confirms. "Off the set he's very funny and relaxed, on camera he freezes up a bit. Ryan can't act *himself* on a movie, he needs direction to do it."

During the location scouting in San Francisco, with Shepherd absent, Bogdanovich and Platt shared an intimate night for the first time since their estrangement. It was to prove a one-nighter, and if Platt had any illusions of a permanent reunion, they were shattered on her return to Los Angeles. Back on the Warners lot, she put a brave face on her situation. "I don't blame Peter," she confided to one of the crew. "If I were a man, I'd have left me for Cybill too." She smiles now as the remark is quoted back to her. "What I meant," she qualifies, "was that if a beautiful man like Robert Redford had come along I might have done the same thing. Anyway, I was no longer the same person I'd been before. On *What's Up, Doc?* I discovered martinis and the pain was much diminished for the time being. I was devastated by my separation from Peter, but refused to admit it. I went around openly saying I didn't mind Peter and Cybill being together, while privately going through hell that alcohol made bearable—for a while, anyway."

CHAPTER 8

Neil Canton was about to go to law school in New York when his father, working in publicity at Columbia Pictures, suggested he take a summer job in Los Angeles with a director about to start shooting a movie at the studio. When this fell through, Canton contacted Bogdanovich to see if there was any possibility of employment with him. "He said he'd be happy to see me," Canton recalls, "and I took a couple of buses out to his place. He asked me if I'd like to work on *What's Up, Doc?* Frank Marshall, who'd been his assistant on *The Last Picture Show,* was moving up to location manager, so I took over Frank's job. It changed my life. I never went back to law school."

Today Canton is well known as the coproducer of such hits as *Back to the Future* and *The Witches of Eastwick.* "I guess I just fell in love with the whole process of making movies. As a student of Peter's I learned from him how they were made—one shot at a time, and cuts here and there. I was incredibly naive on *What's Up, Doc?,* I'd never been on a movie set. Peter had said to meet him on the very first day in San Francisco, where they were shooting at the airport. As his assistant, I would have his script, his notes and his diagrams, and follow him around. I truly loved the experience. Peter was incredibly generous and made me part of the postproduction process as well. Polly came up to me and asked why I'd never said hello to her. Well, I didn't know what production designer meant at that stage, and I didn't know she was Peter's wife, either!"

By the time location shooting was over, Canton had made up his mind that his future lay in movies. Since Frank Marshall and Platt were now his best friends, it was only to be expected that she would offer to put the impoverished young men up in her home on Outpost Drive, where Anna was also staying while she studied for her degree. Canton and Marshall worked with Bogdanovich by day—officially designated "Assistant to the Producer" and "Production Aide" respectively—then went home to Platt's at night. The chores were divided equally; Platt and Anna put the children to bed, while each night the two men cooked for dinner the one dish they knew how to prepare.

For Platt the relationship she forged with Barbara Streisand on the movie was as big a bonus as her hard-won union card. "Barbara is a perfectionist," she declares, "she has unique ideas about everything. We were a fascinating pair. I have strong opinions too and we argued a great deal. I would go home at night thinking I'd convinced her on something, then she'd come in next day and we'd have to talk it through all over again. It would take her hours to decide whether a certain piece of lace on a costume was right or not. I'm the sort of person who sees the big picture, and her attention to detail was fascinating to me. She treated me well, and in the state I was in, I was grateful, for after my split with Peter I got no invitations to any parties and the phone stopped ringing. Peter was with Cybill, and they were the talk of the town. I really was nobody. Barbra insisted on inviting me to her house, where I met Woody Allen and Milos Forman at a party she gave. I guess Woody took a fancy to me. Sue Mengers called next day to say he wanted to go out with me but was too shy to ask. 'Think of all the great movies you could make together. *Polly Allen!'* she urged. I was too proud to call him—I wish I had. Later he asked me to design for him, but I couldn't. I didn't see the potential Woody had until *Manhattan,* I didn't really 'get him' until then. Inviting me was a kind gesture from Barbra; you don't forget these things. I'd do almost anything for her."

Bogdanovich was riding high, the fair-haired, blue-eyed boy on the set of *What's Up, Doc?,* up to his neck in a big-budget movie and loving every minute of it. *Vogue* dubbed his affair with Cybill "Going Steady in Public." Then, to cap it all, *The Last Picture Show* opened in the middle of shooting to extravagant reviews that were brought to him on the set.

As if calculated to set Orson Welles's teeth on edge, *Newsweek* described the film as "The most impressive work by a young American director since *Citizen Kane.*" And in the *New Yorker* Pauline Kael wrote, *"The Last Picture Show* arrives just when it seemed time to announce that movies as pop culture were dead."

Perhaps if Bogdanovich had been able to accept this praise humbly and forgo his references to old movie masters, the backlash that followed might have been avoided. Instead, he continued to produce ammunition for his detractors. "A lot of people have said that *The Last Picture Show* is very much a John Ford or Howard Hawks film," he complained. "They'll say anything, because you've given them a clue that you like a certain director." He then conceded that certain scenes in the movie could be attributed to Ford's influence. "The long shot at the end of the funeral scene is very much a Ford composition. . . . I know I was thinking of him, because I said, 'We've got a Ford sky, let's shoot it.' "

Bogdanovich was demonstrating that Borislav's lesson had, if anything, been too well learned. Anyone else would have shouted, "Cut!" at this stage; not Bogdanovich. "A painter is influenced by centuries of art," he continued, "just as a musician is by everything Bach composed. And since everything in movies came from D.W. Griffith, of course there's that influence. I don't think there's much that's original under the sun, but that doesn't seem to me to be a criterion of merit—certainly not originality of technique. I judge myself by the directors I admire— Hawks, Lubitsch, Keaton, Welles, Ford and Hitchcock. If anything, I thought there was a strange kind of oblique correlation between *The Last Picture Show* and Orson Welles's *Magnificent Ambersons* in that they're both stories about the end of an era."

Tom Milne in *Sight and Sound* was one of the first to read the warning signs and sound the alarm bells. While he admired *The Last Picture Show* enormously, he felt that in discussing his movies in what he felt were "very suspect terms," Bogdanovich was the worst possible advocate for his own work. "So much so," Milne went on, "that one begins to wonder how much Polly Platt contributed to them, considering that the real key to both *Targets* and *The Last Picture Show* is the way they reflect their theme visually. To say this is not to denigrate Bogdanovich's direction, so much as to suggest he may be doing the right things for the wrong reasons."

The Last Picture Show went on to receive no fewer than eight Academy Award nominations, from which Cloris Leachman garnered Best Supporting Actress and Ben Johnson Best Supporting Actor. They both went on to receive the same honors at the British Academy Award ceremony, where Bogdanovich and Larry McMurtry shared the Best Screenplay Award.

In December 1971, an out of town premiere of *What's Up, Doc?* was arranged by Warners in Denver. Although fairly certain they had a smash hit on their hands, they wanted to test the comedy before a live audience. Bogdanovich flew to the preview in the Kinney's Jet Gulfstream II, together with Dick Zanuck, John Calley and the rest of the Warners brass. "If the plane crashes," Bogdanovich thought, "my billing is going to be lousy!"

The reaction of the audience was so good that Warners wanted to release the picture as it stood, at 97½ minutes. Bogdanovich disagreed and insisted on removing 3½ minutes before its opening a few months later at New York's Radio City Music Hall, where its opening day gross was at that time the highest in the cinema's history.

In New York *Esquire*'s Harold Hayes visited Bogdanovich at the Plaza, where he had been put up by Warners for the premiere's festivities. Hayes recalls that Bogdanovich was in his full Jerry Lewis spate on the phone to a hapless PR lady. "What kind of car are you sending? No, no dear. *Not* an Impala. A limousine with a driver. I can't go there in a rental car. It's uncomfortable. You can't stretch your legs and your pants get all wrinkled. No, no, no. Get a Lincoln or a Cadillac and have the driver wait outside."

Bogdanovich was able to walk from the East Side, where *The Last Picture Show* was still playing, over to the Avenue of the Americas, where *What's Up, Doc?* had lines snaking around the block. When he saw his billing above the title, "Peter Bogdanovich's Comedy," he felt the exhilaration of reaching a real peak in his career. A few days later, when the movie was reviewed in *Variety*, even that feeling was topped. "I just burst into tears," Bogdanovich unashamedly admits, "because it was a wonderful review and I was just so happy."

"This picture is a total smash," *Variety* trumpeted. "The script and cast are excellent, the direction and comedy staging are outstanding; and there are literally reels of pure, unadulterated and sustained laughs. Mature audiences haven't seen a film like this in a generation, and younger audiences will recognise *What's Up, Doc?* as a most worthy descendant of the zany old pics watched on TV. The Warner Bros release has nothing in sight but money—by the carload."

Variety notwithstanding, in the U.S. the critical reception accorded *What's Up, Doc?* was much less than unanimously favorable. Stanley Kauffmann, who had wryly noted Hitchcockian overtones in *Targets* and John Ford's influence in *The Last Picture Show*, wrote in the *New Republic*, "Peter Bogdanovich has now made his third imitation," and he went on to describe *What's Up, Doc?* as, "a quick trip through the archives. For those who don't know the comedies of Howard Hawks, Gregory La Cava, etc., it may just possibly seem fresh. . . ."

In the *New Yorker*, Pauline Kael took up the theme. "It's too early in the history of movies for this feeding off the past," she maintained, "and the result is too infantile to be called decadent."

Jay Cocks at *Time* joined the dissenters with a vengeance, characterizing *What's Up, Doc?* as "a comedy made by a man who has seen a lot of movies, knows all the mechanics and has *absolutely no sense of humor.* Seeing it is like shaking hands with a joker holding a toy buzzer; the effect is both presumptuous and unpleasant."

Another mighty blast for the antis came from Peter Schjeldahl in the *New York Times:* "We get the feeling at a certain point," he wrote, "that this movie is not actually a movie at all, that it is some kind of simulacrum of a movie, a celluloid zombie."

Richard Roud coolly summarized the rather overheated U.S. critical reaction in Britain's *Guardian.* "This picture has aroused the anger of many New York critics," he acknowledged, "who seem to feel that, as it is not as good as Hawks's *[Bringing Up Baby]*—which it isn't—then it is no good at all—which it is. Bogdanovich has a wonderful eye, and ear, for casting, and apart from the stars, who acquit themselves surprisingly well, he has found a real gem in the adenoidal Madeline Kahn. *What's Up, Doc?* does provide a very entertaining evening, which in these times is not to be sneezed at, at least not by me."

Bogdanovich decided he had to have the last word. "A good critic is somebody who knows what they are talking about," he declared, "and too many of them don't. If every critic were really brilliant, I'd say fine, but they're rare, the good ones. Talent in any field is rare . . . To me, too many critics are just glorified film viewers, and jaded ones at that because they have to see too many movies."

Just how far he was prepared to go to flatten the critics was demonstrated by the name he gave to Kenneth Mars's plagiarizing musicologist in the movie. It was no coincidence that this particularly unpleasant character was dubbed Hugh Simon; he was named after the acerbic critic, John Simon. "I couldn't think of how to play the heavy," Bogdanovich admitted, "so I tried to think of someone I didn't like!"

Lashing back at the critics was one thing, but dealing with the backlash building up among his Hollywood peers was another. Many saw the fine line between homage and opportunistic name-dropping well and truly breached. Irving Berlin's "Anything You Can Do I Can Do Better" was beginning to sound eminently suitable for adoption as the wunderkind's theme song. And Bogdanovich was more than a little dismayed when even his leading lady—and one of the film's major profit participants—joined the anti-brigade. "I didn't enjoy making *What's Up, Doc?*," Streisand confessed. "I thought it was a silly piece of material. I thought I would be dealing in something very personal and important at first, and what it was finally was a puff of smoke, a piece of fluff. There's room for both things, you know, but I didn't feel I was growing as an artist. I saw *The Last Picture Show* and gave Peter Bogdanovich script approval. I made a mistake. The script wasn't ready until the day before we started shooting. I hadn't worked for nineteen months before that and I tried not to show my real feelings, my hostility, while we were shooting. The picture was trying to be 1940s. It's not. I just felt it wasn't good enough." But she was able to make light of the situation once the profits came rolling in. "Bogdanovich?" she then remarked. "Oh, he's a horny bastard. Arrogant, autocratic—but brilliant."

"She thought we were going to do something else," Bogdanovich conceded. "I suppose I tricked her, but she wasn't really sore when it was all over. She made more money on *Doc* than on any other picture, about $3 million. She could have made more, but she sold her piece for a big hunk of money."

"Barbra was wrong about the movie," says Platt. "Peter didn't trick her. She did it on her own, she really thought *What's Up, Doc?* would be magically transformed into *The Last Picture Show*."

The truth of the matter is that Streisand had *personal* reasons for disliking the movie. She had been having an affair with Warners' John Calley, that ended abruptly when she agreed to do the film, at which point Ryan O'Neal took over in the romance stakes. "Barbra was a tremendous victim of the system here in Hollywood at the time," one insider confided. "She was really used by men."

Jubilant from the movie's success, Warners offered Bogdanovich, Streisand and O'Neal $1 million each to make a sequel. No prizes for guessing that Streisand for one turned up her nose at the proposal. So did Bogdanovich. "What's the sequel going to be?" he asked Calley. *"That's All, Folks?"*

Bogdanovich next toyed with the idea of developing a western with Larry McMurtry, something they and Polly Platt had first chewed over thoroughly as together they had scouted locations for *The Last Picture Show.* Warners was interested, especially with the cast Bogdanovich had lined up—John Wayne, James Stewart, Henry Fonda, Cybill Shepherd, the Clancy Brothers and Ben Johnson. After the studio agreed to pay McMurtry to turn out a first draft script, he and Bogdanovich met at the Hotel Fontainbleu in Miami Beach, where Shepherd was filming Elaine May's *The Heartbreak Kid* close by.

McMurtry later turned in a 350-page screenplay. "Wonderful stuff," was Bogdanovich's reaction, "but way too long." After cutting it down, he sent it back to McMurtry for further work. Two days after Bogdanovich asked Platt if she would care to work on the project, it was scuttled by John Wayne. "It's like a last picture show for westerns," he told Bogdanovich, "and I ain't ready to hang up my spurs just yet." In its place Wayne suggested a couple of other movie ideas, but Bogdanovich was less than keen about them, and disconsolate to see a pet project die. "Fonda liked the script," he maintains, "James Stewart kind of liked it, but when Duke turned it down, it just fell apart. If he hadn't, I'd have made it with Polly and Cybill and it would have been one hell of a picture. I told Larry to forget the movie, just to write it as a novel."

Thirteen years later McMurtry did just that, having cannily bought back the rights from Bogdanovich first. *Lonesome Dove* became his first huge best-seller and went on to win him the Pulitzer Prize.

CHAPTER 9

Flush from the phenomenal success of *The Godfather*, Francis Ford Coppola invited Bogdanovich to join him and William Friedkin in a venture called The Directors' Company, to be co-owned and backed by Paramount to the tune of $31 million. The directors would have complete freedom from studio interference, just so long as their movies' budgets were kept below $3 million each, and they would have final cut, with Paramount not even to be allowed to see the rushes. Each of the directors would produce four films over a twelve-year period, Coppola continued glowingly, and they would all make a pile of money when the concern was floated.

Bogdanovich, who understood little of the business side, agreed to travel to New York to finalize the agreement with Coppola, Friedkin and Charles Bluhdorn of Gulf and Western, Paramount's parent company. What he remembers best about the trip was winning $100 playing blackjack with Friedkin on the journey there, and $100 from Coppola on the way back.

After *Lonesome Dove* fell through, Bogdanovich was talked into doing an adaptation of Joe David Brown's book *Addie Pray* as his initial contribution to the new company. Set in the Midwest of the 1930's Depression, the story concerned two con artists, a father-and-(pretend) daughter team, whose business was tricking grieving families into buying Bibles. At first Bogdanovich liked neither the book nor the script, but then an idea came to him. What if he produced the movie and persuaded Orson Welles to direct? As it turned out, the scheme was clumsily handled, with Welles taking instant umbrage when he thought the offer was linked to a commitment to act in a future Bogdanovich movie. "I'm not being blackmailed into directing any picture," he boomed. Bogdanovich was hurt by an inference he never intended, although he was soon to realize that this reaction was common with Welles and would prove short-lived.

In her belief that Welles was more than a touch ambivalent about Bogdanovich's apparently unstoppable success, Platt had come painfully close to the truth. She feared for her husband, as he adored Welles and listened too often, she thought, to his advice. Welles was only human, after all. Following his meteoric beginning with the Mercury Theatre and *Citizen Kane*, he had endured years of failure in finding major studio backing for his films. Constantly forced to appear in potboilers in order to finance his own independent productions, he had become understandably embittered toward the industry at large—and Bogdanovich was to be a victim of that resentment.

He maintains that the roots of his reverence for Welles and for all "the old masters" were buried deep in the respect he held for his father and his tenets. He claims none of the rebelliousness that Aldous Huxley discerned in sons willing themselves to be disillusioned by that which had charmed their fathers. For Bogdanovich, "attention *must be paid* to this man"—as commanded by Willie Loman's wife in *Death of a Salesman*—held more resonance. "Learn your craft," Borislav had counselled. "*And* its history." This *might* be the simple, innocent source of the homage Bogdanovich accorded Ford, Hawks, Welles and the rest of the industry veterans. But a friend in New York, who knew the Bogdanoviches as a family, disputes Borislav's influence on his son and maintains this represents Bogdanovich's romantic version of the truth: "Peter is far more mother-oriented than he admits. I don't believe Borislav ever really gave him his approval. This may be one of the keys to understanding Peter. I think he had to look elsewhere for guidance and adopted all those movie directors as surrogate fathers. He worshiped them and sought *their approval*. He needed 'successful father' figures and found them in the likes of John Ford, who typified the recognized and accomplished model he needed. Although Borislav was tolerant and giving artistically, he never enjoyed real recognition or success. Sure, there was an element there of Peter turning his back, consciously or otherwise, on his father."

Bogdanovich decided that if he made *Addie Pray,* the title would have to go. He hated it, maintaining that it sounded like a lizard or a snake, and intensely searched for an alternative. Platt showed him a photograph of her father and an old girlfriend taken as they sat on a carnival paper moon. When she suggested the movie contain a similar scene, the idea for the title came to Bogdanovich at once. Wasn't there a great song standard of the period called "Paper Moon"? Paramount's initial reaction was one of dismay. Here they were financing the film version of a best-selling book and Bogdanovich was proposing that they throw the title away! Even when he assured them he would use the song over the titles, they still were far from convinced. From a huddle with script writer Alvin Sargent, Bogdanovich emerged with a more convincing argument for Paramount: he and Sargent had inserted a scene in the movie that featured the song. Paramount's argument remained that the book had sold 125,000 copies in hardback as *Addie Pray.* "Wait a minute," Bogdanovich countered, "if only 125,000 people go to see the picture, we're in real trouble."

With the impending paperback edition of the book he saw his chance to prevail and took himself off to the publisher. *They* should change *their* title to *Paper Moon,* he told them, "formerly *Addie Pray,*" and offered them a still from the movie for the book's cover. "Think of all the cross-promotional possibilities," he urged. With the publisher's agreement, Bogdanovich returned in triumph to Paramount, the name change a *fait accompli.* This time there was no argument. He had his judgment confirmed when he called a contrite Orson Welles in London. "What do you think of *Paper Moon* as a title?" he asked him. There was a long pause. "It's so good," Welles intoned, "you shouldn't even make the picture. Just release the title."

Platt, on board as production designer, suggested Ryan O'Neal's daughter Tatum—whom Bogdanovich had never met—for the role of Addie Pray. At that point Platt saw Tatum's future as troubled, to put it mildly. Once during the filming of *What's Up, Doc?* she had as a favor for O'Neal picked Tatum up at her mother's house and had found her sleeping in the bath tub. "Casting Tatum's a great idea!" Bogdanovich agreed, "because then Ryan could play her 'father'!" Together they drove to O'Neal's Malibu house so that Bogdanovich could check out Platt's choice. The doughty Tatum coolly looked him up and down as they were introduced. "Hey, you're a little on the chubby side!" was her first observation.

But gradually she convinced Bogdanovich that Platt was right. Tatum was cute rather than pretty, extremely precocious and very appealing with her mixture of feistiness, charm and toughness in almost equal measure. There was, however, an obstacle to overcome as Bogdanovich phoned in his casting choices to Bob Evans at Paramount. It seemed that Evans had sworn he would never again make a picture with O'Neal after the star had had an affair with his wife, Ali McGraw. Bogdanovich turned to Platt disconsolately after the call. "He won't do it with Ryan," he informed her. "Yes, he will," Platt promised.

Following the success of Madeline Kahn as Eunice in *What's Up, Doc?* she was signed for a crucial part in *Paper Moon*, the belly dancer, Miss Trixie Delight, whose overtures to Moses would be constantly foiled by Addie's interventions. Randy Quaid, a year away from costarring with Jack Nicholson in *The Last Detail,* was cast in the cameo role of the hillbilly. He had one of the movie's great lines when O'Neal challenges him to a fight and asks if he prefers gloves or bare knuckles. "Makes no never mind to me," Quaid drawls. Many of the small roles were played by the locals in the town of Hays, Kansas. Anxious young men were forced to stand by as their girlfriends, vying with each other for some bit part, flirtingly tried to catch the eye of someone with influence.

Bogdanovich saw the key to the movie in the relationship between Addie Pray and the con man, Moses. "He doesn't want to commit himself on any level," he told Platt, "for he doesn't really love her at all. She's smarter than he is at every turn, but she's at a disadvantage— because she loves him." If there were any ironic echoes here on a personal level, they seemed to be lost on Bogdanovich. But not on Platt.

When in 1964 the couple had made their watershed journey by car from New York to California, the endless miles of flat country in the Midwest had made a lasting impression on them, not least because their car kept overheating and threatening to break down. It was to the Midwest and to Hays in Kansas that they would return to shoot *Paper Moon,* for not only was it a perfect setting for the film, but interior props

such as furniture and exterior props like automobiles and farm imple-
ments were plentiful. None of them could have been duplicated in
Hollywood with much authenticity. To dress the principal actors, Platt
arranged for shipment from Hollywood of hundreds of wardrobe items
for men, women and children. Included were suits originally made for
stars such as Bing Crosby, George Raft, Robert Taylor and James
Cagney. Two of the suits Ryan O'Neal wore in the film had been
tailored for Crosby and Raft, complete with padded shoulders and
deep-pleated trousers.

Once filming started the first problem was with Tatum. "She didn't
have any idea what the hell we were doing and for half the movie she
couldn't have cared less," says Bogdanovich. "I just had to keep Ryan
from killing her. He would shout, 'Goddam it, Tatum, would you learn
your lines? I'm not going to do it again. I did 5,000 *Peyton Places* and I
never went through anything like this!' "

Bogdanovich recalls being on a road in the middle of Kansas with a
rig pulling the car with a camera on it, and about a dozen people
hanging on. "It was a key scene between Addie and Moses, where a lot
of things were implied about their love or need for each other. We
figured the scene would run for about a mile and a half, and two miles
down there was a single place on this narrow road where we could turn
and come back. Since it had to be done without a cut, if they started
down the road and after three lines somebody blew it, we'd have to go
the full two miles before we could turn and start all over again. The first
day we did it 25 times. It was around the nineteenth take that Ryan said
he couldn't do it any more."

Bogdanovich took the distraught actor to one side and walked up the
road with him for about a half mile, trying to calm him down. After this
break, O'Neal was ready to start again, but with several more takes the
scene still wasn't working out. Bogdanovich decided to leave it for a few
days and go on to other, simpler scenes. Later he went back and got the
take he wanted—on the sixteenth attempt, courtesy of Tatum.

"She never had much discipline in her life," Bogdanovich sighs.
"Also, eight-year-old kids have a world of their own. I like that world,
but it didn't necessarily mesh with the world we were trying to create.
There was another time we were shooting a carnival scene at night.
Tatum got there about five o'clock. It took us about three hours to light

the scene. So she did what any kid would do at her age. She started riding the Ferris wheel, eating popcorn, candy corn, peanuts, and by the time we were ready to shoot she was lying on the ground, sick. 'I told you not to eat!' Ryan said. 'Oh, Daddy,' Tatum moaned. 'Get up,' Ryan and I yelled at her. After about five weeks of shooting, she finally got into it and started to like the process and was much better. She almost became professional, thank God."

Problems of a much more personal nature soon surfaced between Bogdanovich and Platt. She was astonished when her normally prudish husband asked her if she would come back to him if he "found a place" for Shepherd. The suggestion spelled "finis" to any misconceived hopes Platt had been harboring that Bogdanovich might give Shepherd up. "I didn't find the idea of three together shocking," Polly claims. "Obviously, he didn't want to let me go, I was important to him. But he couldn't give up Cybill and I didn't want to become an embittered Hollywood wife who knew her husband was with other women."

With Bogdanovich's proposal rejected, the couple entered the last painful stages of their estrangement and divorce, enacted in full view of the *Paper Moon* cast and crew.

A planned visit from Shepherd brought the unpleasant situation to a head. "How can you be so *insensitive?* I am the *mother* of your *children,*" Platt tearfully reminded him when Bogdanovich announced Shepherd's imminent arrival on the set. Shepherd was persuaded to stay away. Bogdanovich's argument, that all three had been scheduled to work together on *Lonesome Dove*, which *Paper Moon* had replaced, ignored the finality of his split with Platt, the door now finally slammed on any chance of a reconciliation.

Polly continued to find solace in martinis, and, toward the end of the shoot, comfort of a different kind from property master Tony Wade, whom she would later marry. "If I had to do it all over again," she says reflectively, "I would not have divorced Peter. I'd have worked harder to make it work, at least until the children were older. Divorce for children is horrible. On *Paper Moon*, Peter blamed me for everything— the project, finding Tatum and our relationship. He tortured me for weeks, saying I was the one who got him into it."

Neil Canton and Frank Marshall both worked on *Paper Moon*, and, together with the rest of the crew, they knew the end had come for

Bogdanovich and Platt. When, back in Los Angeles, Tony Wade moved in with their erstwhile landlady, they were obliged to seek alternative accommodations, though Anna stayed on until she finished her studies.

One day toward the end of *Paper Moon*'s shooting, Bogdanovich took an anxious call from Shepherd. Somehow or other the nude scene from *The Last Picture Show* had found its way into the pages of *Playboy*. "Peter, how could this have *happened?*" she asked between floods of tears. Dismayed, he had Frank Marshall get hold of a copy of the magazine; when he saw the picture, his dismay turned to cold anger. The scene, lasting all of seven seconds in the movie, had been frozen into a single out-of-focus example of "sex in the movies." It turned out that *Playboy* had ordered a print of *The Last Picture Show*, hacked out that particular frame and blown it up. To compound the injury, the same picture was used again the following month—as well as in a later *Playboy* compilation.

Shepherd proceeded to sue Playboy Enterprises, and Hugh Hefner personally, for a total of $8 million. "*Playboy* had been after me for years to pose nude," she angrily declared. "They'd even phoned my mother and offered her $10,000 to persuade me, but I'd always said no. Everybody advised me not to sue, arguing that there's no difference between appearing nude in *Playboy* and appearing nude in a film. My argument is that if there isn't any difference we're in a lot of trouble."

While Bogdanovich gave the impression that the lawsuit was entirely Shepherd's idea, he in fact encouraged and applauded her action. "She's prepared to go all the way with it," he commented. "I don't know if I could go through with it, but I admire her for doing it."

Paper Moon provided yet another resounding hit for Bogdanovich at the box office. If the critics were divided, *Variety* again had no doubts. "Peter Bogdanovich's evocations and recreations of past eras and film genres now includes a Shirley Temple-Damon Runyon plot," they reported. "Alvin Sargent's screenplay is a major contributor to the overall excellent results, while Polly Platt's production design is terrific as are all other technical credits, including Laszlo Kovacs' cinematography. *Paper Moon* is a film for families, teenagers, young adults and older generations. Its heart-warming aspects are conveyed without treacle, and its grittier suggestions of vagabond living are transmitted without vulgarity or tastelessness. Bogdanovich once again has revived another film form, without patronizing and with innovative original work based upon respectful admiration of the screen's past."

When Jay Cocks admitted that he'd liked the movie, Bogdanovich took the opportunity to remind him of his "nasty and uncalled for" remark in reviewing *What's Up, Doc?*: that Bogdanovich had "absolutely no sense of humor." "Maybe you're the one without the sense of humor," Bogdanovich suggested.

Stanley Kauffmann found less to admire than either Cocks or *Variety*. "Bogdanovich mixes a collection of influences and hack work with a few good touches," he conceded, "but the look of the film is all wrong. He has had Lazslo Kovacs shoot it in the black-and-white sententious tones that Orson Welles used on *The Magnificent Ambersons* and *Touch of Evil*, quite inappropriate for this sentimental comedy. I've rarely seen a film look so unlike what it was about, doomed to this schism because this time Bogdanovich has imitated wrongly. He is still a modestly talented non-person."

Stung, Bogdanovich leapt to his own defense. "I even read one critic who said, 'This is Bogdanovich in his Capra mood.' " he raged. "I just wanted to blow up the magazine—it's about as far away from Capra as you can get. I love Frank Capra, but it's me in no mood except my own. Truffaut has used Renoir and Hitchcock in every movie he's made, and they say, 'Ah, Truffaut, *homage* to Hitchcock.' But me, I'm *stealing!* Everybody thought *Paper Moon* was this story about a nice man and this sweet little girl, and I thought it was about this terrible man and misused little girl. I thought they were going off to a life of absolute disaster at the end and everybody else thought, 'Isn't it wonderful?' But that's fine. I think the audience, what I call the civilians, should put their own fantasies into a movie. I don't think it's a director's job to make a movie that can be interpreted in only one way."

Bogdanovich confided to friends that Orson Welles had damned the film with faint praise, wounding him considerably. Once again he was brought face to face with the reality of how much the maestro's professional wounds were still smarting from his treatment at the hands of the establishment.

As the money continued to roll in from box offices all over the world, there was the usual excited talk of a sequel, with Paramount arguing that, after all, a considerable amount of material from the book had gone unused. The studio wanted Tatum O'Neal again, this time partnered by Mae West, no less, who had saved their hide back in the thirties. Bogdanovich turned the idea down. "I didn't see any future in it. Mae West would have been marvelous, but she'd already done her stuff."

Instead, with three solid box-office hits to his credit, he set his sights on finding the perfect starring vehicle for Cybill Shepherd.

CHAPTER 10

After Bogdanovich's return from Kansas, Shepherd announced that she had found the house they had been searching for, a spectacular Spanish-style mansion that in Bel Air terms seemed a steal at $375,000. As the couple wandered around the courtyard at Copa De Oro, with its fountain and stone cherubs, Bogdanovich succinctly summed up the change of fortune that had occurred since he first visited Hollywood in the sixties: "This is the house that *What's Up, Doc?* built."

He encountered several blind alleys and false starts in his search for a new project. Gavin Lambert sent him a script based on John Galsworthy's long short story *The Apple Tree* that Bogdanovich decided needed more work. For a while he had in mind an original story of his own, one in which an Italian visiting the States is smitten by a girl from Texas, but even with Shepherd in mind as the girl he failed to develop the project to his own satisfaction.

In the end a treatment of Henry James's *Daisy Miller*—first suggested by Orson Welles—was deemed interesting enough to draw Bogdanovich to read the novella itself. As he did, he could see it all in his mind's eye—Shepherd as the tragic combination of doomed heroine and misunderstood, innocent flirt, and himself as Winterbourne, her stiff, repressed suitor, with both of them to be directed by Orson Welles. He saw *Daisy Miller* as part comedy, part tragedy, a story that progressed from a light beginning to a sad ending, at Daisy's funeral. "Someone's dead who should be alive," Bogdanovich lamented.

When Platt learned of her ex-husband's choice of material, she was dismayed and felt he was being mistakenly influenced. For his part, Welles seemed intrigued by Bogdanovich's offer; on this occasion, he had insured that there were no "conditions attached." Nevertheless, his mentor dithered and delayed until finally Bogdanovich decided to direct the movie himself, with Barry Brown as Winterbourne. The Hollywood rumor mill sprang into action once again, determined to exaggerate—and aggravate—the acrimony between the master and his supposed pupil. Welles had suggested Shepherd for Daisy, tongues wagged—but in jest, only to find the joke had gone over Bogdanovich's head. A variation on the tale had Welles making the suggestion cruelly, hoping to shock Bogdanovich back to his senses. A third version had Welles offering the casting suggestion quite deliberately, as a time bomb sure to explode in the lovers' faces and end their affair.

In point of fact, Welles was on his best behavior toward Bogdanovich at this time. He needed a place to stay in Los Angeles, while he cut and assembled his footage on *The Other Side of the Wind*, and since Bogdanovich had his own newly-built editing facility at Bel Air, Copa De Oro satisfied both his needs. An earlier incident, when Welles had been a weekend houseguest soon after the couple had moved in, may have prompted some trepidation. Shepherd, the first to smell burning from one of the ground-floor bathrooms, had called through the locked door to find out what was going on. *"Of course* everything's all right—" Welles retorted, even as, to the contrary, smoke from under the bathroom door enveloped Shepherd's feet—"apart from there being no blasted privacy in this house!"

A maid called Shepherd later and showed her what was left of Welles's white terry cloth robe. He had absentmindedly put a still-burning cigar in his pocket, then ripped off the robe as it burst into flames and hurled it into the bath. Half of it had missed and fallen on the rug, igniting a much more serious blaze. Welles had eventually doused the flames by directing the shower nozzle on what was left of the robe and the rug. The incident was not even mentioned until a day later, when Welles presented Shepherd with the gift of a book on opera. Inside was a drawing of a house on fire, with a ladybug in the foreground and the legend, "Ladybug, ladybug, fly away home. . . ."

And if Welles could grow hot, he could also grow cold. After dinner one evening Bogdanovich asked the maid to fetch the quart container of ice cream he had bought that morning. When the maid duly reported that all she could find was an empty carton, Welles turned sheepish, then sullen. "Well, don't look at me," he blurted out, guilt written all over his face. "I certainly didn't eat it!"

Bogdanovich was actively involved in the *Daisy Miller* screenplay, for which he would share credit with Frederic Raphael. They worked out a structure together; then Raphael wrote a script, that Bogdanovich redrafted, incorporating some of Raphael's suggestions into the final version.

With his three substantial successes trailing him, Bogdanovich confidently took the *Daisy Miller* proposal to Warners, where the studio was still counting *What's Up, Doc?*'s earnings. The studio bosses listened to him but were in no rush to put up the money. This was a costume drama, a period piece, after all, and how often did such a film recover its costs? Bogdanovich assured them it would be made relatively cheaply, for around $2 million, but he still failed to elicit any interest, since Warners' impression was that he was hellbent on making another *Death in Venice*, a recent and unsuccessful release. One was enough, they figured.

His fallback position was to transfer the project to Paramount and make it as one of the Directors' Company projects. Francis Ford Coppola had already added *The Conversation* to Bogdanovich's *Paper Moon*, though William Friedkin was apparently suffering from an advanced case of director's block.

Bogdanovich signed Mildred Natwick, Cloris Leachman, Eileen Brennan and Duilio Del Prete for the cast and scheduled an eleven-week shoot in the story's authentic locations, including the Pincio and the Coliseum in Rome, the Château de Chillon on Lake Geneva and the Hotel des Trois Couronnes in Vevey, Switzerland. "I think it will be marvelous to have a costume piece in which nobody behaves as though he's in a costume picture," he enthused as he took off for Italy, leaving Welles in charge at Bel Air. "I don't want the actors to be afraid to be casual about overlapping or stepping on each other's lines. Everybody will talk very fast, and it might as well be *What's Up, Doc?* in terms of pace. I think the whole picture will only play about 95 minutes."

When columnist Rex Reed turned up for an interview with Shepherd and Bogdanovich at the Rome Hilton, he found the room cluttered with albums, scripts and the New York papers Shepherd had brought with her—as well as with three days' worth of room-service spaghetti.

Whatever else Bogdanovich is—writer, director, actor—he remains first, last and foremost a performer, and as such he works best with an audience. If there's someone else in the room when he's on the telephone, he shamelessly plays to that audience, keeping up an endless stream of patter for the benefit of listeners at both ends of the wire. "What do you mean, the driver's downstairs?" Reed found Bogdanovich yelling into the phone. "I've been downstairs and he wasn't there. The guy's an idiot. What am I supposed to do—go looking for the driver? *He* should be looking for *me.*" Just then Shepherd called from the bedroom, "I've got a bee in my bed." Bogdanovich chuckled. "Cybill's got a bee in her bed," he repeated to Reed. "Nothing fazes Cybill." If the reparteé here sparkles with something less than the wit of Nick and Nora Charles, the Bogdanovich persona on view for Reed's benefit owed a debt nevertheless to W. S. Van Dyke and his team of *Thin Man* writers.

Night shooting at the Coliseum followed. Although Bogdanovich had given the authorities a single-digit estimate of the crew required, there seemed to be hundreds trampling through the ruins. When Reed glanced about and saw Eileen Brennan and Cloris Leachman from *The Last Picture Show,* he remarked that Bogdanovich seemed to be building up a repertory company in the John Ford manner. "Jean Renoir," Bogdanovich pointed out, "once said that the important thing in making a movie is gathering round a bunch of friends as though you're preparing a prank. The more friends, the easier it is to pull off the prank!"

Bogdanovich looked around at the massed assembly of cast and crew. "All these people are here because I wanted them," he crowed. "It's a terrific responsibility, but I'm good at faking self-confidence. It's like a war and I'm the general with the whole army waiting for me to tell them whether to retreat or attack."

With a mixture of ingenuousness and let's-hope-I'm-wrong prescience, he mused on the stage his career was entering. "So far I've been lucky, but I know my time is coming. They build you up so they can tear you down. I'm not modest, I'm not humble, and the more success I have the more the critics will resent me. The image they give me is one of arrogance. They say I'm cocky and audacious. But I just have enthusiasm for what I do, and that's not considered cool. They're just waiting for me to have a flop. In a sense it will be a relief—to have my first disaster—because it will make so many people happy."

When Shepherd emerged in her corseted, hoop-skirt costume, ready for the next shot but looking clearly uncomfortable, Bogdanovich whispered, "Now darling, I know this is going to be very difficult for you, but you have to stand up."

"What do I say?" Shepherd asked.

"This is your Mamie Van Doren shot," he smilingly replied. "You don't say a word." A moment later he looked over at her, one eyebrow raised critically. *"Cybill!"* he yelled. "Take that chewing gum out of your mouth!"

The next day Reed found Shepherd eating a tuna fish sandwich in their hotel suite and listening to her album, *Cybill Does It—to Cole Porter!* Bogdanovich's stab at seeking quotes from showbiz legends on Shepherd's vocal performance had already boomeranged. While Fred Astaire had seemed to play along—"Where do these kids get their talent?" he had ambiguously remarked—Frank Sinatra had been less gracious. "Some guys will do anything to ball a broad," he rasped.

"I called Frank Yablans at Paramount," the omnipresent Bogdanovich explained, "and said I'd like to do an album. He said, *'You sing?'* I said, 'No, of course not, it's for Cybill.' He said, *'She sings?'* The whole thing was paid for by Paramount without any of them hearing one song. That's what happens when you have a couple of hit pictures!"

For Reed the hardest thing about interviewing Shepherd was getting her alone, and even when Bogdanovich left the room, it seemed to Reed she still *sounded* like Bogdanovich. When the subject of her impending tussle with *Playboy* came up, Reed suggested that the number of people who saw the nude photo would be miniscule compared to those who would read about her lawsuit. Shepherd promptly let the cat out of the bag. "You think so?" she asked. "I'll let Peter decide." Bogdanovich bounced back into the room a few moments later and proceeded to give the game away completely. "I don't care what the lawsuit costs," he told Reed, "it'll keep other innocent girls from being victimized in the same way." (Bogdanovich had no way of knowing that a full decade later he would be locked in a similar campaign against Hefner and the Playboy organization, under the most tragic circumstances imaginable.) From his visit Reed managed to get one memorable quote that was repeated endlessly over the years. "Cybill started as a whim, an instinct, a little voice in my ear that I listened to," Bogdanovich told him. "Cybill was an itch—and I scratched it."

After the relative smoothness of the Rome shoot, filming at Vevey was held up by unseasonal rain and by problems with Barry Brown, who turned out to be deeply morose, and a chronic alcoholic at 22. "So help me, Barry, if I see you raising a glass just once more, I'll break your fucking arm!" Bogdanovich threatened at one point.

After a downpour which had Shepherd posing for stills to while away the time, he impatiently called out that shooting was about to resume. "OK, Cybill, let's go!" When Shepherd allowed the photographers to finish their snaps, Bogdanovich called again, still friendly, but authoritative as well: *"Now, Cybill!"* Blushing slightly, Shepherd meekly strolled onto the set. On another occasion, when Shepherd turned up late, Bogdanovich burst into her trailer. "How dare you keep us waiting!" he yelled. "I don't care how big a star you are, that's inexcusable!" Shepherd was so upset she burst into tears. She was never late again, having discovered the hard way the difficulties inherent in living and working with her director at the same time. Bogdanovich's arguably over-the-top reaction was at least partly in response to a crew that, he knew, was resentful of the attention and deference he gave her.

Bogdanovich had his usual fixed ideas on everything relating to *Daisy Miller,* but this time there was no Platt to bounce his ideas off. Without mentioning her by name, he clearly missed her. "The big danger in becoming successful," he agonized, "is that people just agree with me. Often in this picture I've found I'm reluctant to give people a direct command, because they'll just do it and it'll be wrong. After all, nobody's infallible. It's not all that difficult to direct a movie—really, it's an overrated job. Orson was the one who convinced me that of all the artistic endeavours, such as writing a novel, composing a symphony or painting a picture, directing a movie is among the easiest."

Bogdanovich still harbors one regret about his stay in Vevey. "The two people I wanted to meet most in the world were Nabokov and Noël Coward, who both lived close by, but I never tried, as I didn't think they'd want to meet me. Years later, after Noël had died and I was trying to get the rights to some play, I was talking to his executor, Graeme Payne. He told me Noël had loved *Paper Moon;* it was one of the last films he saw. I could have gone up there, he'd have loved to have met me, Payne said. It was one of those missed opportunities."

When Bogdanovich and Shepherd returned to Bel Air, they were horrified by the chaos their star guest had wreaked. Not content with merely using the editing facilities, Welles had taken over the entire mansion to continue shooting *The Other Side of the Wind*. Bogdanovich found and paid for rented accommodations in Los Angeles so that Welles could vacate the premises immediately. There was a limit to the hospitality one extended—even to a living legend.

Divorced professionally as well as personally from Peter, Platt teamed up with Ryan O'Neal again at Warners, as production designer on *The Thief Who Came to Dinner*. Between the end of *What's Up, Doc?* and the start of *Paper Moon* there had been talk of the two of them as "an item." Platt, however, denies this: "Ryan is a gorgeous man, but we were never more than friends."

At that time she still insisted that Shepherd might well represent the most important step in Bogdanovich's life. "He had to break out of the mold of seeing and living in movies. Without self-pity, I can say that I had always expected to remain married to Peter for the rest of my life. A lot of people think I'm still in love with him because I talk about him all the time. It's because my whole matriculation is involved with him. I really regretted the loss of Peter as a collaborator. I believe we are both heartbroken about it."

The back-and-forth shuttling of the children was a constant irritant for both of them. "I became more and more angry with Peter for not spending the right amount of time with them. We were both pursuing our careers and it looked to each of us as if the other were being tremendously destructive. I'd go to make a picture and he wouldn't take the children, but then he'd want me to take them when he went on location. They went to Italy with Peter while he was doing *Daisy Miller*, but I had to send my housekeeper along to look after them. When they stayed with Peter and Cybill in Bel Air overnight, they'd call me at eleven in the morning and say there was nobody up and how can they make eggs."

At this stage, Platt, never having harbored any dreams or ambition for herself, simply wanted to find interesting and remunerative work. "I

didn't do a great job as a single mother," she acknowledges, "and I'd
been through deep problems before settling down with Tony . . . Peter
had been the locomotive professionally with me as well as the tracks, so
when he left at first, I lost that drive. We had made a good pair, I was
a good editor and benefited enormously from knowing him. Now I saw
my life opening up in front of me and realized for the first time that I
had nothing to look forward to artistically. I was completely devastated,
demoralized and lonely."

Platt continued to drink, but persuaded herself she could control it
once she switched from martinis to six-packs. And in order to spend
more time at home with the children (the production designer works
longer on a movie than just about anyone, from pre- through postproduction), she began to write film scripts.

After having achieved considerable commercial success and critical
acclaim, Bogdanovich was now in the relatively fortunate position of
being able to regard *Daisy Miller* as a well-deserved indulgence. He had
adapted a small literary gem for very little money and, at the same time,
had provided Shepherd with what he saw as a perfect starring role. It
was a pause between bigger-budget movies, a mere divertissement. At
one time Orson Welles had cynically said of *Paper Moon:* "Let them all
think it's a Capra picture!" Of *Daisy Miller,* Welles might well have said,
probably with a chuckle, that Bogdanovich had brought off a George
Cukor classic. But most of the critics thought differently, Vincent
Canby in the *New York Times* proving perhaps the sole significant exception as he declared *Daisy Miller* "an unexpected triumph" and lauded
Shepherd's contribution. "It's Bogdanovich's best, most original film,"
he raved, burning his boats, while the the rest of the critics mainly sailed
off in a different direction.

"Cybill Shepherd is miscast in the title role. *Daisy Miller* is a dud,"
Variety maintained, before going on to predict, accurately, a thin box
office. *Esquire*'s John Simon decided to zero in on a more personal level,
splashing acid at all concerned. "Bogdanovich was at a loose end," he
theorized, "looking for a subject that might suit his girlfriend, when he
hit on *Daisy Miller.* He decided that Henry James had written the
novella with Cybill Shepherd in mind and that the least he could do to
oblige Miss Shepherd and James was to make the film. It is hard to

determine to whom he has done the greater disservice; to his author, by assuming he could bring him to the screen, or to his inamorata, by assuming he could get her to act."

Being attacked by critics Bogdanovich knew personally made their barbs no easier to endure. Up to this point, he had been accustomed to suffering no more than an occasional unfavorable notice mixed in with a welter of favorable ones, all of them drowned out in any case by the ringing of box office cash registers. Here the dissenters were in the majority and business was negligible. The self-protective line, "They'll understand it better in Europe," turned out to be a vain hope. It is doubtful that what Bogdanovich had in mind was Jonathan Rosenbaum's "understanding" as it appeared in Britain's *Sight and Sound:* "Working for the first time without the talents of Polly Platt," he pointedly noted, "in a period and on a continent where he has to depend more on intuition than experience. . . . the results are sad indeed."

Veteran director Henry Hathaway voiced a particularly wounding remark. "Trying to make that little thing he's with into Daisy Miller was hilarious," Hathaway scoffed. *"God Almighty* couldn't do it. She's so *coy!"*

Bogdanovich and Shepherd's efforts to promote the movie backfired. Featuring the two of them together on the cover of *People* was fine, but the content of the article inside, "Living Together Is Sexy," did little to endear them to the American public. When they appeared on the "Tonight Show," their crassness seemed compounded. Fred Kiel summed up the general reaction in *The Village Voice:* "First of all I enjoy Bogdanovich's films," he admitted, before getting down to the business at hand. "One's relationship to an artist's work is all that should matter, unless that artist pops up hosting the 'Tonight Show.' The very idea shocked me. I would have expected it of Norman Mailer, certainly, but for Bogdanovich to descend from the rarefied atmosphere of Hollywood. . . . Yet there he was, 'He-ee-re's Peter,' and out he sweeps in a Carson swagger and proceeds into a monologue that set the tone for the show, an exercise in giant egoism. Now, many of the jokes fell flat, but he continued onward with an admirable, swinish confidence that, combined with the subject matter, revealed where he was coming from. His greatest accomplishments: *What's Up, Doc?, Paper Moon,* and Cybill Shepherd. Yuk, yuk . . . When Cybill came out he asked her, 'When was the first time you realized I'd made you a star?' "

David Scott Milton caught the TV appearances and disagrees with much of the criticism: "I thought they were kind of fun. Peter will always come across as more serious than he is and Cybill will always come across as more silly than she is. I don't know why, maybe it's an edge of nervousness. Cybill becomes looser and the damn thing works against her. You put the two of them together and it looks a little foolish. Essentially with Peter, it's that old act of his again, for in his soul he's twelve-years old. To deal with the world he developed his other side, which is really a paper-thin act. The reason it comes across as arrogance is that when one is acting something that one doesn't wholly feel, sometimes people are put off by that. Let's face it, though, you can't do an interview and be a twelve-year old kid . . . He's just not playing the public role as well as he might."

"People hated us, just for being young, attractive, successful, and cocky," Bogdanovich says in their defense. "What they didn't know is that it *was* all just an act. We didn't really feel that way. We were just very much in love and enjoying being together."

"We were pretty obnoxious," Shepherd admits today. "We talked like we knew what we were talking about. I don't think you ever know what you're talking about, and certainly not at that age. I'd gone through various personas on talk shows, the first [when] I was a model and was so terrified I couldn't even talk. Then I was so excited I was talking a mile a minute, not making any sense, just mindless chatter. Then I cultivated a persona that wasn't me. I was very insecure. It matched what I was playing in films. I simply didn't know how to be myself. I was living this extraordinary life of getting to know one genius after another—Orson, John Ford, Stella Adler, but it had its element of ivory tower existence. Peter was a kind of rebellion and you have to break away from your roots and find out who you are through rebellion. I'd disconnected myself and got a whole new life, living in a mansion in Bel Air. Believe it or not, there was nowhere cozy in it. I'm a child of the humanities—I like things on a human scale."

Bogdanovich's veneer of cockiness increasingly masked a gnawing assortment of insecurities. Was Cybill good or bad? Was she guilty or innocent? Was she to be trusted? Try as he might, Bogdanovich found himself unable to make up his mind—just as in so many movies, where nobody trusts a beautiful woman for long . . .

Daisy Miller proved to be the end of the much-vaunted Directors'

Company. "Friedkin behaved terribly when it was dissolved," Bogdanovich claims. "He wanted all his money, even though he'd done nothing for the company except break it up. He wanted half a million for himself out of *Paper Moon* when our deal was $350,000. Personally, I wouldn't even have given him that."

Today Bogdanovich is able to place his *Daisy Miller* contribution to the company in perspective. "If I had to do it over again, I'd have done it as a television special for even less money, and it would probably have been a tremendous success. I suppose the subject was not something for the big screen audience."

Frank Marshall, now firmly established at Amblin Entertainment, defends the picture. "I think it was one of Peter's best," he maintains. "Who does Henry James? He took the risk, and he was aware of the risk he was taking. We weren't trying to make a blockbuster movie, we were trying to do something artistic and we did it at a price. I think Cybill and Barry Brown were very, very good in it. And it's shot in a way that gives you the total feel of the period, which is what movies ought to do."

Marshall's view is supported by the increasingly respectful attention the movie has since received in revival. But back in 1973 Bogdanovich and Cybill had brought off the cinematic equivalent of the lovers' leap, take one. Take two was soon to follow.

CHAPTER 11

At one point, early in their relationship, Bogdanovich said to Shepherd, "Look, if you don't like the way I'm behaving, just tell me."

Her response was "I've been brought up to listen to a man!"

"Oh, God," said Bogdanovich, "that'll bring out the *worst* in me!"

To this day he denies that Shepherd was ever a doormat: "The whole Svengali thing, it wasn't like that at all. Cybill was a really strong person with an independent mind. She knew what I was up to and respected it. I encouraged her to sing, to dance and do everything she was interested in, like my mother had encouraged me when I was young. She read a lot on her own, bettering and educating herself. I taught her about movies, as I had Polly. We went through the whole history of films."

David Scott Milton observed their relationship over the years, "I never saw any of that Svengali stuff," he says. "They seemed to have a relationship that was just right. To me Cybill was just delightful, a lot of fun to be with, very lively, unassuming, but with a little streak of toughness underneath and a kind of integrity which she maybe got from Peter. She'll let you know she cares about a certain thing and will fight to get it done in her own way. Pretty unusual for someone in Hollywood."

The integrity that Milton attributed to Bogdanovich is an aspect of his character lost on his detractors. While his friends may have been aware of it, they reflected that if only he were able to combine the quality with an element of humility. . . .

At Long Last Love originated, as did Shepherd's album, from a fateful Christmas present, a volume of Cole Porter's lyrics that she had given her lover. Bogdanovich's prudery was brought face-to-face with the original, unexpurgated versions of Porter's wit and wonder, much of which had been laundered for recorded versions and public broadcasting. The songwriter's trademarks stood out quite clearly amid the poetry—he wrote *dirty*. "I Love Him, But He Doesn't Love Me" was the specific song that inspired Bogdanovich's idea of a romantic musical chairs movie. It would make a perfect thirties musical, Bogdanovich felt, and a superb vehicle for Shepherd.

With any "collaboration" with his ex-wife now relegated to the telephone, Platt's recollection is that Bogdanovich called and asked her reaction to his first thoughts about *At Long Last Love*. Her reply was not what he wanted to hear: "Don't make it a musical," Platt says she advised. "And set it in the present day." Bogdanovich remembers the story differently and years later wrote to Platt accusing her of deliberately encouraging his excesses on the movie because of her "hatred" for Shepherd. "I *never* hated Cybill," Platt says today. "She was the *victim*, and I don't carry any animosity. I never really blamed her, I blamed Peter."

With 20th Century-Fox set to finance and distribute the film, Bogdanovich cast Burt Reynolds opposite Shepherd and signed Madeline Kahn and Duilio Del Prete to play the parallel lovers in his high society quadrille. Eileen Brennan and John Hillerman would provide below stairs support, together with the redoubtable Mildred Natwick as Reynolds's mother. From *What's Up, Doc?* came M. Emmet Walsh, this time as a doorman with a penchant for W.C. Fields impersonations, and Liam Dunn as Harry, the sourpuss newsvendor. To keep everything in the family, Antonia and Sashy were to be featured in one of the musical numbers, with Anna appearing as a Lord and Taylor salesclerk.

In the Hollywood musicals Bogdanovich had grown up with, he had always waited restlessly for the plot to stop to make way for the musical numbers. In *At Long Last Love* he tried to remedy what he considered a failing by making the songs themselves the plot. He intended the film to have not the least suggestion of realism. His interest in making the movie, he claimed, derived from the fantasies that he had entertained as a child of starring in a musical.

Two months before shooting started, Reynolds and Shepherd signed up for daily voice coaching and dance lessons, all too aware that Bogdanovich intended to use live-sound recording: the basic melodies, played on an electric piano, together with Bogdanovich's directorial messages, would be transmitted via FM, through transistorized ear pieces, to the actors, whose live vocal contributions would be recorded by tiny antenna microphones concealed in their hair. "The best moments in any film are the ones that happen by happy accident," Bogdanovich claims. "If I'd prerecorded the whole score I'd have lost all chance of spontaneity."

The drawback of his recording method was the number of takes it required, as anything less than absolute silence from the non-participants meant that scenes had to be shot over and over again. Unknown to Bogdanovich, the FM broadcasts were being made on an unauthorized frequency that was soon picked up by puzzled government personnel unable to make sense of Bogdanovich's cryptic instructions. Once the signal was traced, Bogdanovich and the cast found themselves surrounded by FBI agents who proceeded to photograph and fingerprint everyone in sight. Burt Reynolds was the only one to escape the bust, having left the set earlier to prepare for a dinner in his honor at the Beverly Wilshire Hotel, where he was to accept the 1974 Entertainer of the Year Award. Bogdanovich had been scheduled to give a speech at the event, and when he failed to turn up it was widely interpreted that he and Reynolds had had a falling out over the attention Reynolds was reportedly paying to Shepherd. The truth was that Bogdanovich was in custody, trying to talk his way out of the raid.

As far as Reynolds was concerned, the movie was heaven-sent: "All of a sudden I'm Cary Grant," he enthused, "my lifelong hero, standing in an elegantly appointed room holding a champagne cocktail. Then, very cute, I burst into a romantic song and soft-shoe routine à la Fred Astaire, another idol of mine. No one sets me on fire or throws me out the window!"

The incidental demands of a musical, taken for granted in the days when such films were regularly produced by the major studios—afflictions like sore feet and strained vocal chords—here created conflict and considerable bickering, on a constantly increasing scale, as did what appeared to be Bogdanovich's mountingly arrogant whims. After a contretemps with set director Jerry Wunderlich over the dressing of one particular set: "It's all wrong," Bogdanovich complained. "Ugly, ugly, *ugly*. It looks like it belonged to some diseased 70-year-old faggot in 1912." Wunderlich offered to guide Bogdanovich through 20th Century-Fox's prop warehouse to select alternative furniture. "Show me something with taste," Bogdanovich commanded, "not all this Victoriana. Victoriana reminds me of repression, of Dickens, of what's-her-name, Lady Havisham. No, Jerry, that's pukey. That's too busy . . . that's too cottage . . . that's too Biedermeier."

With Wunderlich's patience near the breaking point, Bogdanovich spotted a couple of pictures he liked, but which were clearly anachronistic. "You don't want to be laughed at for being wrong," Wunderlich commented out of earshot.

"I *hate* those!" Bogdanovich declared of two frolicsome nudes Wunderlich hung on his next set. "Can't we find some other kind of painting? Something with *taste?*" When Bogdanovich left the set, Wunderlich could barely conceal his anger. "He'd better stop using that word 'taste,' " he warned. Bogdanovich's second assistant director, Jerry Ballew, also well out of earshot, voiced his opinion on the difficulties Bogdanovich was encountering—or was it creating? "He's split from Polly Platt," Ballew explained, "and she was a large part of his visual conception of things. Now he has problems he didn't have before. He can't explain what he wants as clearly as she could."

When a particular scene was continually ruined by jets flying overhead, Shepherd repaired to the sidelines, brushing her hair with such furious strokes that the brush broke in her hand. "Find me another one," she told a wardrobe woman. "I can't use this. It'll give my hair *cancer.*" One reporter found Shepherd's fractious temperament confined solely to the set and its many attendant aggravations. Relaxing between takes, Shepherd seemed to be a different person, even when she was asked whether it was difficult to work with a lover. "Of course it is," she answered. "We have two separate relationships. I deal with him at work as a director and at home as a different person—but of course, he isn't."

Shepherd kept breaking out in a rash until she discovered she was allergic to the makeup being used. After one weekend Madeline Kahn turned up with a suntan that didn't fit the elegant black-and-white look Bogdanovich was determined to give *At Long Last Love*. Although it was filmed in color, he had all his principals' outfits designed in varying tones of either black, white, silver or grey, and he even reshot one scene after noticing a cocktail with a red cherry in it, insisting that a black olive be used instead.

"I felt it would heighten the art deco mood of the film," Bogdanovich explained. "Also, it was a technical challenge. Photographing black-and-white is extremely difficult as pure black tends to soak up the light, since you need more lighting for it. In filming, the whites are usually 'greyed down' and the blacks 'greyed up,' but for *At Long Last Love* we're not doing that. We're using pure whites and pure blacks, which is very difficult, but rewarding. Black and white can look gorgeous in color."

Neil Canton, having missed out on *Daisy Miller* because it was deemed too expensive to take Bogdanovich's regular production crew to Europe, caught up with the director during shooting on *At Long Last Love*. What he sensed immediately, coming in as he did halfway through the movie, was the tremendous amount of resistance that had built up between cast and crew on one side and Bogdanovich and Shepherd on the other. The cast felt that the director was paying far more attention to his star than he was to them, thereby making them increasingly short-tempered and nervous. The crew had their own views on the casting. "It's not going to work," they would mutter during a lunch break. "Burt Reynolds shouldn't be singing."

The mood of enjoyment that Canton felt had buoyed *What's Up, Doc?* was here completely absent. "When the movie's going well, you look forward to it," he says, "but this was more like a job for everyone, like they had to get up and go to work. I don't remember anything funny about *At Long Last Love*. Peter was much more uptight. I used to go home at night thinking, well that's one day less to go. Not that Peter was anything less than nice to me. I'd pick him up in his Rolls-Royce in the morning, leave my funky little Volvo at his place, and drive him to work. One night he told me to take the Rolls home, obviously having no idea which district I was living in or where I'd have to park it. I'd have been up all night guarding it! But it was a nice idea, just a little impractical."

After Burt Reynolds collapsed during a particularly strenuous dance sequence, the whole unit had to shut down for a week while he recuperated. Fuel was added to the rumors about his "poor health" and "bad heart" that had already circulated during location shooting of *The Man Who Loved Cat Dancing*. "Burt was sick on the picture and didn't work as hard as he should have," says Bogdanovich in reflection. "He was neurotic." Dinah Shore flew in from New York to look after the star during his week off, thus ending speculation about his "affair" with Shepherd. "And Madeline was difficult," Bogdanovich maintains, "because she wanted to be a glamourpuss in the movie. I just wanted her to be funny."

Even his fascination with Shepherd could be expressed by Bogdanovich in movie-genealogical terms. Alluding to a "morning-after" sequence in *At Long Last Love*, in which Shepherd was required to appear with slices of cucumber plastered on her face, Bogdanovich revealed that he had watched her use that very treatment in Rome to keep her skin moist while shooting *Daisy Miller*. "Audiences will really warm to her at this point in the picture," he predicted, "it's the relief, the shock of seeing a beautiful girl looking really lousy. If you think of it, Marlene Dietrich was a star, but she didn't really connect with audiences until they poured all that water over her in *Destry*." Bogdanovich neglected, as any lover would, to carry the comparison further and note that the film post-dated the influence of Josef Von Sternberg, Dietrich's mentor, by many years.

With a budget of $6 million invested in *At Long Last Love*, 20th Century Fox soon began to express alarm at the peculiarities of the production. Live sound *and* a black-and-white look, with the bulk of the movie shot on the backlot? "The New York of the thirties doesn't exist anyway," Bogdanovich shot back. "You know what Lubitsch said: 'I've been to Paris, France, and Paris, Paramount, and I prefer Paris, Paramount.' Most good movies are made on the backlot. I want to create an illusion of New York, an artificial New York." Sweeping all doubts aside, he confidently predicted the movie would become the landmark of Shepherd's career to date.

CHAPTER 12

*A*t *Long Last Love* had to be cut and assembled with great speed, since Fox wanted it to be the Radio City Music Hall attraction for Easter, 1975. The reviews that greeted the movie were among the most vicious in cinema history. After his virtual solo flight in support of *Daisy Miller*, Vincent Canby was taking no chances this time. *"At Long Last Love* never quite sinks," he conceded, "but then it never really leaves the pier." In the Los Angeles *Times* Charles Champlin described the movie as "The year's most frustrating failure. . . . The damn thing doesn't work." Bad? No, these were the *good* notices.

"The film is an atrocity," John Kobal wrote in *Stills.* "It's the kind of movie one waits years to avoid." David Sterritt in The *Christian Science Monitor* had no doubt where the blame lay. "It all comes down to Mr. Bogdanovich's weary script and tired direction, not to mention his inept use of Cybill Shepherd, his perennial star, in a leading role [for which] her meager song-and-dance skills do not equip her." Bad? These were fairly restrained.

In *Esquire,* John Simon—perhaps still smarting from being sent up in *What's Up, Doc?*—took off the gloves. *"At Long Last Love,"* he sputtered, "may be the worst movie musical of this—or any—decade. . . . Sitting through this movie is like having someone at a fancy Parisian restaurant, who neither speaks nor reads French, read out stentoriously the entire long menu in his best Arkansas accent, and occasionally interrupt himself to chortle at his own cleverness. . . . Cybill Shepherd plays a poor little rich girl with a notion of sophistication that is under-passed only by her acting ability. (I will not even sully my pen by making it describe her singing and dancing.)"

Not even *Variety*, a staunch Bogdanovich supporter until *Daisy Miller*, could find a good word for this movie. "It just lies there," they groaned, "and *dies* there." *Newsweek* described it as "the most amazing combination of adoration and sadism ever seen."

Even the kindest review of all, from Roger Ebert, had a particularly nasty sting in its tail. Agreeing that *At Long Last Love* was no masterpiece, he was at a loss to account for the viciousness of the attacks. "It's almost as if Bogdanovich is being accused of the sin of pride for daring to make a movie in the classical Hollywood style," he wrote. *"At Long Last Love* isn't *Swing Time*, but it isn't *Lucky Lady* either. Bogdanovich has too much taste, too sure a feel for the right tone, to go seriously wrong. And if he doesn't go spectacularly right, at least he provides small pleasures. Cybill Shepherd is a wonder to behold, but she isn't a gifted singer and no regimen of voice lessons is going to make her one. . . . Before Bogdanovich makes further attempts to present her as a singer, he'd do well to rerun *Citizen Kane*, particularly the scene of Susan Alexander's disastrous operatic debut."

When Bogdanovich, looking tired and worried, turned up at the *Village Voice* offices in New York for an interview he immediately noticed the absence of his old compatriot, Andrew Sarris. "Why isn't Andy here? Where is he?" he asked—quite reasonably, since it was Sarris who had originally suggested the interview, which was to run alongside his *Voice* review of *At Long Last Love*. Now, it seemed, Sarris had decided not to do the interview himself. Bogdanovich had figured "that either Andy hated the picture and wanted to give me a chance to defend myself publicly or he loved the picture and wanted to give me some more publicity."

Bogdanovich turned out to be right first time. In Sarris's review the vitriol flowed freely, although he later disclaimed responsibility for the headline "At Long Last Turkey." "Peter and Cybill," he wrote, "have suffered a complete disaster. You may believe it or not, but to me the arrival of a bad movie represents a bit of bad news. And when I know the people involved even slightly, the reporting of the bad news becomes very painful. My initial sentence on this occasion requires my draping a black hood over my head."

In the *Saturday Review*, Hollis Alpert neatly summed up the views of Bogdanovich's detractors: "Bogdanovich wrote, produced and directed *At Long Last Love*, and it demonstrates nothing so much as how easily a fellow can be deluded by his evaluation of his own brilliance. With no experience in writing a musical, he wrote one. With no experience in directing a musical, he directed one. With no experience in producing a musical, he produced one."

Bogdanovich's only comfort was in the film's first-week figures at the Radio City Music Hall: 43,000 admissions was an encouraging start. "Making movies is a bit like [being] a politician," he consoled himself. "You go for the biggest vote. If fourteen critics slaughtered me in New York, which they did, but 43,000 people go to see the movie during its first week in Radio City anyway, who am I to believe? The answer is to take no notice of reviews, whether they are good or bad."

Despite its good start at Radio City, where the take was obviously inflated by the accompanying Easter stage spectacular, the movie quickly bombed elsewhere. Bogdanovich and Shepherd's promotional tour of the U.S. and Canada proved futile; after only a few weeks the run was virtually over. Platt took Antonia and Sashy to a matinee performance. As they waited in the foyer, they heard the music from the end-credits, but then, when the doors opened, not a single person emerged: the movie had been playing to an empty house. Platt felt she owed Bogdanovich a truthful reaction. "I was right," she told him. "You should have made it modern day. And if you hadn't tried to do those Porter songs, if you hadn't tried to make Cybill sing, if you hadn't tried to make her into something she isn't, *and* in a story about you and me and her, about a man who can't make up his mind between two women, it wouldn't have turned out such a silly exercise. As it is, it's just *terrible*."

Bogdanovich and Shepherd traveled to London for the first foreign opening of *At Long Last Love*. There Shepherd took the opportunity to lash out at her tormentors. "The critics have insisted on reviling me personally," she declared. "They've picked a target. And with Peter, who only wanted to give pleasure, they've claimed the film is an attempt to say something in an egotistical manner, that he is taking something from people. You don't have to give in to the critics. You have to make an effort to ignore all that. If the audience responds, then that's what it's all about. The critics were given the chance to attack, because I dared to sing. They hate you for trying to do something different. It's one thing if I'd pretended to be Judy Garland, but there's no pretense in the film. It was done very simply.

"I wouldn't mind if they were objective about me, but they're not. They always write about me and my relationship with Peter . . . I could understand other actresses being jealous. After all, I've walked off with two of the best women's parts in years in *Daisy Miller* and *At Long Last Love*. But why should the critics hate me? It's bad for any actress today; and it's particularly bad for me. Because Peter discovered me, not many other directors want to use me. If they do, you see, that's admitting that Peter was right in picking me and that's something they don't want to do. It's an ego thing. They'd rather find unknowns of their own than use someone else's discovery. That's one reason I continue to work with Peter."

Today Shepherd looks back on *At Long Last Love* and her first album—the whole Cole Porter experience, in fact—with a disarming frankness that distance, and regained success, serve to bring. "The album embarrasses me to this day," she admits. "I was in no way ready for that, or for *At Long Last Love*—but Peter insisted. I shudder when I hear that album or see that movie, and it's been a great hindrance to me. It was an experience, that's the only good thing I can say about it. I felt sorry for myself, but self-pity is debilitating. The only way to survive is to work harder and try not to take it too seriously."

Shepherd had at least one unexpected bonus from *At Long Last Love*, in the form of a telephone call from Cary Grant. "If I was still acting," he told her, "you're the kind of actress I'd like to work with." The sentiment sustained Shepherd through a difficult time. "I'll always love him for that," she says, beaming.

Bogdanovich maintains he was protected from the worst of the reviews. "I had a terribly good secretary who managed to keep it all away from me—under instruction. But I got the general feeling. What really hurt was the venom that was spewed on to Cybill, because she wasn't guilty of anything. She did a good job and worked hard.

"The critics thought I was making a straight musical comedy like in the thirties, and that's something they made up their own minds about without bothering to ask me what I had in mind! That wasn't my intention. None of the people in the story are *supposed* to be singers or dancers, apart from Madeline, and we established early on that even she wasn't supposed to be that hot. I don't know why everyone missed that point. It's *intentionally* bad. I wasn't doing a story about Gertrude Lawrence, or Ethel Merman, or whoever. It would change the story if she were supposed to be a great artist. I wanted it to be loose. If Cybill missed a note, or if Burt got a little off-tempo, that was find, precisely what I *wanted*. That's why I recorded all the numbers live, which was last done in 1932, when they had to do it that way. I was after spontaneity, and you don't get that when the actors are just lip-syncing to something they recorded three months before."

While continuing to write scripts, Platt needed to keep some money rolling in. An attempt to work with director Mike Nichols turned out unhappily. After a series of flops, Nichols was preparing *The Fortune,* to star Jack Nicholson and Warren Beatty. Based on *The Modesse Fortune,* the story concerned two men who were so greedy for an inheritance that they missed the real fortune, the Modesse heiress herself. "Mike and I didn't agree about anything," says Platt. "His ideas about architecture were different from mine. I fought to get my way. I should have let it go, but I didn't and continued to battle. Mike had a very bad way with him in those days, he was very insecure. He'd come in and talk about my ideas and constantly consult the two or three yes men he had with him, who simply agreed with everything he said. It made me so angry."

She stood by helplessly as Nichols drastically cut what she considered a fine screenplay, then disagreed with him on the casting of newcomer Stockard Channing as the heiress. Once Platt had prepared the sets and found all the locations, Nichols called her into his office. She knew what was coming. "You're going to fire me, aren't you?" she asked him. He nodded. "There's no need to tell anyone," he assured her. "We'll just say you were filling in until Dick Sylbert was available."

Platt was enraged and managed to convince herself that was what Nichols had had in mind all along. When she got home that evening she waited for a feeling of shame to overwhelm her in the wake of her dismissal. It never came. "I'd never been fired by anybody in my life. Never! God, I was so angry with him! I decided I wasn't going to work in motion pictures any more. That lasted about a week."

Two spectacular offers changed her mind—the job of production designer on *The Bad News Bears* that reunited her with Tatum O'Neal, and then another real plum, the chance to work again with Barbra Streisand on her production of *A Star Is Born*.

In Britain several critics chose to swim against the U.S. tide of abuse for *At Long Last Love*, neatly raising the question, Had the majority of critics there misread Bogdanovich's intentions, as he claimed? Kenneth Robinson in the *Spectator* felt they had: "The Cole Porter lyrics are performed in a throwaway manner some reviewers have mistaken for amateurishness. I haven't enjoyed a film so much for a long time."

Felix Barker in the *Evening News* also found much to praise: "Bogdanovich shows an infallible feeling for the period, and the parody is somehow improved by having two non-musical comedy players in the leads. Burt Reynolds as an elegant song-and-dance man seems as inappropriate as Clark Gable hoofing in *Idiot's Delight*, but he makes a splendid stab at it, and Cybill Shepherd is a delicious marcel-waved heroine, a melting willowy charmer whom one quite forgives for not dancing like Ginger Rogers. From the beginning to the end it's delightful, it's delicious, it's de-lovely. It's de-Bogdanovich."

The biggest prize of all came from the redoubtable doyenne of British film critics, Dilys Powell, who enthused: "If required to say which of the week's films I would most cheerfully sit through again, I would choose *At Long Last Love*. It breaks all the rules, or seems to. It is a musical, but the plot is strung on the songs, not the songs on the plot. It is in Technicolor, but almost ignores the possibilities of color. Peter Bogdanovich loves the past—the past cinema, I mean. He knows it can't be resurrected. But he thinks something can be done to revive its memory; affectionately he has tried in *The Last Picture Show* and *Paper Moon* to do just that. I don't know about the past cinema, but personally I came away revived. A tribute to Cole Porter then; but also, now I come to think more carefully, a tribute to a kind of cinema no longer fashionable."

Nine minutes that were cut, at Fox's insistence, after the movie's opening, made not the slightest difference to the movie's dire box-office showing. It was painful for Bogdanovich to accept that, after all his efforts, the chapter was closed on *At Long Last Love*, with the picture withdrawn from release, having failed to recover even its advertising costs, let alone its budget. So Bogdanovich had produced two box-office bombs in a row with Shepherd.

Burt Reynolds spoke up after he had ample time to reflect on his involvement. "I'd waited 20 years to make a movie like it," he admitted. "When Peter asked me to do song and dance it was not like jumping from square one to square two; it was like jumping from square one to square ninety-nine. It was a terrible mistake because we all sank together. My audience, which is a big audience, let me know right away that they didn't want me to sing and dance. They practically picketed the theaters; it was frightening. I'm not going to take the entire blame for *At Long Last Love*, I think Peter and Cybill should share some of it. Ironically, I came out with better reviews than anybody else, but that's like staying afloat longer on the Titanic. I still drowned. However, it was not as bad a film as it was reviewed. What was reviewed was Peter and Cybill's relationship. You see, Peter had done something that all critics will never forgive him for doing. That is, stop being a critic, go make a film, and have that film, *The Last Picture Show*, become enormously successful. Well, what he did then was go on talk shows and be rather arrogant and talk about how bad critics are. That was the final straw. So they were all waiting with their hatchets and knives. And along came Peter, and gave them something they could kill him with. Unfortunately, there I was between Cybill's broad shoulders and Bogdanovich's ego. And I got buried along with them. The danger is that Cybill's had such bad notices that Peter may set out to prove he's right and the critics are wrong. I just hope he doesn't spend the next three films trying to show she can be Anne Bancroft. *That* would be making a mistake."

At least one *At Long Last Love* cast member, Eileen Brennan, makes no bones about being a Bogdanovich supporter. "The movie turned out to be lots of people's favorite. I don't give a shit what the critics say! Does *anybody?* I needed money after becoming a single parent after my husband walked out on me, and Peter gave me a check *and* a job! He can be hilarious. After *The Sting* he wagged his finger at me and said I *must not do* a part like that again—I'd been *supporting* Paul Newman and Robert Redford, he scolded me! I said I'd always supported *Cybill*—what was the difference?! That's why I love him. I can poke him and make him laugh. He's very quick to laugh at himself."

The indomitable veteran Billy Wilder summed up the depth of Hollywood's feeling against Bogdanovich with a fair degree of accuracy:

"There is a canard that Hollywood is full of bitterness and dissension, envy and hostility. It's just not true! I've lived here for 40 years and I can tell you that it took one simple event to bring all the factions together—a flop by Peter Bogdanovich. Champagne corks were popping, flags were waving. The guru had laid an egg, and Hollywood was delighted."

Prior to the release of *At Long Last Love,* Dennis Stanfill, president of 20th Century-Fox, had thrown a lavish red carpet and black tie party following a private screening of the picture. As hundreds of guests had gulped and guzzled the finest food and drink Hollywood could provide, all the talk was of the total disaster the film would prove. One local wit had observed, "What they should have done was shelve the movie and release the party!"

To Bogdanovich the failure of *At Long Last Love* was all the more devastating in that he regarded it as his most personal picture to date. "In lots of ways it was a musical version of my divorce, about the difficulty of breaking up with Polly. In a way Madeline was Polly and Cybill was Cybill and I was both guys. How can you choose between two people, one who makes you laugh and the other who's romantic?"

Bogdanovich was ready to take Otto Preminger's advice—"Forget it," the old warhorse told him. "Go and make your next film."—but accepting that was one thing and finding someone to back the film was quite another.

CHAPTER 13

With the cacophony from the reception of *At Long Last Love* still reverberating in their ears, Bogdanovich and Shepherd spent several months in Europe trying to console each other. Back home they had felt almost tangibly that certain people were turning their backs, as if afraid of somehow being tainted by the movie's failure. Although Bogdanovich realized better than most that what had happened to him had been endured by scores of other directors before him, it was still hard to come to terms with no longer being the hottest director in town. But he was, after all, only 37, and surely far from being finished.

Meanwhile, Columbia Pictures was having jitters of its own. The studio, intending to finance Bogdanovich's new movie, *Nickelodeon*, had watched in dismay as first *Daisy Miller* and then *At Long Last Love* had died in the dust. Were they about to stuff money into a third turkey? David Begelman at Columbia decided that damage control had to be the order of the day.

Nickelodeon had started life as a script by W.D. Richter, a comedy about the early days of filmmaking, much of which was dramatized history of the early patent wars between studios and wildcat producers. When the producing team of Robert Chartoff and Irwin Winkler hired Bogdanovich to direct, he proceeded to rewrite the script extensively, with Shepherd in mind as his star and with making *Nickelodeon* an ode to silent movies as his aim. Lighter on the comedy and heavier on the abrasive realism than Richter's original script, Bogdanovich's contribution laced the movie with anecdotes related by the likes of Fritz Lang, Allan Dwan, Raoul Walsh and John Ford.

One by one, from the beginning he was forced to make compromises. When he announced that he wanted to shoot in black and white again, Begelman suspended the picture and agreed to restart only after Bogdanovich had backed down and agreed to make it in color. Shepherd? Forget it. But it was written for her, Bogdanovich protested. *Forget* it! Jeff Bridges and John Ritter for the two male leads? Begelman turned both down and insisted that major stars be cast. Bogdanovich picked Burt Reynolds for the country bumpkin who becomes an overnight screen hero and Ryan O'Neal for Leo, the lawyer-turned-director, à la the veteran Leo McCarey, reasoning that here at least were two stars he knew. And then, whenever Bogdanovich had O'Neal's character appear tougher, Begelman proceeded to cut these scenes from the script. John Ritter was relegated to one of the supporting roles. Orson Welles for the studio boss? No, Brian Keith. Even before the movie had begun shooting, the list of concessions forced on Bogdanovich seemed endless.

At the same time, also for Columbia, Martin Scorsese was casting *Taxi Driver*. He had heard the rumor mill only too well and spent six months trying to cast someone else in what he had originally seen as "the Cybill Shepherd role." "I'd heard she was trouble," he admits. When, having exhausted every other possibility, he finally asked Shepherd herself to read for the part, the role was hers for the taking. Whereupon, with all the considerable charm and tact of which he is capable, David Begelman presented her with a straight choice. "He told me I couldn't do both *Taxi Driver* and *Nickelodeon*," she recalls. "And because Peter and I had such enormous flak from working together, I chose *Taxi Driver*." She pauses and gives one of her most engaging smiles. "Was I *really* given a choice?" A tinkling laugh. "Maybe, maybe not."

Begelman's charm was noticeably absent from the more direct ultimatum he handed Shepherd's lover: If Bogdanovich made any waves over being denied Shepherd for *Nickelodeon*, she would not be allowed to make *Taxi Driver* either.

Although hurt by the implication that he could produce his best work only when kept apart professionally from Shepherd, Bogdanovich was in no position to defy Begelman. On Shepherd's recommendation he picked a friend from her modeling days, Jane Hitchcock, to play the role of the blonde silent movie star. Tatum O'Neal joined the cast as the young Anita Loos-type character, who at fourteen has sold her first script to D.W. Griffith for a Mary Pickford film.

As the budget for the movie climbed, largely because of the studio's own demands, Columbia nervously searched for other investors to share the risk. At the last minute they landed British Lion/EMI, whose team of Barry Spikings and Michael Deeley came in for $3 million, half the total budget. Without their contribution, Columbia might well have chosen not to proceed.

Location filming, in Modesto, California, got off to a sticky start. If Tatum O'Neal had been a wild, untutored kid on *Paper Moon,* her experience on that movie had served only to make her into a first-class pain in the neck, Bogdanovich found. After a few days' shooting he took her to one side. "Love," he said, "we're just not getting along."

"I know," Tatum agreed, "that's because you're picking on me."

"That's because you're being such a nuisance," Bogdanovich countered. "You've got to know your lines. Stop picking on the other actors, and don't be so clever. Be a *professional,* and stop blaming everyone else when you screw up."

Tatum heeded Bogdanovich's advice, so much so that only a few days later he was able to tell her father, "She's doing great now. She's more controlled, more natural. She's doing it without a lot of tricks."

The out-of-the-way location and an early start to the twelve-hour shooting day may have been appropriate for a picture about the early years of movie making, but it proved too much for Burt Reynolds—especially with the edgy atmosphere that quickly developed on the set, and that Reynolds felt emanated from Bogdanovich. He collapsed after one particularly strenuous scene, sending waves of panic all the way from Modesto to Hollywood amid reports that had him dead, dying or, at the very least, suffering a severe heart attack. As it turned out the doctors who examined Reynolds back in Hollywood could find nothing wrong and discharged him merely with the advice that he take it easy for a few days.

Bogdanovich assured him this would be no problem, that without impeding the production they could shoot around him and use Reynolds's stand-in, Hal Needham. Reynolds gratefully stayed home, only to be shattered to hear, a few days later, that Bogdanovich had reported his illness to the producers and was claiming insurance money on him. In fact, Columbia had filed the claim without Bogdanovich's knowledge. Determined to prove to the world that he was fit, Reynolds then subjected himself to a battery of tests, including a heart catherization, an extraordinary painful procedure in which a tube is inserted through an artery in the arm and slowly pushed to the heart. The tests proved conclusively that Reynolds was well, enabling him to return to the *Nickelodeon* set. But relations between Bogdanovich and his star remained tense for the rest of the shoot.

Neil Canton saw the strain of the production take its toll as the weeks rolled on. "We had to get this balloon up . . . and shoot before 7:30, before the winds got up, which we kept missing, since we had a 40-minute drive to the location every morning. The production manager asked me to call Peter early and lie about the time to get him here before 7:30; that way we eventually got the shot. I don't know if Peter ever knew that! Peter was always professional, though; he always cared about the movie and his actors. He would never print a shot and move on to the next one unless he felt it was there. He loved *Nickelodeon,* but he clearly felt compromised. Cybill wasn't there and Peter spent a lot of time on the phone talking to her. We were falling behind schedule, the crew were getting disgruntled and I can only speculate that Peter was beginning to feel the pressure of his films not being successful. He'd gone from being the darling of the critics to everyone attacking him. During lunch breaks the crew would start playing rock 'n' roll music. Peter would yell at them to turn it off, he wanted to sleep. I always ended up defending him, but the whole thing was kind of edgy."

Once when Shepherd did visit, intending to spend the weekend; she flew back to Los Angeles a day early instead. "I was suffocating, I needed air," she told friends. Although she was referring specifically to the windowless motel room in Modesto, the reunion with Bogdanovich was not a happy one. He was brooding and appeared distracted, his sense of humor noticeably absent. His total involvement with production problems made Shepherd feel like an outsider coming in half way through a particularly complicated and annoying puzzle from which she was totally excluded. As for Bogdanovich, her presence served only to remind him how far he had fallen. He had re-written *Nickelodeon* with Shepherd in mind—and now, here she was, a mere observer.

In any case, as filming progressed on *Taxi Driver,* Shepherd had distractions of her own. There was a moment in shooting when she became totally paranoid, deciding that a particular scene Scorsese wanted her to do was just another way of Hollywood degrading her. "It was where Bobby De Niro takes me to see a pornographic movie. We shot it in a real porno movie house on 42nd Street, late at night. I had to have bodyguards because of the crazies on the street. I'm overwhelmingly repulsed by pornography anyway and for five or ten minutes I was sure, I *knew*, that asking me to make the picture was just another way of humiliating me."

During a break in filming *Nickelodeon*, Bogdanovich spent a weekend in Los Angeles that proved a welcome respite from the rigors of Modesto. Visiting an all-night newstand on Santa Monica Boulevard at three o'clock one morning, he caught sight of a familiar figure. "Hey, Sal Mineo!" A passerby waved and shouted as the actor left his parked Volkswagen to join Bogdanovich in his Rolls-Royce. Mineo's magnificent Bentley and luxurious Santa Monica home from the time he and Bogdanovich had first met were long gone, and as film offers had dried up the star had been caught in the time-honored back-taxes trap. Home was now a $75-a-week West Hollywood apartment. Since his last, ignominious screen appearance in *Escape from the planet of the Apes*, Mineo was seizing whatever acting opportunities came his way; occasional television and dinner theater now typically paid the rent.

The Mineo that Bogdanovich happened upon in 1976 was nonetheless the same uncomplaining, outgoing and delightful companion he had always known, with little trace of the bitterness he was perhaps entitled to feel. He was as handsome as ever, and at 37 still looked barely more than a teenager. Having played the part of a bisexual burglar in the San Francisco production of the James Kirkwood play, he told Bogdanovich he was about to direct *P.S. Your Cat Is Dead* at L.A.'s Westwood Playhouse.

Back in Modesto, two weeks later, Bogdanovich spotted several grim-faced crew members as he and Neil Canton alighted from their car. "Who died?" Bogdanovich joked. "Sal Mineo" came the unexpected reply.

Returning home from a rehearsal of the play, Mineo had been stabbed to death by an unknown assailant. A neighbor had heard his last words—"Help! Help! Oh, my God"—followed by a scream, and had found him lying in a pool of blood. Mouth-to-mouth resuscitation was attempted, but the blade had penetrated his heart, causing massive hemorrhaging. He was on the brink of death by the time paramedics arrived. A boy walking his dog nearby and two other witnesses reported having seen a white male with long blond hair running from the scene.

Mineo was a well-known member of Hollywood's gay community and there was much fevered speculation as to the motive for the crime. Had he been murdered by a hustler? A jealous lover? One of the ex-cons he'd befriended? Bogdanovich himself contributed to the conjecture when asked about Mineo's alleged fondness for sado-masochistic ritual. "Sal had some strange tastes," he told *Newsweek*, but added, "he was totally unaffected by them. The murder was so shocking because as a person he was so innocent."

The tabloids enjoyed a field day. "Shadow of Fear as Sal is Murdered," one headline blazed. Movie idols and pop stars, the story ran, were locking their doors, loading their beside guns and unleashing their guard dogs, as Mineo's death set off a wave of terror as intense as the panic that followed the killing of actress Sharon Tate by the Manson "family" seven years earlier. The crime was seen by many as a drug hit carried out against the wrong party, with Mineo the unintended victim of a swindled cocaine dealer.

The rumors appeared to be finally scotched with an arrest and conviction more then two years later. "The sheriff's bulldogs have done it again," Sheriff Peter Pitchess told a news conference before announcing the arrest of 21-year-old Lionel Williams, a Los Angeles man who had spent the last eight months in a Michigan jail on a separate charge. "The Sheriff's bulldogs" had been considerably aided and abetted, it transpired, by Williams's wife and a fellow-inmate, who in fact had simply turned him in. Several puzzling discrepancies remained. Williams was black—but surely the blond man described as running from the scene by no fewer than three different witnesses was Caucasian. Pitchess's reply was that they had caught only "a fleeting glimpse," and he added that, in any case, Williams was "light-complexioned for a Negro." At the time of the murder Williams was nineteen and he claimed to have no idea who Mineo was. The police concluded that the actor had been killed for his money, $38 that was left in his wallet after Williams had become frightened and fled.

In 1979 Williams was found guilty of second-degree murder and ten armed robberies and was sentenced to 51 years to life which is likely to be reduced to fourteen years, with eligibility for parole in 9 years.

In the beginning, police detectives had declared, "It's a mystery. We know it was not robbery. Mineo still had his watch and ring and there was money in his pocket book. It looked as though whoever did it *knew precisely* what they were doing." Now, although the mystery of Sal Mineo's murder appeared to be solved, two intriguing possibilities remained. Was Williams a hit man? Or simply a fall guy?

Former underworld figure Mickey Cohen had come forward immediately after Mineo's murder. "He was my friend," he acknowledged. "I just spoke to him seven or eight days ago. He was such a fine young man. It's unbelievable." Almost as unbelievable, perhaps, as the subsequent death of Mineo's friend and producer, William Belasco, with whom the actor had just signed to make a movie. After Mineo's murder his friends planned a memorial service at Belasco's home. It was never held. The night before the service Belasco was killed in an automobile accident. If the Los Angeles Police Department ever investigated a possible connection between the two deaths, it was never reported.

An example of Bogdanovich's ability to airbrush "disagreeable" truth came in his otherwise cogent and moving tribute to Mineo, in which "gay" and "bisexual" were notably absent from the 2,500 words he used. Many wondered why, if Mineo had been honest enough to acknowledge, and take pride in, his sexuality during his lifetime, Bogdanovich chose to ignore it after his death? Mineo's friends regarded Bogdanovich's closing of the closet door on the dead actor as something of a disservice. And touching as Bogdanovich's eulogy was, with its theme of the artist on whom Hollywood had turned its back, wouldn't it have been more convincing had he seen fit, in more than six years of filmmaking, to find a part for the friend who had handed him *The Last Picture Show* on a plate?

According to Bogdanovich, Mineo had never expected a role in *The Last Picture Show*. "At one time I'd like to have played in it, but I'm too old, now, I guess," he claims the actor told him. "Greg," an Englishman who was one of Mineo's last lovers, recalls otherwise: "One of Sal's biggest disappointments was that Bogdanovich hadn't given him the chance for a comeback in *The Last Picture Show*. Bogdanovich thanked him repeatedly, but didn't give him a part." At the same time, Greg provides a fitting epitaph for the irrepressible Mineo. "Sal would have hated that the robber didn't know who he was! As for all the scandal published, he'd probably have been amused. Sal never cared much what the public or the neighbors thought. His peers' approval was what counted. He wanted less to be a star than to do good work and be acknowledged as a craftsman. He played hard, worked very hard and he still had a lot of potential. . . ."

When delays on *Nickelodeon* made budget overages a certainty, Bogdanovich was urgently asked to prepare a 90-minute roughcut for viewing by Columbia's nervous executives. After screening it, they flew out to Modesto to lay it on the line: Bogdanovich was given a choice of either wrapping the movie quickly or having the extra costs deducted from his fee.

One scene in the movie has Ryan O'Neal, on being told that he's behind schedule, exasperatedly brandishing the script, ripping out a dozen pages and then declaring, "There! I'm back on schedule." An answer like that may have crossed Bogdanovich's mind, especially since the scene was based on a real-life incident involving John Ford, but, exhausted as he was after the grueling location shooting, he knew that he had to carry on until the film was properly finished. If the adage "You're only as good as your last picture" had any truth to it, how much more would it have when applied to two—and possibly three— movies?.

CHAPTER 14

Back in Hollywood when shooting on *Nickelodeon* was finally completed, and with Columbia having informed him that the $500,000 overage would be deducted from his salary of $750,000, Bogdanovich worked day and night on the editing of the movie while the studio awaited the final print. At least he had Shepherd to cool his overheated brow, since shooting on *Taxi Driver* was now also over. "Cybill's a *witch*," he gratefully confided to a friend at that time. "She knows what's bothering me before I do. Yesterday I was in some kind of mood. 'Let's take a swim right now,' she said. 'We can't,' I replied, 'I'm right in the middle of editing a scene.' I resisted. I always resist, and she's always right. I finally gave in, and after a swim everything was better, the scene cut together beautifully. You know, I've got so much to be grateful to Cybill for. She's made me more easygoing, more open to things, less narrow in my taste, more patient—while she's hardly changed at all. The main difference with Cybill now is that she's simply no longer afraid to show who she is."

In the film community anticipation was high. Was Bogdanovich going to clamber back to safety with *Nickelodeon*, or was he going to suffer another, and perhaps fatal, battering on the rocks? Advance word on the movie, fueled by reports of friction from Modesto, was bad. "I hear it's awful," a publicist confided. When asked where he had heard this, he replied, "Well, from some people I met at the beach last Sunday." Bogdanovich shook his head in despair when this was repeated to him. "It's people with their knives out," he raged, "talking about a film nobody has seen, *hoping* it won't be any good."

While editing continued, rumors soared when Columbia postponed the scheduled release date. The picture was too long, the stories went. It was being drastically cut; it was being permanently shelved; Bogdanovich would never make another picture in Hollywood—all these tales and more were rife as the weeks of delay passed.

Before the official opening, Bogdanovich arranged private screenings for the Hollywood veterans who had inspired many of the characters in *Nickelodeon*. Allan Dwan in particular seemed too frail to laugh so much. The screening was a great success, he declared afterwards: "I've lived it all over again, I'll never need to see another film." There was another less happy screening, for a preview audience at the Gramercy Theater in New York. It was left to the manager to explain to Bogdanovich that the audience reaction had been less than enthusiastic. "Are *you* happy with it?" he asked the director. "It's a good picture," Bogdanovich replied, somewhat distractedly, "but I'm too close to it right now."

Columbia released the movie simultaneously in 400 theaters across the country, with an opening-day charity gimmick of charging only a nickel for admission; their hope was that thereafter good word-of-mouth would do the rest. Within days, however, the movie was playing to near-empty houses. "It's a lead balloon," Clancy Sigal wrote, in his American column in *The Guardian*. "Almost nothing clicks. Technically the film falls apart because of a bad script. In the past Bogdanovich has shown a willingness to dare; maybe next time he should try making a picture that's a tribute to nobody but himself as a genuinely talented, if perilously nostalgic moviemaker."

Would there even be a "next time?" Not necessarily, according to the *New York Times*, whose devastating headline ran, *"Is This Bogdanovich's Last Picture Show?"*

Bogdanovich's third fall from grace left Polly Platt with mixed emotions. "I'd be less than honest," she admits, "if I didn't admit that for a long period of time Peter's fame was a slap in the face for me. I'd be in bed at night and all of a sudden he would come on TV talking about his films and leaving me out. What happened then, though, was *equally* horrible. As Peter's films became less and less successful, my stock in this town began to go up. Although I contributed, I still hate it when people say I was *responsible* for his successful films. It's simply not true."

Bogdanovich flew to London for the British opening of *Nickelodeon*, hoping that the critics would evaluate the picture differently, as they had to some extent with *At Long Last Love*. In a burst of candor, he told the English press that his last three movies virtually represented "The Peter Bogdanovich Story:" *"Daisy Miller* was the story of a guy trying to decide if a girl was one thing or the other. Next was *At Long Last Love*. I don't know how I had the nerve to make it. And *Nickelodeon*, of course, is the story of every director who ever lived. I'd like to have worked in the old Hollywood system. Warner Brothers, in its heyday, would make 45 to 50 films in a year. Next year they're going to make 7! Hollywood's finished. The whole idea of the way we thought of movies has gone forever and it'll never come back. It's sad, because it was a very exciting period but there's no way to bring it back. I just regret that I missed it, but that's what I like about *Nickelodeon*. It celebrates the invention and spontaneity of movies. It has a freshness, a lack of calculation, and an innocence that I miss. The industry is no longer geared to just say, 'Hey, let's go out and make a movie.' I miss that and I think that movies have been diminished because of it. *Nickelodeon* is a better picture because of my mistakes on *At Long Last Love*. I learned from them and when I had pressures to shorten *Nickelodeon* I resisted them."

This time the publicity tour of Britain made no impression on the critics. Nigel Andrews in the *Financial Times* deemed *Nickelodeon* "the comic nadir of the week," and Patrick Gibbs's *Daily Telegraph* review was headlined "Slapstick Without the Laughter." Russell Davies in the *Observer* acknowledged that he had been pleased to meet Bogdanovich at the excellent lunch EMI had laid on in his honor. "But truly," Davies added, "some sort of human diversion was a necessity rather than a luxury after such a disappointing morning at *Nickelodeon*. It isn't even funny peculiar. A characteristic of filmmakers of this kind is that they work with casts they have personal fun with. If this ever worked for Bogdanovich, it had now ceased to do so."

"Its touch is lumpen," Derek Malcolm declared in the *Guardian*, "its length inordinate and its zaniness so obviously manufactured as to be embarrassing at times. Bogdanovich seems almost permanently hooked on making movies about movies. Maybe the way back is to make a film about real people instead. This celebration threatens to become a wake."

Alan Brien in the *Sunday Times* detected "a perverse, pedantic literalism that is almost beyond belief." Bogdanovich, he maintained, "misdirects his own script, defuses his own squibs and gets kicked by his own horseplay."

Back in Hollywood, Ryan O'Neal was having his say. *"Nickelodeon* is a disaster," he told one reporter, "and it was unbelievable agony to make as well. I love Peter, but I think he's been unlucky, he's made some mistakes in terms of choices. If he has, I have too, for I've been in a couple of them."

"Ryan had personal problems on *Nickelodeon,"* Bogdanovich says today. "I think it was around the time that *Barry Lyndon* didn't do very well, and he was disappointed in that. He'd got the part because Stanley Kubrick had seen *What's Up, Doc?* and his kids fell madly in love with the picture. Then he met Ryan and thought he had Cary Grant. What he didn't realize was that Ryan had to be very carefully directed to do that kind of stuff."

Burt Reynolds was tightlipped about the movie, and refused to comment on his strained relationship with Bogdanovich. "I didn't have any fun on *Nickelodeon,"* was all he would say. "I was ill—and it showed."

Bogdanovich was pointedly asked if he saw any career parallels between himself and Orson Welles. "There aren't any," he snapped. "Orson's never been in a situation comparable to mine, except before he made *Citizen Kane.* I'm not as good as he was, and he's never been as successful as I am. Look, there's no point trying to draw any tragic or even sad overtones from my personal situation. I made three pictures that were successful. I made a couple that weren't, [and] I made this one that I still hope will be. If it is, I'll make other pictures. If it isn't, I'll still make other pictures. If I ever do get into a situation where I can't do what I want the way I want to, there's no point in making pictures any more; it'll no longer be fun. I'd rather write a book, get a job as an actor, direct in the theater, anything. *Nickelodeon* is about the obsession of moviemaking and yes, it *is* an obsession, but I'm not going to do it if I can't speak for the work. There's always going to be somebody who'll give you a few bucks to make a picture when one has had the successes I've had. I've turned down four pictures, so it's not that I'm wanting for work. If you have to, you can make a picture for peanuts."

With his asking price for a movie now settling at a reported $600,000—compared to the $750,000 he had received for *At Long Last Love* and had been due to collect for *Nickelodeon*—he talked frankly about the major studios. "They try to undercut you," he railed, "but if you want to do the thing, you'll take less money. No one can guess what it's like to deal with these people who run the studios and handle the money. The patrons of our profession cannot be described. Or if they can, there's no substitute for the actual experience."

Bogdanovich continued to demonstrate a near-infallible ability to alienate even his most ardent supporters, frequently rising to the Shepherd bait when silence would have served him better. "My affair with Cybill is the reason many people want me to fail," he claimed. "It's not just that I've been successful, but that I'm in love with a girl who is beautiful. I put her in my films and I'm living with her and I make no secret of it. They talk about me in Hollywood as being a Svengali and of love having made me blind. It's been a wounding, depressing, hurtful business. I suppose in a sense I have been naive and innocent. I realized that if I made a hit early on with *The Last Picture Show* people would ask whether I could repeat it. What I hadn't suspected, and neither had Cybill, was that the criticism of me would take the form of attacking my relationship with her. Candidly, it's been a tough year, but my personal life is good with Cybill and my two daughters. What our critics can't swallow is that Cybill is beautiful, she's talented, and we're in love. People in Hollywood are jealous of me and envious of her."

Asked if *Nickelodeon* would be the end of his obsession with cinema and the start, perhaps, of a more fertile preoccupation with life itself, he poignantly replied, "I've heard that since I was fifteen and I don't know what it means. Cinema is my whole life!"

CHAPTER 15

During 1976 Shepherd decided she wanted her own beach house, where she could get away from time to time, her version of Virginia Woolf's *A Room of One's Own*. Bogdanovich would go down and spend an evening with her in Malibu and occasionally stay the night. He sensed that Cybill was working hard to keep their relationship going, while he in his usual way was content to let matters drift. "Cybill taught me a lot about relationships," he admits, "about all that male and female stuff." What Shepherd herself then refused to acknowledge was that when one reaches the stage in any relationship where one has to work *too* hard at it, something is basically wrong.

An actress friend recalls Cybill auditioning at this time for director Richard Brooks for the role in *Looking for Mr. Goodbar* that later went to Tuesday Weld. "She was very serious. This was one of her first steps away from the Bogdanovich umbrella, but he undermined her with his mindgames before she even went in. Peter tried to manipulate her, choose her friends, her clothes, her looks. He really *was* Svengali, no matter what they say today. And Sue Mengers was totally on Peter's side in all of it. Sue was wonderful at getting everybody to confide in her, then she would play one against the other. Cybill was trying to live her own life and she would tell Sue something, and Sue would run to Peter with it."

Shepherd continued her jokey, flirting ways, even when confronted by a future American president, as she was at a cocktail party she and Bogdanovich attended at the Beverly Wilshire Hotel in honor of candidate Jimmy Carter. Flanked by Warren Beatty and 200 of Hollywood's finest, Cybill took in Carter's peanut lapel pin as they were introduced. "My," she crooned, "I just *love* your peanut." Carter turned beet red.

Remembering the incident, Bogdanovich suggests that "Cybill puts on a frivolous attitude because it amuses her, but the men ended up disliking both of us for episodes like that. I was always amused when I saw how ill at ease they became."

Beatty introduced the couple to Hugh Hefner at the Carter reception. "Oh, we're suing you," Bogdanovich cooly informed him when they were left alone. Soon after, Cybill received a letter of apology from Hefner, thus setting the stage for a resolution of her long-standing lawsuit against *Playboy*.

In 1977 Bogdanovich decided not to work for a while. He had, after all, made almost a picture a year for seven years—three that were extremely successful, three that were not. He knew he had lost his way, and he was well enough versed in Hollywood careers to know that his own was in poor shape. Although offers still came in, he said "no" to everything. Instead, he and Shepherd did more traveling—to the Far East, Australia and Europe. If Bogdanovich had arguably failed to catch the Henry James flavor in *Daisy Miller*, the couple captured it together as disillusioned expatriates.

With Shepherd off in Europe making *Silver Bears* with Michael Caine, Bogdanovich received an offer from Warren Beatty to direct *Heaven Can Wait*. Since Beatty was already starring in and producing the movie, from a script by Elaine May, Bogdanovich told him he should direct it himself. "If you need any help, call me," he volunteered. Instead, Beatty sent him the script and asked him to reconsider.

Bogdanovich's distinct impression was that at first Beatty simply wanted to pick his brain, and he duly obliged. "Get Buck Henry to do a rewrite," he suggested. "And if you've made up your mind not to direct it yourself, get Elaine May to do it—and Cybill, not Julie Christie, to star."

The fact is that Beatty did want Bogdanovich to direct, but at a fee he would name, and forgoing the possessive "Peter Bogdanovich's"

Peter Bogdanovich behind the camera, 1971

Tim O'Kelly, the anti-hero of *Targets*, 1968

Their credo is violence...Their God is hate...and they call themselves 'THE WILD ANGELS'

AMERICAN INTERNATIONAL presents

PETER FONDA · NANCY SINATRA

STARRING IN

THE WILD ANGELS

PANAVISION® & PATHECOLOR

CO STARRING BRUCE DERN and DIANE LADD

PRODUCED AND DIRECTED BY ROGER CORMAN

WRITTEN BY CHARLES GRIFFITH

WITH

MEMBERS OF HELL'S ANGELS

OF VENICE, CALIFORNIA

Lobby card, 1967

Orson Welles directing *Citizen Kane*, 1941

Howard Hawks, with Rosalind Russell, during the filming of *His Girl Friday*, 1940

John Ford, with George O'Brien to his right, c. 1930

Cybill Shepherd and Timothy Bottoms in a moment of teenage angst

Bottoms hears words of wisdom from Ben Johnson

Cloris Leachman being reawakened by Bottoms

The Last Picture Show, 1971

Shepherd, suspiciously, with Jeff Bridges

Shepherd and Bogdanovich (Trilby and Svengali?)

What's Up, Doc?, 1972

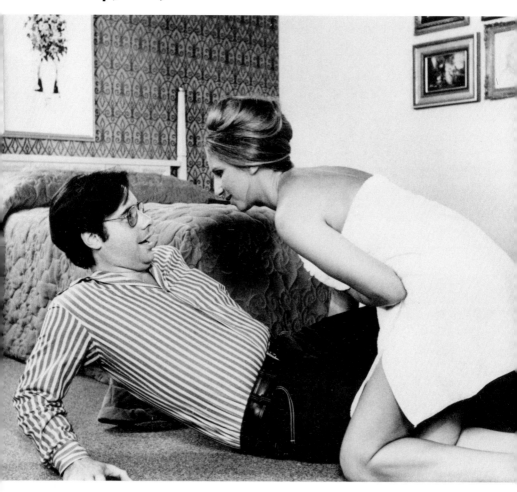

"You're the Top": Bogdanovich to Barbra Streisand

Bogdanovich with Tatum and Ryan O'Neal

PJ Johnson and Tatum looking on as
O'Neal goes off with Madeline Kahn

**Paper
Moon, 1973**

Bogdanovich
conferring on
design matters
with Polly Platt

Sal Mineo

A teenage heartthrob, c. 1955

Coming clean in a stage production of *Fortune and Men's Eyes*, 1969

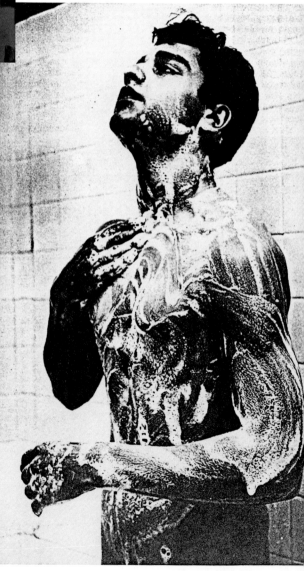

His murder as reported in London's *Daily Telegraph*, February 14, 1976

SAL MINEO STABBED TO DEATH

By IAN BALL
in New York

SAL MINEO, 37, the actor who became known as "the Switchblade Kid" for his many roles as a knife-wielding teenaged tough, was found dying of stab wounds in a pool of blood outside his Hollywood apartment house late on Thursday.

His murder remained a mystery to police and friends yesterday. Robbery was not the motive—cash was still in his wallet and his flat had not been robbed—and Mineo was known to neighbours as a man who lived alone and led a quiet life.

The one lead police have is a rough description of a man with long blond hair whom wit-

Daisy Miller, 1974

Cybill Shepherd, American
"innocence," with (above) Duilio Del
Prete, Italian "experience"

At Long Last Love, 1975

Mildred Natwick carries the ball.

Tatum O'Neal, John Ritter, Jane
Hitchcock, Ryan O'Neal and
Stella Stevens in a scene from
Nickelodeon, 1976

Tatum and Bogdanovich, with a
nickelodeon-type camera
between them

Bogdanovich with Ben Gazzara during the Singapore shooting of **Saint Jack,** 1979

They All Laughed, 1981

Dorothy Stratten
and John Ritter

They all posed: (l. to r.) Colleen Camp, Blaire Novak, Patti Hansen, Ben Gazzara, Audrey Hepburn, Ritter, Stratten and George Morgofen

Stratten and Bogdanovich, discreetly together, in New York during the filming of *They All Laughed*, spring 1980

Two years earlier, in May 1978, a wedding photograph of Stratten and Paul Snider

Mask, 1985

Cher, here an attentive listener
to Bogdanovich, on the set

Cher comforts Eric Stoltz as her
son in a shot that captures the
pathos of the film

Illegally Yours, 1988

(L. to r.) L.B. Stratten, in her film debut, with Rob Lowe, Kenneth Mars and Colleen Camp

The hunted and the helpless, Lowe and Camp

Texasville, 1990

Cybill Shepherd and Jeff Bridges, older and a whole lot wiser

Friends and lovers: Bridges, Shepherd and Annie Potts

Reunited for the first time since *The Last Picture Show* rocketed them both to fame: Bogdanovich and Bridges

above the title. Bogdanovich was having none of it. "So you can't afford my price, is that it?" he asked Beatty.

"That's right."

"How about your salary, Warren, as producer and star? What are you getting?"

"What's that got to do with it?" Beatty asked, looking distinctly uncomfortable.

"A lot. Look, I'm not lowering my price, nor am I changing my billing. If you want me, give me some of what you're getting."

"That's outrageous!"

"Why? You've had three hits out of 20 pictures. I've had three hits out of six, so I figure I'm doing better than you."

"That's a ridiculous way of looking at it. Look, Peter, there's no point in falling out over this. Let's talk about the football scene in the movie. How would you shoot that?"

"Very tight, right in there."

"Oh, I thought I'd do it from the stand with a 1,000mm."

"Really? That's how everyone sees it on TV, Warren. Listen, back in '69 I was about to make a picture with Sergio Leone, who was the last person to tell me what lenses to use. I told *him* to go and fuck himself, and in those days I *needed* the job!"

Beatty shook his head. "Peter," he said, "you're *unbelievable.*"

Bogdanovich concedes today that there are times when his practice of public relations proves sadly lacking. Most of these failures, he believes, stem from his frustration over his father's disappointing career and represent anger taken out occasionally on the wrong people.

It was Orson Welles who inadvertently became the catalyst in the resolution of Shepherd's lawsuit against *Playboy*, landing Bogdanovich a new project at the same time. Welles had read Paul Theroux's novel *Saint Jack*, which he was keen to turn into a movie. "Fine," said Bogdanovich, "let's try to get it done. I'll produce it for you." When it turned out that *Playboy* owned the rights, the possibility arose of both settling the suit and acquiring a property for Welles. Shepherd agreed in principle: she was to get half the film rights and payment of her legal fees. Her victory, however, had a wider ranging effect in that subsequently a clause was inserted in all Screen Actors Guild contracts stating that no nude photographs from a film could be used elsewhere without written permission from the actor.

Since Hefner's organization was ostensibly to produce *Saint Jack*,

Bogdanovich had taken his first, relatively innocent steps on the Playboy treadmill. "Cybill, Orson and I went to a football game with Hefner and his crowd," he recalls. "They were really nice to us. We had dinner there one night, no sex stuff, just very pleasant. Hefner asked if I'd like to come along and play monopoly on Mondays—*not* strip monopoly—but Cybill said she didn't particularly care to go. So I went there on my own . . . I know it sounds like bullshit, but it was just guys playing monopoly. Sometimes a girl would join us, but it was very harmless. You had to pay ten or twelve bucks if you lost and winner took all."

With *Saint Jack* having been secured for Welles, the maestro again became difficult. Whenever Bogdanovich tried to set up a meeting to advance the project, Welles would cancel out. He said he had Jack Nicholson in mind for the part of Jack Flowers, but each time Bogdanovich set up a meeting with the actor, Welles would postpone it. Then, after a few weeks, he announced that he no longer found Nicholson suitable; Dean Martin had become his ideal choice.

While Shepherd was, naturally, eager to realize some money from the project, it soon became obvious that Welles was "chickening out." That she and Bogdanovich had both watched this happen before in no way reduced the frustration of seeing it happen again. Then when Bogdanovich finally declared that he was ready to direct the movie himself, Welles became furious and broke off all diplomatic relations. "John Houseman," Bogdanovich wryly points out, "once remarked that Orson thought every property was his, no matter what. There was never a truer word spoken!"

Bogdanovich had seen and admired everything Ben Gazzara had done on Broadway, including *End as a Man, A Hatful of Rain* and *Cat on a Hot Tin* Roof. He met him in 1977, on the set of John Cassavettes' *Opening Night,* and was immediately struck by Gazzara's humor, gregariousness and warmth. Here, he decided, was the perfect Jack Flowers, Theroux's Saint Jack.

David Scott Milton had spent a lot of time with Gazzara, having become his closest friend during the actor's run in *Hughie* and *Duet,* a Broadway two-parter that had won rave reviews from the critics and a 1975 Tony nomination for Gazzara. "Ben has this incredible voice, he's so striking on stage, but he's never translated successfully to film," Milton acknowledges. "My feeling was that he'd never had the right chances with the right directors, the ones he should have worked with.

He was supposed to do *Wild River* with Elia Kazan—they'd worked together on *Cat on a Hot Tin Roof*—and when Kazan cast Monty Clift instead, it really cracked Ben up. It was a terrible blow to him, and he never forgave Kazan. . . . When Peter asked me what I thought of Benny for Jack Flowers, I assured him he'd be terrific."

Denholm Elliot not only came highly recommended by Shepherd after his work with her on *Silver Bears,* but Bogdanovich had never forgotten his performance in *None but the Brave* back in the sixties. James Villiers, Joss Ackland, Rodney Bewes and Mark Kingston joined Elliott to complete the movie's quintet of British expatriates. Charles Grodin was set for the role of Eddie Schuman, the army's sinister Mr. Fixit.

The first draft of the script was written by Shepherd, reworked by Bogdanovich and author Paul Theroux and finally overhauled by playwright Howard Sackler. Theroux recalls being mightily encouraged when *Playboy* bought film rights to the book before it was even published, only to be told later, when he asked if he could write the screenplay, 'Oh, we're trying to get someone *really good* for this!'

Bogdanovich was originally under the impression that *Playboy* would put up some of the money for the picture, but its investment proved to be limited to the funding of one publicity party! When no major studio would take on the movie with Ben Gazzara as its star, Bogdanovich turned to his old friend and mentor, Roger Corman, who agreed to back the project. "Roger thought he was doing me a big favor," Bogdanovich laughs—not ungratefully—"because he thought I was unemployable. He went around making speeches that he'd always believed in me!"

Gazzara was fascinated by the Saint Jack role and looked forward to developing the character with Bogdanovich in Singapore, where the movie was to be filmed. "I think every actor should risk his life once," he said at the time, pointing out that he'd be making *Saint Jack* for "the lowest fee I've ever been paid—but with a *big* slice of the cake."

Unsure for a while whether to shoot *Saint Jack* in color or black and white, Bogdanovich heeded Jean Renoir's advice: "Do it in color. If people go to see a picture set in Singapore, they'll want to see the *colors* of Singapore." For his cinematographer it was suggested that Bogdanovich look at the work of Robby Muller, much praised for his contribution to Wim Wenders' *The American Friend.* He asked Shepherd to check it out. "The movie's lousy, but the photography's fine," she reported, and Muller was hired.

Bogdanovich recognized that it was clearly time to stop emulating his favorite directors and to make a picture that was one hundred percent himself. If he was to save his reputation, he had, as never before, to succeed on his own terms. No more Hitchcockian overtones, as in *Targets;* let John Ford rest in peace following *The Last Picture Show* and *Paper Moon;* give Howard Hawks a break with *What's Up, Doc?* now out of the way; leave Cukor classics to Cukor after *Daisy Miller;* and perhaps even set Mark Goodrich free since *At Long Last Love* had been exorcised. Few directors in Hollywood history had set themselves up as targets as thoroughly as Bogdanovich had. But was he deep enough a thinker, he pondered, or even interesting enough a person, to stamp his own mark on a movie?

Despite the braggadocio, private doubts remained, quickened now by a sense that his relationship with Shepherd was beginning to fall apart. When she spoke of marriage and a baby, Bogdanovich was never entirely sure whether she meant specifically with him or whether such talk was part of a broader yearning that did not necessarily include him at all.

There was another element at work that Bogdanovich could scarcely confess even to himself. As for many men, marriage and its constraints ran counter to his idea of self-development and freedom. The mixture of desire for the institution and parallel fear of it had manifested itself first in his initial unwillingness to settle down with both, then in his eagerness to escape the marriage contract.

Moreover, despite the public denials ("Criticism has has only brought us closer," Bogdanovich claimed at one point), his relationship with Shepherd *had* deteriorated after the reception accorded *Daisy Miller* and *At Long Last Love,* and perhaps Shepherd had absorbed all that he had to give. It was time to move on or stagnate. . . .

With *Saint Jack* Bogdanovich returned to his expatriate theme. It tells the tale of an Italian beached in Singapore who pimps to supplement his daytime job of ship's chandler assistant, but who in the end refuses to compromise his principles when lured by corrupt establishment money. The idea of an anti-hero who turns out to be more of a hero than any of the authorities held great appeal for Bogdanovich, who could easily identify with Jack Flowers. He felt that *Saint Jack* dealt with integrity and morality in a world that was fast losing both. The choice, and the parallel for Bogdanovich, was clear: whether to continue (studios permitting) to make large-budget Hollywood movies or try to recapture a sense of his own first principles and to trust in his instincts.

To shoot the movie in its authentic locations, he had to resort to subterfuge. The novel had not been well received in the island republic, portraying Singapore, as it does, as virtually a floating brothel. The authorities, under Premier Lee Quan Yew, had indeed banned the book and they were not, Bogdanovich figured, about to give warm welcome to a crew that was to make a film of it. What he did, therefore, was to concoct a fresh synopsis of the movie especially for the authorities, retitling the project *Jack of Hearts* and presenting it as an acceptable, and totally false, mixture of *Pal Joey* and *Love Is a Many-Splendored Thing*. "I knew we had no chance if we leveled with the Singapore government, and we had to have their assistance to film at the airport and post office and places like that," he recalls. "So the only thing to do was to write this other story, taking in all our locations, but leaving out anything controversial. And that's the script they okayed."

With the cast and crew wearing *Jack of Hearts* T-shirts, Bogdanovich stayed at the plush, old-colonial style Goodwood Park Hotel where he kept the faith by using other hotels as settings for the rendezvous of his various characters. Filming at the Goodwood Park was limited to the as yet undeveloped area at the back of the hotel.

Learning that Charles Grodin had decided against the role of Eddie Schuman—he wanted to play leads, not supporting heavies—Bogdanovich decided to do the part himself. His rationale, apart from the fact that he was caught in Singapore with no extra money to recruit anyone else, is disarmingly self-deprecating: "I thought I'd just do it because at that point everybody in Hollywood thought I was a shit anyway. So it was good casting."

Two days into shooting, Bogdanovich became aware of a problem with his leading actor. Concerned, he sought out his coproducer, George Morfogen. "I think Ben's scared," he confided, "and it's coming across, I can see it through the lens." Following Morfogen's advice,

Bogdanovich asked Gazzara out for a few drinks that evening. "Ben, I think you're wary of the camera," he told the actor. "I believe you're scared. You seem to think it doesn't like you."

Gazzara, initially resentful, stiffened. "I won't let you down if that's what you're worried about," he assured Bogdanovich.

"I know," Bogdanovich replied, "but it's more than that. Look, you're a guy I know has no trouble with the ladies. What you have to realize is that the *camera* is a woman. If you just remember that, then the closer it gets the more relaxed you'll be."

Whether the advice sank in or whether it was just that Bogdanovich had made the effort, Gazzara never looked back after that and proved more than equal to the task. He even went on to direct Bogdanovich in his Eddie Schuman scenes with considerable panache.

Bogdanovich set a hectic pace. *Saint Jack* was filmed on the run, using doorways and alleyways instead of caravans and dressing rooms. "Cut the cute" was the watchword. If a scene appeared to be written in a traditional or sentimental manner, the opposite would be filmed. Midway through shooting a Bogartian sense began to surface. "If Rick's joint in *Casablanca* had been a cat house," Gazzara told Bogdanovich, "this is what it would have been like. Jack's a tough guy in a tough world, supposedly amoral, who at his core is more and more open than the others." Gazzara would describe his experience on the movie as "the most creative I ever had. I was never so deeply involved in the structuring of a character and the writing before. *Husbands* came close to it, *Saint Jack* went further."

To the rest of the cast, the Bogdanovich/Gazzara collaboration was just a little too cozy. The sight of their matching cigars and the sound of their often matching instructions jarred on Joss Ackland for one. "You'll love working with Peter," Shepherd had assured him, but the actor found it hard to associate the author of the sensitive eulogy for John Ford that he had read with the bumptious, egotistical, insensitive individual he found in Singapore.

Every weekend Bogdanovich, Gazzara and Morfogen would sit around the Goodwood Park and rewrite. One of the scenes Bogdanovich had fun with had Gazzara telling Denholm Elliot how Singapore got its name. Much of this was taken from a guide book which recounted a time when the island had been overrun by tigers. "They were up to their asses in tigers," Flowers was to explain, perfectly deadpan. "So guess what they named the island? Singapore—Lion City!"

"This is bizarre," Bogdanovich declared at one point. "Here we are doing a film about prostitution and pimps and there's no scenes with women. They're around, but there aren't any *scenes.*" Bogdanovich and Gazzara began to do a lot of research to fill the gap, and as it intensified shooting was suspended for a week so that everyone could catch up with the new dialogue that kept being added to the script.

"I went to many brothels, sometimes in the afternoons outside business hours," he freely admits, "noting conversations for screen dialogue. My impressions of these places were sometimes touching, sometimes pathetic, but never sordid. All the scenes with women were written in Singapore; there was hardly any of that in the book. Sure, I met a lot of hookers, every nationality I could imagine. Many, many scenes that happened between me and several of them ended up in the movie, like that wonderful moment at the end when the girl says to Ben, "I look for you in Ceylon," and he says, "Sure." A Thai girl had said the same thing to me. When Gazzara finally met Theroux, he asked, 'Did you go to any whorehouses? I mean, did you ever go to any whorehouses when you were in Singapore, Paul? How many years were you there, Paul? Well, there's nothing in the book, Paul.' He's subtle, you know, is Ben!"

While Bogdanovich was busy filming, the final chapter of his affair with Shepherd was being written. Following her meeting David Ford, a car service manager in her home town of Memphis, she flew to Singapore to join Bogdanovich, but the visit proved to be a disaster on several levels. She had little to do but shop and lie about the hotel pool as Bogdanovich shot the whorehouse scenes in the area behind the Goodwood Park. Ben Gazzara turned unexpectedly resentful at the temporary break in the close working relationship he had established with Bogdanovich. He didn't want Shepherd around and made no attempt to hide his feelings. When she told Bogdanovich she had an offer from England to appear in a remake of *The Lady Vanishes,* his advice, although as well-intentioned and prophetic as it was ignored, could have been rendered with more diplomacy. "For Christ's sake, don't do it," he told her. "It'll be a piece of shit, and there's no way it will get anything other than a bad comparison with Hitchcock's version." And Shepherd could tell when Bogdanovich had been out carousing with Gazzara. Enough was enough.

Although she had planned a two-week stay, Shepherd tearfully checked out of the Goodwood Park Hotel after a week and headed home to Memphis and David Ford's waiting arms. "Perhaps I should have followed her," Bogdanovich said later, "but when you're making a picture it's just so tough. You're right in the middle of it, eating it, sleeping it. It's totally consuming. I was spending every waking hour trying to make the movie work, thousands of miles away from home and with a very small, inexperienced crew, trying to do it without the usual Hollywood bullshit. Cybill was the sacrifice for *Saint Jack.*"

Sacrifice or not, Bogdanovich tracked Shepherd down in Memphis as soon as the completed filming in Singapore in August. His entreaties were in vain; he was still too high on the whole *Saint Jack* experience, and Shepherd made it clear that she was aware of his affairs with Singapore women. "Peter, it's no good," she told him. "I want out." Bogdanovich was nevertheless shattered when Shepherd had David Ford and not him accompany her to England where she was to film *The Lady Vanishes.* "There was a lot of misunderstanding," Bogdanovich claims. "When she first said she wanted out I really thought she meant it, then later on I began to think maybe she hadn't. Perhaps I should have followed her to England. It just happened so quickly in the end."

With *The Lady Vanishes* completed, Shepherd and Ford were married, in November 1978, in the Gloucestershire village of Winchcombe. Back home, they moved into a converted cotton warehouse in Memphis, with a matchless view of the Mississippi. Shepherd looks back now on her split with Bogdanovich with a considerable degree of equanimity— and affection. "Even when there was no sexual relationship left, when Peter and I broke up, he remained a friend, even when I married David. I think one of the reasons my relationship with Peter ended was because I needed to be on my own to discover who I was. I needed to get back to basics, to do theater, face the world alone and prove to myself that I didn't need his validation. Peter's very powerful to be around, very intense, and I was so young . . . I'd never been a *child* growing up, I'd been an *adult* early on. I always had to be in charge. I don't believe time has anything to do with knowing someone. My parents were married for 25 years before they suddenly got a divorce. Now they're both remarried to terrific people who make them happier. You can live with someone for years and not *know* him. Or you can meet someone and your life can change in an afternoon. That's the way life is. While I was with Peter my development was arrested . . . [in terms of independence], so it was important for me to get away from him. I was miserable and just going nowhere. His being on location didn't break up our relationship, but it was an opportunity. When I went to Singapore, the die was cast from my point of view."

CHAPTER 16

A fter *Saint Jack* was completed and the authorities realized how Bogdanovich had tricked them, the Singapore High Commission felt constrained to issue a rebuke: *"Saint Jack* depicts Singapore as one big whorehouse. It shows only the seedy side of the island and is therefore very unrepresentative. We believe people who have been here and know the city would agree. Obviously, we are not pleased with the way Mr Bogdanovich resorted to subterfuge. Equally obviously, the picture will not be shown in Singapore and Mr. Bogdanovich will be prohibited from returning to the island."

Bogdanovich tried to have the last word. "I suppose it was a bit deceitful, but what could I do?" he protested. "The picture is much more critical of America than of Singapore. A pimp is generally considered on the lowest level of society. A president, on the other hand, is thought of as being on the highest, yet at the time the movie takes place, which is in the same period as Watergate and Vietnam, a poor American pimp in Singapore behaves in a way our highest officials didn't behave, and with a sense of morality no one in the U.S. government had at that time. Hey, don't get me wrong, I still feel bad about having to fool these people in Singapore. What we both got out of it, though, is a wonderful document of the island in the seventies, the last gasp of Singapore as a kind of Oriental, exotic place. We captured the color and texture of the place at a certain period in time. Unfortunately, I'm scared to go back there. I'm sure they'd let me in—" he offers a lopsided grin—"getting out might be a problem, though."

But Bogdanovich had more serious concerns than the government of Singapore. He had turned his back on Hollywood and made a film completely outside of the system. Would it be another bomb or could he bring this one successfully home? Private screenings for friends were reassuring. "One of the major surprises of the movie is going to be Ben Gazzara's performance as Jack," Bogdanovich told his friends. "Nobody's ever seen Ben the way he is, not even in Cassavetes' films. He *is* Jack." Gazzara reciprocated in his own way. Having made three movies with Cassavetes, he called his friend: "John, I want you to come over and see the best movie I ever made." And even when Peter Falk and Cassavetes agreed *Saint Jack* was terrific, Gazzara couldn't resist drumming it in: "The *best* movie I've made, right?"

Paul Theroux helped things along. "Bogdanovich," he declared, "used people who had never done anything but make noodle soup, kids who'd worked in stalls, transvestites and old amahs who were used only to wash children's clothes. In Singapore, where everyone is brought up to believe that the world is going on somewhere else, [Bogdanovich's] idea was revolutionary. Ben and the [other] actors are all marvelous, but it was the prospect of an old lady, who'd never been before the cameras, delivering her lines expertly that reduced me to tears."

At this stage of a film's history, its director is of all people the least able to judge it objectively. The reactions of colleagues help, but they are far from infallible, and dearest friends especially are not likely to tell a director if they think a film is poor. Dan Talbot remembers sitting through an advance screening of *Nickelodeon* with increasing dismay and with Bogdanovich at his side, knowing that as soon as the screening was over, his opinion was going to be anxiously sought.

Bogdanovich ran and reran *Saint Jack*. To him it was his best picture and he felt confident that he had put everything he had into it. He knew that it wasn't going out on wide showcase release through a Columbia or a 20th Century-Fox. Major studios can often achieve playdates for their smaller pictures by trading off their potential blockbusters and offering theaters a package deal, but New World, Corman's distributor, was not in a position to do this.

The reviews were in the main extremely favorable, with some really outstanding notices among them. Frank Rich at *Time* was not, however, one of the enthusiasts. In an early review he described the film as "bargain-basement Graham Greene. When a director's three latest films are commercial and critical bombs, where does he go next? In Peter Bogdanovich's case, it is back to basics. *Saint Jack,* the director's first film since 1976, is a sharp departure from the projects of his Hollywood heyday. The movie has a small budget, no big stars and not a single reference to a classic screwball comedy. Cybill Shepherd is nowhere in sight. Still, some habits die hard. If *Saint Jack* is not another complete embarrassment for Bogdanovich, it nonetheless reveals his deficiencies as a filmmaker. Again he describes emotions without ever feeling them. He flogs tired ideas to death and gets bland performances from his cast. *Saint Jack* shows off Bogdanovich's considerable skills, but it has the look of a high-minded movie, too empty to arouse any emotion other than indifference. No doubt it is healthy for Bogdanovich to be adventurous, but for now his new directions all appear to be wrong turns."

To the rescue came *Variety,* though with qualified praise and doubtful about *Saint Jack*'s commercial prospects: "The film is extremely well crafted, finely acted and conjures up a positively intriguing milieu . . . Bogdanovich has made *Saint Jack* an object lesson in making a seamless, effortlessly fluid piece of work, reeking of atmosphere but in need of a stronger narrative. . . ."

The review tide began to turn as Rex Reed rose to be counted among the film's admirers. "Cancel those epitaphs and throw away the eulogies," he wrote. "Peter Bogdanovich is back, not from the dead, as the Hollywood gossips predicted, but from Singapore, with a brand new movie. *Saint Jack* is unlike any movie he's ever done before. It's a tough, tight little film with a two-fisted performance from Ben Gazzara that ignites the screen."

After this the reviews became more and more encouraging. Jack Kroll in *Newsweek* found the film, "offbeat, raffish and ironic," adding that *"Saint Jack* returns Bogdanovich to the sweetness and finely tuned sense of loss which are his true qualities. Gazzara makes Saint Jack one of the most appealing characters in recent movies."

Judith Crist joined the supporters and noted an interesting comparison, echoing Ben Gazzara's observation: "Squint a little, and in Gazzara's Jack Flowers you'll see Humphrey Bogart's Rick of *Casablanca*

. . . Bogdanovich's triumph is his refusal to sugar-coat the pill. He has, instead, placed it on a rich and vibrant tapestry of truth. His Singapore is a glowing, squirming, rhythmic blend of nationalities, his characters rounded and real."

Bogdanovich flew to London for the movie's opening there and found time to open an exhibition of his father's paintings and drawings at the Aberbach Fine Art Gallery in Saville Row. The painting they chose to hang in the window was one of Bogdanovich as a young boy in 1950. He chuckled as he recalled his father painting him at various times as "a cowboy, an actor, a clown and playing the flute, none of which I could do properly." The British critics almost unanimously decided, on the evidence of *Saint Jack,* that directing a movie was definitely one art the grown-up Bogdanovich *had* mastered.

"It's a pleasure to catch up with *Saint Jack,*" Felix Barker enthused in the *Evening News.* "Gazzara gives a perfect study of a man living dangerously on his wits. Wonderful photography and finely executed by Peter Bogdanovich." David Castell agreed: "This fine, vital movie puts Bogdanovich right back on course and offers once-in-a-career acting opportunities, which Ben Gazzara and Denhom Elliott match gratefully."

"The director's best film to date," Patrick Gibbs maintained in the *Daily Telegraph,* while Nigel Andrews in the *Financial Times* found *Saint Jack* "the brightest surprise. Bogdanovich has found rejuvenation in Singapore."

Alexander Walker topped them all in the *Evening Standard.* "A real triumph for this filmmaker," he wrote. "Instead of plastering his movies like *What's Up, Doc?* or *Nickelodeon* with appliqued bits of other directors' styles and talent, Bogdanovich has this time returned to base form. No fingerprints on this one but his own—in a story whose every minute unpacks a revelation, minor and major, on a scale that makes most films seem famished of novelty. Ben Gazzara gives one of the best performances of any screen actor in recent years, I have seldom seen an actor so much at the service of his director, yet so totally in charge of his part. This is real filmmaking."

There was a sting in the tail of Bogdanovich's London week. In one of those odd coincidences almost impossible to stage manage, Louis Malle's *Pretty Baby* opened on the same day as *Saint Jack.* One of the few who noticed was Philip French in *The Observer,* who also spotted the full circle that *Saint Jack* represented in Bogdanovich's career. "Produced by

Roger Corman, who gave Bogdanovich his start in pictures," he wrote, "*Saint Jack* is something of a comeback for its director, while *Pretty Baby* is written and produced by Bogdanovich's ex-wife Polly Platt, who designed and helped script his best early pictures."

Soon after the U.S. premiere of *Pretty Baby,* Platt imparted some idea of what the movie meant to her. "What I've done now is terribly important to me," she declared. "At last, I've written on my *own.* Something of my *own. All mine.*" She found *Saint Jack* a total revelation. "Peter's flaws were always in not knowing himself and in needing to develop personally. With *Saint Jack* I knew he was on his way. I loved it, even though I thought it was frightening in its sexuality. Peter had always been prudish, sheltered, didn't drink, didn't do dope—and what was *this?*"

In a new Burt Reynolds movie, *Hooper,* Bogdanovich had to confront the portrayal of a particularly unpleasant director whose manner of speech and physical appearance were unmistakable. An English reporter brought up the comparison, and in his response Bogdanovich chose to ignore his own earlier lampooning of critic John Simon in *What's Up, Doc?* "I don't expect loyalty from *actors*—or should I say *stars?* Most of them, quite frankly, are a bunch of pathetic people. Warren Beatty asked me to direct *Heaven Can Wait,* but I turned it down because after our first meeting it was clear that he and I could never work together. He wanted to do everything his way, so I said, 'Why don't you do it yourself?' And he did. As it turned out, I could have done a terrific job on it—much better than the slipshod one he did. I don't want to make big budget movies any more and I definitely don't want to work with superstars. They're just a pain in the ass."

When asked if this included Burt Reynolds, Bogdanovich snapped, "*Especially* Burt Reynolds! I mean, when you work with someone like Burt what you're basically up against is a king-size ego. And he's not alone in this; Ryan O'Neal has it and so has Warren." Bogdanovich paused for a moment, then smiled and shrugged. "Come to think of it," he admitted, "so have I!"

Bogdanovich's presence in London may have helped *Saint Jack* get off to a good start in the West End, but the film was never distributed outside the capital. The reason for this was that Roger Corman had closed his New World distribution office in London when it became evident that it was losing money every week it was open. Back home, despite the good run *Saint Jack* enjoyed in major American cities, it had great difficulty in finding playdates elsewhere. "All the theaters had already been booked for the summer in January for pictures that exhibitors hadn't even seen," New World's sales manager complained, "and I don't have the edge of an *Alien* or a film with Barbra Streisand to bargain with."

While *Saint Jack* lost money in its theatrical release, among critics Bogdanovich was back in business with an extremely well regarded movie, one that completely restored his standing, in Europe particularly. It prompted an extended article in France's *Positif* magazine, "Bogdanovich, the Misunderstood," and went on to win the Critics' Prize for Best Film and the Best Actor Award for Ben Gazzara at the Venice Film Festival.

"Somebody once said there's only one thing more difficult to handle than failure," said Bogdanovich at the time, "and that's success. They're both tough. Having been through both success and failure and survived, in a funny way I think success is tougher. But it's more encouraging! I look back on these last ten years and it's a blur. Things were moving so fast I didn't have time to think about it. I was shooting one picture after another. I was also very young. Everything was happening at once—a lot of guilt from my divorce from Polly, my kids, then my father dying. It's only in the last few weeks I've been able to sort it all out. I think I'm still in shock. Even when I was with Polly, I never liked the idea of being married. I used to express this thought to Cybill and she said she felt the same way. I was dumb enough to believe her, when what she really wanted was marriage and a baby. Today I'm not involved with anyone and I'm not going to be."

These protestations notwithstanding, and though he still carried a huge torch for Shepherd, Bogdanovich had returned from Singapore with a beautiful girl from Sri Lanka, whom he introduced to Platt. Then, after a whirl with actress and singer Colleen Camp, he asked to meet model Patti Hansen (shades of Cybill!) after seeing her on the cover of *Esquire*. Together they enjoyed what Bogdanovich describes as "a brief, weird sort of relationship."

The death of Bogdanovich's mother in 1979 from cervical cancer temporarily stopped him in his tracks. He felt as if his last European tie had died with Herma. The cancer had first been diagnosed in 1975 and then had gone into a period of remission. Anna, after a failed marriage in her early twenties, devoted herself to her mother as nurse and companion for four years, watching as Herma grew ever more emaciated. Contact with her brother was limited during that time. "I just didn't relate to Cybill," she recalls. "I felt Peter had really changed. We were so wrapped up in our own worlds that we really didn't know what was going on with each other. I'd been in and out of hospitals myself, had very bad health."

"Herma had a horrible life," Platt mourns, "and really died through neglect, in that she'd never gone to a gynecologist. She was everything you could possibly want in a mother and mother-in-law. I'm not deifying her; I just don't believe there was an evil bone in the woman's body. She was very loyal to me."

For Bogdanovich not only was his European link gone, but his sexual anchor was weighed, heralding a new era of promiscuity. He became a regular at Playboy's Mansion West, situated a mere two minutes from the Bel Air home he now occupied alone.

CHAPTER 17

Bogdanovich claims that most of his visits to the Playboy Mansion were completely innocent, involving nothing more than a game of pin ball, a sandwich, a closed circuit fight on TV—and waiting for something to happen that would fill the void Shepherd had left. He says he was uncomfortable with all the sex so openly offered and turned off by the idea of group sex and such items as the endlessly adjustable "fuck chair" that Hefner had specially built for himself and his clients.

He admits to a couple of incidents in the mansion, however. On his very first visit he tried to coax a nineteen-year-old into going home with him, hoping, according to his later account, "first to make her trust me, then talk her out of the Playboy idea." Unfortunately, he had picked as his subject Hugh Hefner's date for the evening. "I thought I was the guest here," he mumbled as "Tammy" was spirited away. "I'm not *that* good a host," Hefner snapped.

Another involvement was with a girl named Lee, Bogdanovich claiming he was lured by one of his friends, "Bob," into a compromising position with her in the mansion's Jacuzzi grotto. A few months later, Lee moved into Bogdanovich's home for a few days, leaving with $5,000 and a cashmere sweater for her trouble. The story that circulated had Bogdanovich, who denies it, paying Lee the money to sleep with him and "Bob."

He admits to over a score of conquests, mostly under Playboy auspices, in the year after Shepherd left. If he can be seen as looking for love in all the wrong places, he was not the only one to ride a sexual merry-go-round in the permissive climate of the late seventies. The boys' camp atmosphere at Playboy, and probably the sight of some all-too-familiar faces, like Warren Beatty, Ryan O'Neal, Jim Brown and James Caan, soon began to pall. He was different from the "regulars," he told himself, who only went there for the sexual fun and games. He was, he says, looking for something deeper, a lasting relationship that would remove the sour aftertaste of the endless run of one-nighters and short-term flings.

In October 1978, while still cutting *Saint Jack*, Bogdanovich was introduced to the model tapped to become *Playboy*'s 25th Anniversary Playmate, eighteen-year old Dorothy Stratten. She was tall, blonde, blue-eyed, and a breathtaking beauty. "I'm casting a picture right now," he told her. (He wasn't and knew it was one of the oldest lines in the business.) "Why don't you call me?" he asked, scribbling his phone number on a piece of Playboy notepaper. "I'll bet he's a fake," Dorothy told a friend. She didn't call, and it would be a year before she and Bogdanovich would meet again.

Dorothy Ruth Hoogstraten was born in a Salvation Army hospital in Vancouver, British Columbia, on February 28, 1960, to Dutch immigrants Peternella (Nelly) Schaap Fuchs and Simon Hoogstraten. A brother, John, was born two years later. Nelly's third child was stillborn, prompting the discovery that she was an Rh-negative mother. By the time Dorothy was three years old, Simon Hoogstraten had deserted his family.

Having grown up in an orphanage back in Holland, Nelly Hoogstraten was no stranger to privation, but she now had two children to look after as well as herself. She found jobs as a housekeeper and became pregnant by an employer when Dorothy was six. Abortion was then a legal option in Canada on account of her Rh-negative condition, but approval for such a step took four months. Finally, with the abortion due to take place that very morning, Hoogstraten felt her baby kick. She decided to have the child after all and checked herself out of the hospital. Dorothy and John's half-sister Louise Beatrice was delivered by Caesarian section on May 8, 1968, and survived a complete blood exchange.

The summer Dorothy was fourteen she began part-time work at the local Dairy Queen restaurant on East Hastings Street and decided to keep the job in September when high school started. A year later Nelly moved her little family from Vancouver's East End, one of the roughest areas in town, to Coquitlam, a more desirable suburb east of Vancouver. Although they were still on Social Assistance, she now worked in the local hospital while she trained in practical nursing and studied for her secondary school equivalency. Dorothy took the bus into Vancouver on the weekends to work at Dairy Queen.

Her transformation from a gawky teenager into a voluptuous young beauty was a source of wonderment to all around her. Soon the boys were flocking around. She chose one in particular, but it was to be a difficult relationship. Although they slept together, Dorothy gained no pleasure from it. "If this was love," she wrote in her journal, "then love was a pretty big letdown." She blamed herself for her lack of responsiveness. By the time Dorothy turned eighteen she had broken off the romance.

Paul Leslie Snider entered her life ordering a Strawberry Sundae Supreme while eyeing Dorothy up and down in her abbreviated red and brown outfit and obligatory pigtails. "What's *your* name?" he asked her, while the blonde he had arrived with fumed. To the ingenuous Dorothy, Snider's mustachioed good looks, stockily athletic build and confident, streetwise manner came over as the very essence of sophistication. As for the rest of his hustler-on-the-make accoutrements—the long leather coat with fur collar, the sideburns, the snakeskin boots and the bejewelled Star of David that dangled on a chain round his neck (and earned him the nickname, "The Jewish Pimp")—they were to Dorothy all part of his air of glamour, just like the gleaming black Corvette with red leather upholstery that waited outside in the parking lot. And he at 26, eight years older than she—though hardly a father-figure, was the perfect combination of suitor and substitute for the father she had scarcely known.

The cuddly charm that won Dorothy over was another, more endearing aspect of Snider's stock-in-trade. He had also grown up in the raw environment of Vancouver's East End and had watched his parents split up when he was still a boy. Electing to stay with his father, he quit school in seventh grade and for a while worked by day as a leather cutter in his father's sweatshop and from some bikers he befriended learned how to customize automobiles. At night the skinny kid hung around the streets, watching pimps as they hustled, before falling into their circle. "Paul took to it real quick," one of his early friends testified, "like a duck to water. When some of the chicks laughed at him for being short and skinny, he took up body-building and gave himself a new torso."

Snider left his day job behind and became a promoter of whatever he could find to promote—automobile and cycle shows, wet T-shirt competitions, "exotic" male and female go-go dancers. When more money was needed, there was always pimping. He told a friend he had married and divorced by the time he was 21. His wife had left with their child, he claimed, and he swore that nobody would ever walk out on him again.

By 1977 Snider was sneeringly regarded by Vancouver's notorious "Rounder Crowd" as a third-rater, more typically prey than predator. "He never handled drugs," one Rounder scoffed. "He used them, but wouldn't peddle. He was scared to death of them. He swore he'd die first before he went to jail." When the leader of one narcotic gang was in prison, Snider moved in with his girlfriend, borrowing heavily from loan sharks to give her a silicon breast implant. After claiming he was unable to repay the loan, he was dangled by his ankles from a hotel room 30 floors above the street.

Humiliated and broke, he took off for Los Angeles, his girls and promotions in tow, searching for the one big break that would catapult him out of the nickel-and-dime rut in which he seemed stuck. Maybe he could be an actor, or discover and promote his very own star. Or he might take up producing movies. It was all a matter of getting in with the right crowd. Wasn't this Hollywood—Dreamland itself, where everything was possible? After a year, with his dream fast becoming frayed around the edges, Snider beat a tactical retreat back to Vancouver and his meeting with Dorothy. "That girl could make me a lot of money," he is allegedly to have declared shortly after he first met her.

Dorothy's family loathed Snider, whom they saw as a loud-mouthed, obnoxious braggart. Unable to understand why Dorothy was spending so much time with him and not with them, Louise berated her older sister. After Dorothy's gentle explanation that Snider was the first person who had made her feel important and loved, the sisters cried together and made up. But Nelly's suspicions were unallayed. She had had to slave for every penny she had ever earned. How could someone have so much money to throw around without a steady job?

Apparently blind to Snider's faults, Dorothy was not totally unaware of what was happening. She was being sweet-talked by an expert, she recorded in her journal. But she had also experienced her first orgasm in his embrace.

Dorothy's best friend, Cheryl, was another who tried to warn her of Snider. "Why do you put up with him?" she asked one night at a downtown disco, as Snider danced with a succession of girls. "When Paul says 'Jump!' you ask 'How high?'" Cheryl, soon forbidden by Snider to talk to Dorothy, predicted at that time, "In a year we're going to find Dorothy dead in an alley."

Her first step toward the Playboy Mansion was taken when Dorothy agreed to pose naked for photographs Snider intended to submit to the magazine. Its quest to find the 25th Anniversary Playmate was almost over when Dorothy's pictures were received by *Playboy*'s VP Marilyn Grabowski and forwarded to Hefner. His response was immediate; Dorothy was invited to fly to Los Angeles as a strong contender for the anniversary honor. Taking time off from her new job at BC Telecom as a clerk/typist, and without her mother's consent—Nelly was in Europe—Dorothy took her first-ever plane trip on August 13, 1978. Miffed that *Playboy* had provided only one airline ticket, Snider was consoled by the speed of their response. The prediction he had made soon after meeting Dorothy was coming true. "You may have to sleep with Hefner," he now cautioned Dorothy, "but don't worry about it. I'll still be around for you afterwards."

Dorothy felt secure looking back on the nights of candlelit dinners and wine with Snider, when he would play his guitar and sing for her. With their "lifetime agreement" to share Dorothy's earnings, come what may, he would always be there to look after her interests.

As soon as she landed in Los Angeles, Dorothy was taken to a photo session with *Playboy*'s master photographer, Mario Casilli. Dorothy went on to spend the weekend at the Playboy Mansion before returning briefly to Canada. She had to go back to Los Angeles almost immediately, she excitedly told Snider. She was on a short list of sixteen for the 25th Anniversary Playmate honor and was being given a modeling contract by *Playboy*. They decided the name "Hoogstraten" was too clumsy—how about "Stratten" instead? If Dorothy was dazzled, so was Snider. Everything was going according to plan.

Within days "Dorothy Stratten" was back at the mansion, having lost her job at BC Telecom. She had been secretive to John and Louise, making no reference to *Playboy* but mentioning a "modeling job" in Los Angeles, where she would spend the next three weeks. When Stratten returned to Vancouver in September, to shoot some pictures on location, she put off informing her mother that she was modeling for *Playboy*, certain that she would not approve.

At the time Bogdanovich first met Stratten, Snider was in the process of relocating to Los Angeles, fed up with Stratten's long absences and distinctly apprehensive that he was in danger of forfeiting his meal ticket. He joined her at the home of Patrick Curtis, a man she had met at the Playboy Mansion with whom she had been lodging. Later, the couple moved into a small apartment of their own in Westwood and, the following summer, into a two-story house in West Los Angeles, near the Santa Monica freeway.

Thrilled even to be allowed inside the mansion's hallowed gates, Snider proudly escorted Dorothy to Playboy's Halloween party. Although pleasant to his face, everyone from Hefner on down regarded him with disdain. "He has a pimplike quality," Hefner blithely informed Stratten, illustrating a somewhat blinkered view of his own standing in the community at large.

Perhaps influenced by Snider's omnipresence, Hefner finally decided that Stratten lacked sufficient "experience with the press" to qualify as the 25th Anniversary Playmate. He determined instead to feature her as the August 1979 centerfold, holding out to her the possibility of being selected Playmate of 1980.

Put to work as a bunny in the Los Angeles Playboy Club, Dorothy began to study acting and enrolled at Richard Brander's twice-weekly class in Sherman Oaks. Brander immediately discerned a star quality in his new pupil. Soon she was offered a leading role in a movie, albeit a cheap soft-porn effort, by a Canadian company. In *Autumn Born* she would play a strong-willed seventeen-year-old girl kidnapped by a gang of mindbenders and beaten up, starved and raped by both men and women. Then she was to appear in a series of color reels destined for *Playboy*'s video and cable outlets.

With demand for Stratten's services reaching this level, Snider became increasingly anxious and decided the time had come to legitimitize their relationship. His marriage proposal threw Dorothy into new confusion. For months she had been on Librium, prescribed to calm her nerves and ease the depression and blinding headaches to which she was often subject. But the pills, on which she had come to rely, were having several disagreeable side effects causing bouts of crying and irritability; moreover, to achieve the initial calming effect required an ever-increasing dosage. She did try to stop taking Librium, but then the headaches and depression came back. Or were they now withdrawal symptoms of the drug itself?

Unable to think clearly, she sought advice from several sources: Should she marry Snider? Hefner told her he had "serious reservations," enough to have a check run on him with the police in Canada. They reported no trace of a record. Nevertheless, marrying Snider could hold back her career, Hefner advised. "But he cares for me so much," she told one friend. "He's always there when I need him. I can't ever imagine myself being with any other man but Paul." She agreed to marry him.

Stratten's first *Playboy* promotion was to be held in Las Vegas at the beginning of June. Snider flew to Nevada with her and they were married in the Silver Bell Wedding Chapel in Las Vegas on June 1, 1979. Dorothy's working honeymoon consisted of several days posing for *Playboy*. Their wedding reception was held in Los Angeles (in the Van Nuys home of actor/producer Max Baer, Jr.), a doctor friend of Snider's dispensed Quaaludes to them both, almost in a mockery of a blessing. Snider's father had flown in from Vancouver for the occasion and was photographed posing beside Stratten. So, eight months after Bogdanovich had met her, she became Mrs. Dorothy Ruth Snider and entered the realm of forbidden fruit.

A tour of Canada for *Playboy* was organized a few weeks later. "Aren't you worried about being exploited by those people?" one Vancouver newshound asked. "I see the pictures as nudes, like nude paintings," Stratten cannily countered. "They're not made for people to fantasize about." Her reply was largely for her mother's benefit, for Nelly had finally received the news of her daughter's involvement with the magazine with the expected stone-faced disapproval. "At first," Stratten would tell Lydia Lane of the *Los Angeles Times*, "I hesitated to come to

Hollywood for fear of what the people in British Columbia might think. But when I went back they treated me like a celebrity—and my mother was so relieved."

Stratten's secretiveness and confusion had begun to assume worrying proportions. *Playboy* had been anxious to keep her marriage from becoming instant public knowledge, since the attraction of a sex bomb who was single and attainable would be that much more powerful, but no such restriction applied to informing her family. Yet for almost a month she chose not to, feeling that the *Playboy* revelation had been enough of a shock on its own. She did confide to a friend that she had refused to let Snider near her for more than two weeks after the wedding. His touch "revolted her," the newlywed explained.

CHAPTER 18

For his next movie Bogdanovich hit upon the idea of a bittersweet tragi-comedy, based on the adventures of a team of private detectives specializing in the shadowing of married women. After Howard Sackler drafted an outline of what would become *They All Laughed,* the two had a falling out and Bogdanovich decided to write the script himself. He had Ben Gazzara in mind for the role of the disillusioned ex-romantic paid to follow Audrey Hepburn, with whom he unexpectedly falls in love. Bogdanovich originally saw himself in the part John Ritter was to play, that of a second detective mourning the death of a love affair that ended because of his inability to commit to marriage and a family. It was autobiography again, an attempt this time to exorcise Shepherd's still-lingering ghost.

Time-Life, already filming their first two movies—*Fort Apache, The Bronx,* with Paul Newman, and *Loving Couples,* with Shirley MacLaine and James Coburn—agreed to back Bogdanovich's submitted treatment of *They All Laughed* as their third venture. They put up $7.5 million, and with David Susskind acting as producer, location filming was set to start in New York in April 1980.

Bogdanovich's second meeting with Stratten came in October 1979, in the entrance hall of the Playboy Mansion. He listened enrapt, thinking how utterly exquisite she looked, as she told him about *Autumn Born* and the bits she had since done in *Skatetown USA, Americathon, Fantasy Island* and a planned appearance in *Buck Rogers*. The response to her August centerfold had been overwhelming, she went on, and based on the volume of her fan mail she was certain to be designated 1980's Playmate of the Year. Bogdanovich mentioned that he would soon be shooting a movie in New York. Would Dorothy like to read for him? She would love to, she replied.

Bogdanovich had been about to leave the mansion, but now he decided to remain for dinner. Afterwards he met Stratten again and asked if she was staying on for the movie. "I'll call home," Dorothy replied, "and if my husband isn't there, I'll stay."

"Oh," said Bogdanovich, "you're married?" When he went on to ask if she was *happily* married, Stratten replied that there were a few problems, but they were not her husband's fault. Had she had many boyfriends before she got married? Bogdanovich persisted. Stratten shook her head. "Only one," she replied.

Bogdanovich was back at the mansion a few days later, attending a pajama party Hefner was taping for a TV special. His hopes of talking to Stratten again were dashed on this occasion, but he did view her, in company with Hefner, as the Playboy boss proudly showed scenes featuring Stratten from the previous week's party. On the big screen, in this the first photographic image Bogdanovich had ever seen of her, she looked stunning. She was on stage with the disco group The Village People as they sang their anthem for the coming decade, "Ready For The 80s." Bogdanovich later complimented Hefner on the footage. "The blonde girl," he murmured, "seemed interesting." Perhaps there might be something for her in his new picture . . .

At the mansion the next day, watching Stratten again from the sidelines, Bogdanovich was approached by Nicky Blair, a friend of Hefner's. "She's quite something, isn't she?" Blair remarked. Aware of the risk he was taking, Bogdanovich asked the question that was uppermost in his mind: "Is she Hefner's girl?" Blair shook his head. "Nah," he replied, "once in a while one gets by him. But she's married to a real prick . . . He comes round here, dressed in tank tops, flexing his muscles . . . I don't know how she can stand him. She's such a sweet person, a real sweetheart. Hef can't stand the guy. He puts up with him because of Dorothy, but otherwise no way. The guy is horrible."

There could be a part for Stratten in his new picture, Bogdanovich explained. "Really?" Blair asked. "I'll mention that and put in a good word for you." A couple of days later he phoned Bogdanovich: Stratten was looking forward to their meeting.

When Bogdanovich phoned Stratten's agent, David Wilder—to whom Hefner had entrusted the fortunes of several other Playmates— the sales pitch continued, clearly having been passed from Hefner to Blair to Wilder. He repeated Hefner's description of Stratten as "a very special lady," then went on to explain how she needed someone to guide her through the showbiz labyrinth and choose her roles for her. It had to be someone who knew the ropes and could help her avoid the pitfalls, someone who could build her career as an actress. Snider, he told Bogdanovich, was "a pain in the ass . . . A real creep, who stuck his nose in everything. Don't say I said anything, but that marriage is not going to last. I don't know how she can stand him."

A few days later Wilder drove Stratten over to Bogdanovich's house for her first reading. As the electric gates swung open and they entered the courtyard, Stratten may have reflected on how far she'd traveled since leaving the shelter of her mother's tiny frame home in Coquitlam only fifteen months earlier. Now here she was in Bel Air, about to read for a famous movie director—and for a real movie this time, not an exploitation special. Bogdanovich's secretary welcomed her at the door, Wilder drove off and she was led through the hall and the enormous rectangular living room, a giant-screen television at one end, a grand piano and bookshelves at the other. Chunky armchairs were arranged round an open hearth, while cream-colored walls formed a serene backdrop for Borislav's oil paintings. The floors throughout and the staircase that led from the hall up to the bedrooms were covered in magnificently burnished hexagonal Spanish tiles. Sunlight filtering through from the palms outside lent a cool airiness to the house.

Stratten was barely seated in a tan leather armchair in Bogdanovich's book-lined office when he arrived and greeted her. Instead of sitting behind his desk he chose the blue couch, determined to keep their meeting relaxed and informal. She was to play the part of a secretary in the movie, he explained, as his maid appeared with a tray of tea and cookies.

After her reading, they discussed the problem that had cropped up regarding Stratten's new surname: another actress was registered with the Screen Actors Guild as Dorothy Stratton. Her husband wanted her to change it to Kirsten Shields, Dorothy noted. Why not consider D.R. Stratten? Bogdanovich suggested.

His performing zeal got the better of him as soon as Stratten's reading and the business side of the meeting was over. He picked up a copy of Noël Coward's *Private Lives* from the coffee table and did some reading of his own, quoting from the second-act love scenes. Bogdanovich was smitten, and for him this was as far removed from a one-night stand as it was possible to get. Perhaps Frank Sinatra, one of his favorite singers, provided the theme for the next four months— "Nice and easy does it every time"—for it would not be until March 1980, in New York City, that the couple would consummate their love.

Bogdanovich began to rewrite *They All Laughed* in earnest. Unable to build up Stratten's role of the secretary any further, he decided instead to cast his own secretary, Linda MacEwen, in that part and create another, bigger role for Stratten. In the original draft John Ritter's character was to follow a 37-year-old married woman until he discovered within the first dozen pages that she was cheating on her husband: end of case. With "Mrs Martin" transformed into young, blonde "Dolores," whose marriage was in trouble and who was soon to divorce, John Ritter now had someone to pursue throughout the movie and to fall for, just as Ben Gazzara was to do in a parallel affair with Audrey Hepburn.

When Stratten returned for a second reading six weeks later, Bogdanovich had part of the new script ready. Aware by now that he was mirroring real life, Bogdanovich had written several scenes showing Dolores quarreling with her on-screen husband, who he admits was based on Snider. "I knew she was unhappy in her marriage, although I didn't know why then or in what area," he says today. "All she told me when I was writing the script was that he was a guy nobody had anything very nice to say about. Dorothy was unhappy, but wouldn't say why exactly. She could see the part was based on her when she read it, and she sort of smiled privately to herself. She understood how to play it, but never said [real life] was better or worse than what I'd written."

On this occasion, instead of *Private Lives* with tea and cookies, Bogdanovich produced a book on occult science, *What's Your Card?*, based on birthdays, charted "life spreads" and personality traits. As they compared each other's horoscopes, Bogdanovich had no idea that

Snider was impatiently waiting outside, having chauffeured his wife over in the Mercedes she had bought for him. The license plate Snider had chosen, "Star 80," represented his own prediction for the coming year.

A few days later Stratten was back, this time on her own, and clearly depressed. She was concerned about a part in a science-fiction quickie, *Galaxina*, that Wilder was promoting: what did Peter think of it? As he read through the script, Stratten began to weep. She felt she was being pressured into the movie, she tearfully explained. And she was having more problems with her husband; he wanted her to sign over 50 percent of her earnings to him for life. Everyone else was telling her she would be crazy to agree, but Paul was her husband. He had discovered her, she argued, and without him she would never had made it to the pages of *Playboy*.

Would that have been such a bad thing? Bogdanovich asked. She could have made just as much of a splash with "legit" modeling, he pointed out and, come to that, "old Hef" was no philanthropist. For their modeling fees of $500 a day—about a third of the going rate— Hefner's girls often worked eleven or twelve hours at a stretch and then had to throw in free sex as well. While Stratten had served as a waitress at the Playboy Club in Los Angeles, she had been obliged to hobble around on 6″ heels, her breasts and buttocks spilling out of the scanty, demeaning costume. "If any one of us had trouble closing our zippers," Stratten had told Lydia Lane at the *LA Times*, "the chaperone would warn us to reduce. And if we did not we had to go on suspension." As the bunny ears flopped and the tail twitched, a nonstop series of passes had been made by both men and women. In contrast to *Playboy's* highly-paid writers, the girls were strictly ten-cents-a-dance. ("What would I have without them?" Hefner once joked. "A literary magazine!")

Stratten was back at the Bel Air house on Christmas Eve, once more enabling Bogdanovich the performer to emerge and to show off the leaf he had taken from the Frank Sinatra songbook. He followed a rendition of "Too Marvelous For Words" with the theme from *Love Story*, "Where Do I Begin?"

When they next met, in January, Stratten told Bogdanovich she had been bulldozed into doing *Galaxina*—and that problems with her husband were escalating every day. Although she did not mention Snider's offensiveness on the movie set, it was transparently obvious to the cast and crew.

She had first been introduced to James David Hinton, one of her costars in *Galaxina*, in the office of the president of Crown Pictures. Hinton, a tall, ruggedly handsome actor from Texas, had the usual preconceived "Playmate" expectations and was taken aback when Stratten walked in with her sister, Louise. She was dressed like a school-teacher, Hinton noted, in a tweedy plaid skirt with a rainforest green top. He found her extraordinarily beautiful, and later as he walked with her through a roomful of crew, he saw ample evidence that he was far from alone in his opinion. Sheila Manning, who had cast Stratten in *Galaxina*, observed the same reaction as they walked together down the street. "God, I must look wonderful today," Stratten joked to her companion.

The next time Hinton met Stratten was on *Galaxina*'s first day of shooting. Since the costumes were late in arriving, Stratten was first presented with her proposed outfit on the set. The skirt was cut so short that the her buttocks showed. "I'm not wearing this," she quietly protested. Another, less revealing costume was quickly substituted.

When Snider was absent, Hinton found Stratten a sweet, guileless nineteen-year-old Canadian girl. He gained the impression that Holly-wood success was not necessarily *her* ambition, that she was there because of circumstances which others had set in motion for her. On the set she was a lot of fun, dancing on her own to songs on the radio and quietly passing the time with the rest of the cast. With Snider around it was different: Stratten immediately tightened up, and a cur-tain descended.

Hinton took Stratten for dinner several times when the day's work was over. They enjoyed a "game" in which Hinton would light a cigarette and hand it over to her; that way she could "overlook" that Snider had forbidden her to smoke. "It really gets me when people imply what a loose life I must be leading," Stratten told him, "while all the time I've got girlfriends back in Canada who could show me a thing or two!"

On one occasion Hinton accompanied Stratten and Snider to dinner and dancing at the Jockey Club Marina. With heads turning at every table, Dorothy seemed oblivious to the attention she was generating. That same evening Hinton was shocked and annoyed when Snider did some overt flirting with a couple of the girls at the club. What made such behavior particularly galling was his insistence that Stratten constantly call in and report on her whereabouts to him, while he himself would often return home in the early hours, after the Jockey Club had closed.

All the time Hinton knew Stratten, there was never a hint of her becoming familiar or flirtatious. She undressed and dressed privately, well away from the set. No one even saw her unbutton a blouse or dress in public. Hinton was invited to attend Stratten's 20th birthday party—she was particularly keen to have him see a Marilyn Monroe spread she had just completed in a "Blonde Movie Goddess" series—but he chose not to go when he learned that several Playboy people were going to be there. He wanted to show up for Dorothy's sake, but he had found the atmosphere of previous parties with Playboy representatives uncomfortable; so in the end he decided to stay away.

Hinton found Stratten's connection with his image of *Playboy* a total—and bittersweet—contradiction.

Bogdanovich introduced Stratten to his daughters when they visited and watched, gratified, as they frolicked like three children. The sight of the people he loved most in the world together in one room filled him with a glow of contentment. He could scarcely credit the miracle of Stratten's arrival in his life, just when he'd given up hope of ever again experiencing a deep and lasting relationship. And as every day passed, he was sure she felt the same way. A lingering hug and kiss on the beach at Santa Monica preceded a location scouting trip he made to New York; on his return, another rendezvous was arranged in Bel Air. After lighting a fire in the living room hearth, the couple kissed passionately. When Bogdanovich indicated he wanted more by laying his hand on Stratten's breast, she gently removed it. She was right, Bogdanovich agreed, the kissing was enough . . .

It was down to earth with a thud the following day, thanks to Bogdanovich's house guest, Blaine Novak. A sometime dabbler in film distribution, Novak had helped cement the deal for *They All Laughed* in exchange for a role in the movie as Arthur, the street-smart hipster, a character not far removed from the doughty Novak's own personality. Novak was mainly concerned that the rapid expansion of Stratten's part had left considerably less for the ostensible stars. But he was also worried about Stratten's role in Bogdanovich's private life. Bogdanovich was being set up, he told him—Hefner, Blair and Wilder had maneuvered her into *They All Laughed*. Bogdanovich, after all, was known to have a weakness for blonds as strong as Hefner's desire for his very own movie star. And everyone was putting Snider down and encouraging Bogdanovich's romance with Stratten. "After two hours of necking last night, you sent the girl home to her husband?" Novak remonstrated. "Do I have to draw a picture of the risk you're running?" Novak went further, making no bones about his belief that Stratten herself could well be in on the 'plot."

Novak's theory sent Bogdanovich into a tailspin. After expressing his interest in Stratten to Hefner, he hadn't thought to question Nicky Blair's remarkably helpful attitude. And Wilder had followed Blair's lead in badmouthing Snider. An icy blast of stark reality had suddenly penetrated the roseate fog Bogdanovich had built around his relationship with Stratten. Any image he may have cherished of himself as the white knight riding to the rescue of the damsel in distress was shattered. Was this instead a case of the hunter being captured by the game? And the fact was that Stratten had never actually discussed *leaving* Snider . . .

Shortly after Novak dropped his bombshell, Stratten phoned Bogdanovich from the Playboy studio and he told her they had to meet and talk right away. When she said she was in the middle of photo sessions, he was unable to contain himself and proceeded to deliver his ultimatum over the phone. Of course he wanted her in *They All Laughed,* he assured her, whatever other decision she made. But she was a married woman and his message, though clearly anguished, was brutal: she had to choose between Snider and him. He could no longer handle the situation as it stood, he was "going crazy," and until she made her choice they could only meet again professionally.

Playboy's photographers were accustomed to seeing Stratten cry after phone calls from Snider and they assumed he was the cause of her tears when she returned to the set. She was unable to work again that day. She thought Bogdanovich was saying goodbye, that it was all over, although he had promised to call her the following day.

When he did, it was to apologize abjectly for losing his head. Still he felt constrained to mention Novak's conspiracy theory. Surely, Stratten asked, he didn't think she was involved? Bogdanovich assured her he didn't. Did Novak? He was a naturally suspicious type, Bogdanovich replied, and he was very concerned about everything to do with *They All Laughed*. Stratten meekly conceded that the situation "wasn't fair to Peter."

During their next meeting, on the eve of Bogdanovich's departure for New York, the couple for a second time came close to making love, only to draw back at the last moment. Again it was Stratten who resisted, this time by getting up and walking out onto the balcony of the master bedroom. Bogdanovich repeated how difficult it would be for them until Dorothy decided whether or not she was leaving Snider. Why had she married him in the first place? "I didn't want to have an argument," Dorothy replied. "My *Playboy* issue was coming out and I guess maybe he was getting insecure. I felt sorry for him and I loved him. I still love him. But it isn't the same anymore. I don't know what's wrong." Bogdanovich told Stratten that it sounded to him as if she did not love Snider any more.

With a month ahead of them before she would join him in New York, the couple felt poised in that tremulous moment when lifelong vows are exchanged. "I wouldn't leave my husband for anyone but you," Dorothy promised.

CHAPTER 19

On Saturday, March 22, 1980, Stratten flew first class from Los Angeles to New York, where Bogdanovich met her at the airport. With Snider very much in mind, it had been decreed that *They All Laughed* would be shot on a closed set, no visitors permitted. When her husband protested that he still wanted to accompany Stratten to New York, she was ready with Bogdanovich's explanation: she was performing a difficult role in the movie and would suffer if she was in any way "emotionally upset."

For appearances' sake, Bogdanovich booked himself into the Plaza Hotel, overlooking Central Park, while Stratten stayed at the nearby Wyndham, on 58th Street. The four months of courtship and foreplay were almost over. After Stratten insisted on sleeping alone the first night, the couple finally made love the following afternoon in Bogdanovich's suite at the Plaza. Bogdanovich would describe it as "the purest experience he ever had, as natural as breathing."

That weekend they were spotted by a William Morris agent strolling through Central Park. Were they an item, Stratten was asked? Despite her blushing denials, or maybe because of them, the couple's secret was out.

Blaine Novak was not the only one concerned about the changes *They All Laughed* had undergone. The more Bogdanovich deviated from the original script, the leerier Time-Life and producer David Susskind had become. By now the project had been changed out of all recognition. And who were all these new people Bogdanovich was bringing in— Stratten, Colleen Camp, his secretary Linda MacEwen, model Patti Hansen, Blaine Novak?

A party Bogdanovich threw to smooth Susskind's ruffled feathers only served to alienate his producer further. Audrey Hepburn was unable to attend, John and Nancy Ritter turned up late, Bogdanovich later still. Although Ritter asserted afterwards that the party had united the entire cast against Susskind, that had not been Bogdanovich's intention.

Bogdanovich maintains that in making a movie, the people involved must check out of the "real world." The trouble with *They All Laughed* was that the real world kept intruding, with Snider's constant calls to his wife and the problems vis-à-vis Susskind that were soon to come to a head.

Even in the script the real world encroached as Dolores/Dorothy was wooed and won by Ritter/Bogdanovich. In Stratten's three scenes with her jealous husband, the temperature escalated with each confrontation. One scene Bogdanovich had concocted between the lovelorn Ritter and Stratten had Ritter using his knowledge of her marital situation to promote his own prospects. Winningly spoken in the movie, the dialogue was uncomfortably prescient:

RITTER: This line here, this is your heart line. It shows you're very emotional. Emotions are terrific—besides, nobody can help how they feel. Oh, oh, here's a problem.

STRATTEN: What's that?

RITTER: You're married, right?

STRATTEN: Right.

RITTER: Well, that line's a little short, it's weak, but that's not what I'm worried about.

STRATTEN: No?

RITTER: There's a bad romance here.

STRATTEN: Really?

RITTER: Very bad. You see this line? It goes nowhere.

STRATTEN: Boy, that doesn't leave me with much, does it?

David Susskind's success in other media had made him determined to crack the movies as well, and with *Loving Couples* and *Fort Apache, The Bronx* already completed under his stewardship, he saw no reason why *They All Laughed* should depart from the formula moviemaking he felt comfortable with. The rallying cry of Bogdanovich and his cinematographer, Robby Muller—"We did it in Singapore, let's do it in the streets of New York"—was not what Susskind wanted to hear. "You've improvised enough with the script since we bought it last year," he told Bogdanovich. "I want no further improvisation when you start shooting. This is not an experimental movie, Peter, for Chrissake."

Bogdanovich was furious. If he, as author of the script and director of the movie, couldn't improvise, who could? Some of the wacky comedy situations in *They All Laughed* simply demanded it, he argued, bearing in mind that the framework of the film had been well and truly hammered out.

Susskind and Bogdanovich disagreed even about the color process to be used. "We'll shoot New York in Fuji color, like *Saint Jack*. They'll never know what hit 'em!" Bogdanovich had exclaimed to Muller. But Susskind's reaction was predictably negative. "He was less than liberal," says Bogdanovich, "and felt that Fuji was a bad thing. He was against it just because I wanted it. So I said to Robbie, 'Let's see what we can do to make Eastman look like Fuji.' He did it by fooling around with the filters."

As Bogdanovich worked his way through the ten-day rehearsal period and began the thirteen-week shoot, it soon became clear that he and his producer were never going to find common ground. Under Susskind's watchful eye, a regular union crew of 50 stood by their trucks and equipment, while Bogdanovich would be busy setting up scenes several blocks away, shooting from a car or on the street with only a half-dozen crew present. After several days, Bogdanovich could tolerate the situation no longer and phoned Austin Furse, the head of Time-Life's film division. "Austin, you have a choice," he told him, "David or me." When Time-Life reluctantly accepted Susskind's "resignation," Bogdanovich was free to go his own way.

"Peter was incredible," Colleen Camp recalls. "He'd write as he went along. On a scene on Fifth Avenue, where John Ritter and I were in a shoe store, he'd give us the lines right before we had to shoot. He'd say, 'Here's two pages.' I'd say, 'Wait, can't we rehearse?' He'd say, 'God, no. It's war outside!' You had to be on your toes, but that's what's so great about working with Peter, he's so spontaneous about the way he lets his actors contribute."

Bogdanovich was bearing in mind something Orson Welles had passed on. "He told me this terrible thing about pictures being 'canned.' Anything that comes in a can can't be fresh, right? I thought that was an interesting analogy. Things [should be] canned at their peak of freshness, so that's what we tried to do with this picture."

One of Bogdanovich's favorite scenes, shot in the Algonquin Hotel, had Ritter watching Stratten across the room. "Wouldn't it be funny," Bogdanovich mused, "if the waiter came in and interrupted your reverie while you're staring at her?"

"What'll I say?" Ritter asked.

"Whatever comes into your head."

With the scene rolling, Bogdanovich signaled the waiter's entrance when Ritter was least expecting it. The waiter's innocent "Can I help you, sir?" startled the actor and sent him off into a burbling "Oh-oh-sure. Let's see now—do you have a special? I think—uh—I'll just have a soda," all accompanied by a look of the most acute discomfort.

"Cut," Bogdanovich ordered.

"Was it any good?" Ritter asked, clearly anxious.

"Oh God," Bogdanovich replied, "it was hilarious. Nothing you could do would be any better!"

Bogdanovich was gratified by the warmth of the reception Stratten got from the cast, with the single exception of Patti Hansen. "I don't like blondes," she explained to Bogdanovich. The last remark she made to Stratten before leaving was *"Jesus,* you've got big tits!" Audrey Hepburn, on the other hand, described Stratten's beauty as "translucent, like an angel," and when John Ritter was asked how he managed to look so convincingly lovesick, he dreamily replied, "All I had to do was look at Dorothy." As for the crew, their impression was of a quiet, reserved young woman who spent much of her time between scenes reading everything from Dickens to diet books to Dostoievsky. They knew she was dieting quite severely, suffered from headaches and took

Valium to relax. For much of the time, they also knew, she and Bogdanovich were "together," though this was seldom flaunted. April produced a pleasant surprise for Stratten when she was named Female Star
of the Future by the United Motion Picture Association.

A particularly unfortunate consequence of filming *They All Laughed*
was the director's falling out with Ben Gazzara. Much as he loved the
actor, Bogdanovich now found him impossible to work with. Professionally, Gazzara was upset by the split in focus of the movie, so that
he and Audrey Hepburn no longer had center stage to themselves.
David Scott Milton was to compare the situation to the many games of
racquetball he'd played with Gazzara, where theoretically it was of
crucial importance to take over midcourt. Although a good player,
Milton had no natural inclination to do this and would always happily
yield the center to Gazzara. On *They All Laughed*, with four major roles
to be juggled, Bogdanovich was neither able nor prepared to follow suit.

On a personal level, Gazzara was experiencing intense pain and
anguish as his 20-year marriage to actress Janice Rule was about to
collapse. Although he had a formidable reputation as a womanizer,
Gazzara had assured friends he could never imagine being married to
anyone else. Now he was in love with another woman, who had given
him an ultimatum: if he wanted her, he must divorce his wife. Milton
saw the decision tearing his friend apart. "He was so unhappy one day
in my apartment that I was afraid he was going to kill himself. He had
a look of such palpable pain; he just sat for two hours staring at the wall.
Thank God, he got over it. I've seen him since the divorce and he seems
very happy now. But the filming of *They All Laughed* was agony for him."
Bogdanovich looks back with regret at the lack of understanding he
showed Gazzara at the time: "I didn't appreciate what he was going
through. I do now."

Gazzara's daughters in the movie were charmingly played by Antonia and Sashy Bogdanovich, during their spring vacation from school.
They were both delighted to be working with their father again, for the
first time since their debuts in *At Long Last Love*. When in 1989 Antonia
saw her contribution to *They All Laughed*, she pronounced it "weird."
"That really was me," she says with a rueful smile, "the bossy and
bitchy elder sister! Seeing the movie again really took me back. I could
see back then how happy Dorothy and my dad were, and I cared about
her too. She was sweet and she treated us like adults. And she was

beautiful. She didn't need to have makeup on—her *face* was beautiful."

In all, the filming of *They All Laughed* was for Bogdanovich like old home week. Apart from his daughters, his cast included two old flames, Patti Hansen and Colleen Camp; his current girlfriend, Dorothy; his secretary, Linda MacEwen; and buddies Blaine Novak and George Morfogen. More significantly for Linda, since she was immediately moonstruck, Audrey Hepburn's nineteen-year old son, Sean Ferrer, was in the movie as well.

Even with the "perfect prank," as Jean Renoir would have described it, there was a downside. Not for the first time, despite Bogdanovich's popularity with the cast, many of the crew reportedly found him a "selfish, mean-spirited megalomaniac." And a hint of lurking danger was on one occasion introduced into the mix. Bogdanovich had given a small part in the movie to a black actress, Rosanne Katon, whom he had first met in the Playboy Mansion. Katon knew Paul Snider. She confided to Colleen Camp that she saw him around the mansion all the time. He was a real creep, she said, and he was dangerous. *He was the kind of guy who might kill Dorothy and Peter and himself.*

CHAPTER 20

A month after her arrival in New York, with her filming to be resumed later, Stratten left on a *Playboy* tour of the U.S. and Canada, where in Vancouver she attended her mother's wedding. Back in Los Angeles, her discretion slipped a little when one day she picked Antonia up at Platt's house. "She's Daddy's new girlfriend, Mum, but we're not supposed to talk about it," the girls had informed their mother when they had returned from New York. Platt saw in Stratten a confused, unhappy girl. "I knew she'd been a Playboy Bunny. My husband Tony had told me. She looked so . . . bedraggled that day, her hair was limp and sad and fell round her face in clumps. I remember thinking she looked like those awful pictures of Marilyn Monroe in the elevator after she'd attempted suicide. She was all sort of wilted, not at all the beautiful girl in the movie . . . I just felt so sorry for her. I didn't know she was married to anybody; I didn't know anything about her except that her relationship [with Peter] was supposed to be a secret. She was just a poor, sad girl, driving an old car which looked as if it had been through a sandstorm."

On another occasion, Stratten stopped at her house, on the way to a movie with Antonia and Sachy, to pick up a bag Antonia had left behind in New York. While Sashy waited in the car outside, Stratten introduced Antonia to Snider as "the director's daughter." Snider was lounging around in a vest and boxer shorts, rolling a joint. "Care for one?" he asked Antonia, then laughed as Stratten angrily ushered her outside.

"She was embarrassed," Antonia recalls. "For me, it was no big deal. He was surly to me, I guess, because he knew Dorothy was having an affair with my dad. Dorothy never once talked about Paul to me. I reckon she thought I was old enough to realize . . . why she was with my dad. My impression of Paul was evil and scary. He looked creepy. I couldn't believe Dorothy could have lived with someone like that. She had a signed picture of my dad in her bag, but she told me to keep it in case Paul found it. We had a really good afternoon after that. She said she would give me a quarter for every cigarette she smoked but at the end of the day she gave me $50."

When a friend noted that Stratten had taken up smoking again, she replied, "I don't know what to do about Paul. I wake up in the morning and I'm so unhappy. He makes me so nervous. I need a cigarette to calm down. It's all I have." The same friend saw Snider in action one day. "Once you walk out that door," he shouted at Stratten—striking at her deepest fears of abandonment—"you can never come back!"

At the end of April Hefner threw a press luncheon to announce officially that Stratten was *Playboy*'s Playmate of the Year. A total of $200,000 in cash and prizes was attached to the honor. "For you, Dorothy, with a great deal of love," Hefner said as he handed her a check for $25,000. (The balance of the gifts were later described by Bogdanovich as "overvalued" and most of them had to be sold to pay an estimated $80,000 tax bill that came with the prize.)

Following the luncheon, Stratten taped a guest appearance on the *Tonight Show* with Johnnie Carson. One of her gifts, she told him, was a $13,000 brass-lined rosewood bathtub that seated ten people. To which Carson's lightning response was "What are we going to tell the other eight?"

Stratten invited James David Hinton to come over that evening to watch her on TV. "Hey, I'm sorry I didn't come to your birthday party," Hinton told her on the phone. "I wanted to avoid some of the company you were having, but I should have called and told you the reason."

"That's all right," Stratten assured him. Hinton felt a need to say something more, and although their telephone conversation could hardly be described as clandestine, he first asked whether Snider might be listening.

"Yes," she answered in a whisper.

"I love you," Hinton said.

"I love you, too," she replied.

They both knew—as did Snider, for that matter—that they were merely giving tender expression to a deep fondness and regard for one another. (*Playboy*'s later contention that the actor had fallen in love with her was, he says, in error.) To this day, however, Hinton is thankful he was able to say what he did, for it was the last time he would ever speak to Stratten.

Snider then came on the phone to announce that a group of people was coming over to watch the Carson show. Why didn't he come over too? When Hinton did, he discovered that Stratten was elsewhere. For the first hour, in fact, the "party" consisted of himself and Snider, who presented him with a copy of the just-released Playmate-of-the-Year issue of *Playboy*. "What do you think of it?" Snider asked. Hinton felt he was in the strangest situation he had ever known, without a clue as to how to respond. Snider broke the silence. "I think her tits look real good, don't you?" he asked.

The root of Hinton's problem with Snider lay in that remark. Although he knew Snider was totally immersed in the whole *Playboy* mystique, he found it hard to believe that Stratten's husband could be so crude and boorish when discussing his wife. Hinton's impression of Snider was of the kind of person who, in an unflagging effort to make people like him, actually drove them away. Snider, sensing Hinton's reaction, was more careful in what he said as the evening wore on. He showed the actor a scrapbook he was compiling on Stratten as well as the contract he had with her. Basically, however, he was marking time until the *Tonight Show* started. In the end five people attended the "party," Stratten not among them.

By the end of May Stratten had returned to New York to resume filming. She admitted to Bogdanovich that she had slept with Snider "a couple of times" while she'd been in Los Angeles but said that "it had made her flesh crawl." It was time to acknowledge, Bogdanovich told her, that she and Snider had gone beyond the point of no return. The joint bank account that Stratten had opened had been cleared by Snider of the $15,000 she had deposited in it.

A letter of intent to separate, clearly spelling out that the breach would be both physical and financial, was drafted and sent to Snider by Wayne Alexander, a lawyer Bogdanovich had found for Stratten. When Bogdanovich offered to put up $50,000 or $100,000 to pay Snider off once and for all (Snider could then start his own talent agency, he suggested), Stratten demurred. Once she filed for a divorce, she pointed out, Snider would get half what she had earned during the marriage anyway.

Shortly thereafter, Stratten began to suspect she was being followed. Clues appeared in several forms. After she was briefly hospitalized for a minor operation, Snider phoned and asked what her problem had been. When she asked how he had known about it, Snider replied that he "had his ways." On another occasion, in New York, according to Bogdanovich's account, there was a knock on the door of his Plaza suite one morning while he and Stratten were in bed together. When Stratten got up to open it, she found Bill and Susan Lachasse standing there. Months earlier, Snider had commissioned the two photographers to take a series of shots of Stratten in roller-skating regalia, one of which he intended to market as a poster. Could Stratten select the best picture, while they waited, and then give them the go-ahead? Bogdanovich was livid when Stratten came back to the bedroom with the photographs. Who *were* these people? he raged. And how had they *known* where to find Stratten? Under her breath, she explained that they were working for Snider and had specially flown in from Los Angeles. After giving the pictures a cursory glance, Bogdanovich declared them to be "cheap and ordinary" and he left Stratten to turn them all down "diplomatically."

Bogdanovich's recollection of the incident was off, Bill Lachasse later maintained: "It was three or four in the afternoon. There had been a cast party the night before. Dorothy answered the door in her pajamas and said, 'Oh, my God. What are you doing here?' She shut the door and when she came out again she explained that she couldn't invite us in, there were people inside. When she'd looked at the photos in the hallway we could tell she liked them, but after she came out she said, 'Look, my tits are hanging down.' Somebody in there was telling her what to do. She said, 'Look, I'm confused. Have you shown these to Paul?' I said, 'Dorothy, you're divorcing Paul.' And she said, 'I don't know, I just don't know.' "

A week later, Lachasse maintains, he called the suite again, while Bogdanovich and Stratten were still there; a woman answered the phone and told him, "We don't know Dorothy Stratten. Stop harassing us."

Bogdanovich and Stratten came up with two theories as to how the Lachasses located Stratten at the Plaza—either she had been followed or they had been redirected there from the Wyndham—but neither was correct, according to Lachasse. He had simply asked for them at the production office of *They All Laughed* and had been told to try Room 1001 at the Plaza Hotel. In any case, if Snider hadn't been sure that Bogdanovich and his wife were together before, he certainly was now. Soon he was telling everyone, including people at *Playboy,* that Bogdanovich and his wife were "shacked up at the Plaza." While the couple had been priding themselves on their circumspection, Mario Casilli at *Playboy* had first heard whispers back in early May. Now, although he had kept the news to himself, Hefner and half of Hollywood knew.

One night Stratten unburdened herself to Bogdanovich about a series of incidents that had occurred soon after she first arrived at the Playboy Mansion from Canada. Once Hefner had surprised her in the Jacuzzi and had made a pass at her. After she had protested that she was soon to be married, he had left her alone, only to become insistent, angry and threatening later. On another night James Caan had invited her to his room and in front of her had begun to make love to another Playmate. "I was so mad at Jimmy," she told Bogdanovich, "that he would think I'd want to be involved in something like that. He was never very nice to me afterwards." There were other incidents involving a lawyer *Playboy* had recommended, a relative of a top Playboy executive and Vince Edwards, TV's Ben Casey, all of whom had tried to take advantage of her. Patrick Curtis, Raquel Welch's ex-husband and manager, had been "one of the only gentlemen" she'd met. Bogdanovich assured Stratten that all this was now behind her.

As filming drew to a close, they planned a trip to Europe on the Concorde. It would be their "honeymoon," Bogdanovich told Stratten. Snider was informed that his wife was traveling abroad "with some girlfriends."

In London the couple went to see plays by Dario Fo and Harold Pinter—and, almost as if it had been preordained, a revival of *Private Lives*. A jarring moment in this idyll came during a graphic rape scene in a production of Marlowe's *Faustus* that they attended. "I'm not going to watch this," Stratten cried, and promptly walked out. Later, in tears, she refused to discuss why the scene had upset her so. Bogdanovich had already been given clues, and a few days later Stratten would give him a few more. Hefner had pursued two of her girlfriends from *Playboy*, she told him, neither of whom was initially willing to surrender. First one had been maneuvered into his bed, then another. Stratten's signals—as Bogdanovich would later interpret them—went over his head at the time.

Although her mother had been kept in ignorance of the Bogdanovich affair, she was told of her daughter's impending breakup with Snider. "He could ruin your face," she warned when Stratten called her from London. Despite this, Stratten assured Bogdanovich that Snider would never hurt her. Such a thought being inconceivable to him, Bogdanovich chose to believe her—while he remained convinced that Snider could be bought off.

Meanwhile, with the help of a bodybuilding friend, Paul Snider was spending part of the summer making exercise benches with the metal-working tools he had kept from his days of customizing automobiles back in Vancouver. The benches were to be sold through health spas and local ads. Snider also spotted an S/M bondage contraption in a Santa Monica Boulevard sex shop, the Pleasure Chest, which he then duplicated—metal frame, padded boards, velcro tape restraints and all—in his garage. Later that summer a dozen or so exercise benches lay around the house, while the bondage device sat in a corner of Snider's bedroom.

The lovers' return to the U.S. began badly. First they had a problem at immigration in New York because of Dorothy Stratten's expired visa, and this then served to undermine their plan to arrive in Los Angeles unheralded. Stratten put through a call to Playboy's immigration lawyer, charging it to Snider's number, thereby letting all parties concerned know at a stroke of their imminent arrival. "I'm scared," she told Bogdanovich, and she cried as the plane began its descent into Los Angeles. "I don't know why."

When Hefner learned of Stratten's return, he assumed that, as Playmate of the Year, she would agree to attend his annual Midsummer
Night's Dream Party the following evening. Fully aware of her affair
with Bogdanovich, and displaying every ounce of the delicate sensibility
long attributed to him, he decreed that Snider must not be allowed to
attend—unless he came with Stratten. The fuse had been lit.

Crazed with anger at the news of his banishment, Snider made his
way to Bel Air and stood outside the electric gates of Bogdanovich's
mansion, a loaded .38 revolver in his pocket. When no one appeared,
he drove up to Mulholland Drive. Later, he told friends he had thought
of ending his life there and then. Instead, he fired two shots into the air
as a token of his impotent rage, and then drove back home, still seeth-
ing. In any event, neither Bogdanovich nor Stratten attended Hefner's
bash.

Two days after their arrival in Los Angeles, Stratten agonized over
whether or not she should telephone Snider, Bogdanovich having said
the decision was "up to her." Clearly dreading the call, she decided to
put it off for a while longer. Days later, when Stratten left on Monday,
August 4, for a brief tour of Texas, she had still not made the call.

After her departure, Stratten's new lawyer, Wayne Alexander, called
Bogdanovich, the man who had chosen him. Could he have a final
decision on Snider's roller skate posters? Unaware that he was lighting
a second fuse, Bogdanovich informed Alexander that Stratten, with his
encouragement, had left definite word to pass on the deal. When this
message was relayed to Snider—through his lawyer, Michael Kelly—he
contacted Alexander and angrily demanded to know Stratten's whereabouts. He was "not at liberty to divulge that information," Alexander
told him.

Stratten's call to Snider that night, from Houston, had a calming
effect. "I love you," Snider whispered, after they had arranged a lunch
meeting for Friday, August 8. "I love you, too," Stratten replied, "but
I haven't changed my mind about wanting my freedom." Unknown to
her, seventeen-year-old Patti Laurman had just moved in with Snider,
bringing her waterbed and cheerleader outfit with her. Laurman was
another of Snider's "discoveries," whose career as an actress and model
he was hoping to develop along the lines of Stratten's.

After leaving several messages for Hefner at the Playboy Mansion
during the week of his return, Bogdanovich finally got a callback, and

for the first time he told Hefner about his love for Stratten. "You always did have a weakness for blondes," Hefner said with a wry chuckle. Though clearly annoyed by the couple's failure to attend his "Dream Party," he went out of his way to assure Bogdanovich there would be no problem in their visiting the mansion in the future. "If you're worried about her husband," he said, "I'll just make sure he's not allowed in without her." He had banned him once, he explained, and he could do it again. Bogdanovich asserted that Snider was "not the only issue," but he did nothing to stop Hefner from lighting the third fuse.

Snider's elation over Stratten's impending visit was boundless. "I've really got to vacuum the rug," he told friends. "The Queen is coming back!" The couple's lunch together on Friday, August 8, their first meeting since May, went cordially enough—until Stratten faced Snider with an admission that she was in love with Bogdanovich. This was Snider's cue to pull out every card in his deck. Didn't she know how Bogdanovich had walked out on his wife and two kids to shack up with Cybill Shepherd? How he'd ruined her career? And how he'd paid a girl $5,000 to screw him and a friend? Was this Stratten's idea of a dream lover?

Realizing that his diatribe was having a negligible effect, Snider broke, sobbing pathetically. Then he tried, unsuccessfully, to embrace and kiss his wife. For Stratten, it was over, and before she left she cleared the closet of the clothes she wanted. The rest she left for Patti Laurman, who appeared just as Stratten was promising to phone the following Sunday. "His eyes looked so sad," Stratten told Bogdanovich later.

The following day, Snider heard from *Playboy* that he was now totally banned from entering Hefner's mansion on his own. That day, too, Stratten had to pick Louise up at the airport. She was no longer with Snider, she told her half-sister, but was staying with Peter. No, he wasn't her boyfriend, but Louise was not to mention his name to their mother.

Polly Platt met Louise when she took her and Antonia out for the afternoon. Louise seemed to her an extremely introspective, incredibly shy and quite beautiful child, with a distracting if obviously unintentional habit of staring at people endlessly. "I knew somehow that this was the kid sister of Dorothy, Peter's new girlfriend," says Polly. "She was about the same age as Antonia and in spite of the fact that she was so shy, she was extremely alert and attentive to the circumstances around her. It struck me that this was the way she'd learned to survive in what was probably a difficult family environment."

Stratten and Louise drove together on Sunday, August 10, to the Mojave Desert, where Stratten was to shoot some commercials for *Playboy*. "We went to the Mohobby Desert," twelve-year-old Louise wrote to Julie Fisher, her friend back in Vancouver, "and while we were down there we saw 10 raddle snakes, 5 jack rabits. I have a grate tan and at Dorothy's place I have my own room, portable television, my own bathroom, a pool and a movie projector."

Stratten phoned Snider from the Mojave and immediately felt the full brunt of his rage at the apparent campaign to destroy him. A week ago—barred from Playboy's "Dream Party"! Monday—his dream of selling a million posters of Dorothy shattered! Saturday, the day *after* their lunch—permanently barred from the Playboy Mansion! *She must have known about this!* If she was counting him out, she was making a big mistake! He'd show *everybody!*

Stratten was taken aback at the fury of Snider's attack. She'd known about the posters, she told him, but had no idea that he had been barred from the Playboy Mansion. Bogdanovich, feeling "vaguely guilty," had neglected to mention it.

Louise overheard only fragments of the conversation, but it was enough. Stratten cried, "Please, *please*, Paul, don't *be* like that! *Don't do this to me."* Promising to phone him when she got back to Los Angeles, Stratten put the phone down. All she revealed to Bogdanovich later was that she had had a "very unpleasant conversation with Paul."

Bogdanovich drove over to Mansion West on the afternoon of Tuesday, August 12, perhaps deciding that some fence-mending was in order. Hefner gave him a brisk, formal greeting, followed by a tour of the mansion's latest installations. Later he confirmed that the ban against Snider was in force. "Now you can definitely feel free to come over anytime," he told Bogdanovich.

"Well, we still don't want to be seen [together] in public."

"This isn't public here, it's *private*," Hefner corrected him.

"If we're seen here together," Bogdanovich insisted, "it'll be all over town tomorrow."

Instead of riposting, "It was all over town *months ago*, Peter!"—as he may well have been tempted to do—Hefner indicated that he had no more time to chat by extending his hand in farewell. The meeting was over.

On Wednesday, August 13, Wayne Alexander presented Stratten with the array of alternative settlements that Snider could be offered. Should he proceed with divorce proceedings? "Not yet," she replied, "give him a little time." She had secretly arranged to meet her husband the next day, at 11:30 A.M.

When Douglas Dilge, another of Bogdanovich's *They All Laughed* associates, entered the kitchen at Copa De Oro that fateful morning, Stratten had obviously just hung up the phone, and she put a finger to her lips to indicate he was to say nothing. Later when Bogdanovich got up for their morning swim, she told him she had two appointments that day: a meeting with her business manager and a sitting for *Playboy*. Only to Louise did she confide that between the two appointments she had planned a visit to Snider.

When her sister failed to return home by 6 P.M., Louise told Bogdanovich of Stratten's secret appointment. He had had a feeling of dread all day: Stratten always called; what could have happened to her? "What's the matter?" Blaine Novak had asked him earlier. "Are you worried you're never going to see her again?" Douglas Dilge had his own down-home explanation: "Any girl I ever knew that didn't show up when she said she would was out getting laid!"

All of Bogdanovich's inherent insecurity came rushing back. Had Stratten left him? Had she gone back to Snider? Wasn't that what Novak and Dilge were hinting? After a 7 P.M. call to Snider's apartment went unanswered, Novak offered to drive over to check it out. "No, don't," Bogdanovich pleaded, "that might make matters more difficult for Dorothy." As he put Antonia, Sachy and Louise to bed at 9:30, he held them a little longer than usual as he gave them their goodnight kisses. "I'm really angry at Dorothy," Louise said. "She *said* she'd be back by 2:30!"

Shortly after 11:30 the phone rang. Almost giddy with relief, Bogdanovich picked it up as Novak and Dilge grinned, shrugged and turned the TV volume down. It was Hefner. "How are you?" Bogdanovich began.

"Haven't you heard?"

"No—heard what?"

"Oh, God . . ."

"Hey, what's the *matter?*" A pause.

"Dorothy's dead."

Bogdanovich got up from his chair, dropped the phone and began to stagger forward. "What happened?" Novak asked, as he watched his friend fall to his knees. "What *is* it?" Dilge echoed.

"She's dead," Bogdanovich mumbled. He saw his friends look at him incredulously, then uttered the words again, this time in a desperate scream: *"She's dead!"*

He threw himself on the ground and began to bang his head against the floor. Antonia and Sashy still remember his badly bruised forehead when they were finally permitted to see their father several days later.

CHAPTER 21

It was Patti Laurman who discovered the nightmare tableau in Snider's bedroom. Stratten, naked, lay half-crouched across the bottom corner of her husband's low bed, the left side of her face blown apart by a single blast from his Mossberg 12-bore pump shotgun. In a last, desperately futile attempt to save herself, she had raised her left hand for protection and lost the tip of her left index finger. Blood was spattered all over the east wall of the apartment, a television set and curtains near her head. A trail of black ants performed grisly sentry duty around the gaping hole that had been her cheek and eye socket.

Snider had been propelled forward by the force of the blast he'd trained on himself a few hours after killing Stratten. His naked body lay rigid on the floor at the bottom of the bed in a crimson pool that had attracted another procession of ants. An entrance wound gaped on the right side of his head; there was an open exit wound between his eyes and a drain from that wound behind his left ear. His left eye was bulging from its socket.

Nearby was the bondage machine Snider had built, set for rear-entry intercourse. This, combined with the bloody handprint on Stratten's buttocks and left leg, led to newspaper reports that Stratten had been raped and sodomized.

A private detective hired by Snider had arrived at the apartment before the police and had called Hefner at the Playboy Mansion. A suicide note from Snider blamed his lawyer for "not keeping an eye on me." Stratten's purse, found by the police lying open in the middle of the living room floor, contained a note from Snider saying he had no green card, was in financial distress and needed her help. They also found documentary evidence of Stratten's settlement offer, a flat sum of just $7,500, said to represent half her total assets after taxes. She had $1,100 cash in her purse, perhaps intended as a downpayment.

The apparently straightforward murder-followed-by-suicide scenario was subjected to challenge from several sources. Snider's friends contended he had bought the gun only to scare Bogdanovich. A Los Angeles psychic attributed the deaths to an unemployed actor friend of Snider's who had been involved with him in drugs. Snider's private detective, apparently suspecting a double murder, demanded that fingerprint evidence and paraffin tests be released. His requests were turned down, the police department claiming they were unable to determine scientifically whether or not Snider had fired the shotgun, since his hands were coated with too much blood and tissue for conclusive tests to be conducted.

Although the coroner initially returned an open verdict—"questionable suicide, possible homicide"—a later report by former Los Angeles County Chief Medical Examiner, Thomas T. Noguchi, seemed to correct this. "Paul Snider shot [his wife] in the head," he ruled, "then put the gun to his own head and pulled the trigger."

Antonia walked through the house the morning after Stratten's murder. It was too quiet; she could tell something was wrong. When she heard voices from the living room she hid behind the door to listen. Her father's lawyer was there. At eight o'clock in the morning? That was weird! The first thing Antonia had done after getting up was to run outside and look for Stratten's car. When she didn't see it, she somehow knew that Stratten was dead. It was the only possible explanation that occurred to the twelve-year old. "I knew there was no way a woman of that beauty could stay out all night and be alive," Antonia says today. "I still can't believe I thought that at twelve, but it was instinctive. I called my Mum after that and she told me what had happened over the phone. She told me not to tell Louise, because she was going back to Canada. And not to say anything to Sashy until Louise had gone."

When Anna was notified, she rushed to Bel Air immediately. She had met Stratten only once, in the garden of her brother's home—just two weeks before the murder: "It was Peter's birthday and I'd brought him a present. We were a little estranged. He was preoccupied and I was in my own world. I tried to talk to him, but he was distracted. Dorothy seemed very anxious that day. Now here was this sudden, shocking thing out of the blue. I left my own apartment and found Peter hysterical. My heart went out to him as a brother. All of the men were hysterical, in fact. They were being very protective of Peter. Blaine started screaming at me—I guess they had to scream at somebody."

Anna called Platt later that day to ask her to speak to Louise, since Bogdanovich was under sedation and she, Anna, was unable on her own to tell Louise what had happened. As Louise was about to be flown home to Vancouver, and Platt could only talk to her on the phone, all she could do was prepare the ground. Dorothy had disappeared, she told Louise; people were very frightened for her, Paul may have done something bad, maybe something very bad; it was her place to be with her mother. "She mentioned to my children . . . how kind I was," Platt recalls. "They were calling me for information, but I couldn't get them out of there, they were so fascinated and horrified—worried for their father and grieving for Dorothy—that they wanted to stay. I felt tremendous compassion for Louise, as well as for my own children. Peter's home was sealed up like some kind of tomb."

In the Playboy limousine that took Louise to the airport newspapers were kept out of sight and she was told that Stratten had had to go to New York unexpectedly. It was back in Canada, where Nelly was told of her daughter's death by a reporter from CBC-TV, that Louise's friend, Julie Fisher, finally broke the news to her. "Do you want the truth or a lie?" she asked, after Louise had exasperatedly demanded to know why she wasn't being allowed to see newspapers or television. "The truth," said Louise.

Two days later with her mother she was back in Los Angeles for her half-sister's funeral. Bogdanovich was devastated by Nelly's decision to have her daughter cremated, but at least with her consent he was able to have Stratten's ashes interred at Westwood Memorial Park, the cemetery where Marilyn Monroe had been laid to rest. Before leaving for the ceremony and before Nelly met him for the first time, at the funeral, Louise told her mother of Stratten's affair with Bogdanovich.

Nelly found it difficult at first even to assimilate, let alone acknowledge, the information.

Bogdanovich had an epitaph from Hemingway's *A Farewell to Arms* carved on Dorothy's headstone:

> . . . if people bring so much courage to this world the world has to kill them to break them, so of course it kills them. It kills the very good and the very gentle and the very brave impartially. If you are none of these you can be sure it will kill you too, but there will be no special hurry.

The mourners (excluding an "emotionally drained" Hefner) later congregated at Copa De Oro for meditation and refreshments. Bogdanovich issued a statement soon afterwards:

> Dorothy Stratten was as gifted and intelligent an actress as she was beautiful, and she was very beautiful indeed—in every way imaginable—most particularly in her heart. She and I fell in love during our picture, and had planned to be married as soon as her divorce was final. The loss to her mother and father, her sister and brother, to my children, to her friends and to me is larger than we can calculate. But there is no life Dorothy's touched that has not been changed for the better through knowing her, however briefly. Dorothy looked at the world with love, and believed that all people were good down deep. She was mistaken, but it is among the most generous and noble errors we can make.

Playboy's statement was brief, perhaps in an attempt to minimize the impact on the organization:

> The death of Dorothy Stratten comes as a shock to us all. She was a beautiful and talented woman. As *Playboy*'s Playmate of the Year and with a film and television career of increasing importance, her professional future was a bright one. But equally sad to us is the fact that her loss takes from us a very special member of the *Playboy* family.

Nelly spent some time at Platt's house in the days following the funeral. "She never mentioned Dorothy or her death," Platt recalls.

"She was very friendly to me, very admiring of my house—and in a state of complete and utter shock. I think now she was trying to figure out what had gone on . . . who Peter was . . . She drank coffee and smoked a lot, desperately trying to blank everything out."

The press reaction to Stratten's murder was predictable. It heavily emphasized the *Playboy* angle—'Playmate Shot To Death'—and a bizarre coincidence: "Galaxina Star Found Slain on Day Film Opens." John Finken, a senior investigator for the coroner's office, declared that it would be several weeks before test results would be available indicating whether Stratten or Snider had been under the influence of drugs at the time of death. As it turns out, there were no traces of drugs found—and in Stratten's case, the coroner's report clinically added, "No drugs stash was found."

Frantic but futile efforts were made to remove photographs of Stratten from *Playboy*'s October issue. There was time, however, to substitute another Playmate on the 1981 calendar, and to scrap a Christmas promotion that had Stratten posing in the nude with Hefner. Snider's body was returned to Vancouver for burial—and permanent exile from Hollywood's Elysian Fields.

For a while Bogdanovich would see and speak to no one. Stunned by Stratten's tragic death, he locked himself away, running and rerunning her scenes in *They All Laughed,* watching a performance that augured so well—for a career that would never be realized. Bogdanovich, his whole life called into question by the cataclysm of Stratten's murder, began asking himself all sorts of questions. What was a number? What was a color? If someone said it was Wednesday, he'd think, "What does Wednesday *mean?*" He began to read books on early Christianity, mythology, numerology, astrology—anything that might allow him to come to terms with the loss. "I almost went crazy," he admits, looking back on this period, "maybe I *did* go crazy." As far as Platt was concerned, he did—for five solid years.

Working on *They All Laughed* and coping with the memories it brought back with such desperate poignancy might have proved too much for him, but Bogdanovich knew he had to complete the movie for the sake of Stratten and all she had meant to him. It would be his testament to her, his record of her, and in an odd way the editing process began to have a palliative effect, gradually helping him live with his torment. Without the movie to work on, what else was there but the very abyss of despair? "I'm a widower," he grieved to friends, "I don't know if I can ever love again as totally as I ever loved Dorothy. I'm still a hopeless romantic, without that there's just emptiness. She was the finest, kindest, most decent human being I've ever known. She made me change for the better. The movie will show her beauty and luminosity, her promise." At John Ritter's suggestion, the opening frame of the film was to carry an inscription: "The company dedicates this picture to Dorothy Stratten."

Polly Platt had her own preoccupations in the months after Stratten's murder, but fairly quickly she began to gain a perspective on events. "We were all victims," she reflects, "all of us. Peter was always a person who ignored strangers and it wouldn't have occurred to him that this man could have been that dangerous. [Dorothy] sneaked out to meet Paul that day without telling Peter, and that's what you have to do with him, because he's very controlling over what you do. Dorothy had to lie to him . . . You are forced to lie to Peter if you are one of his girls, because he doesn't want you to go anywhere or do anything, and it's very confining. I used to call him the Pumpkin Eater—'Peter, Peter, Pumpkin Eater, had a wife and couldn't keep her.' And I used to call that house 'the Pumpkin' way before Dorothy died, because you can't get away from Peter."

Just as Platt had taken the beating for Bogdanovich in the parking lot after the filming of *The Wild Angels,* Dorothy Stratten, it was remarked, played the same role in this far more horrifying act of violence. Newspaper columnist Liz Smith put the case this way: "Some of those who witnessed Peter Bogdanovich's ongoing love affair with Dorothy Stratten are blaming the movie director for not protecting the Playmate of the Year from being killed . . . Bogdanovich, everybody's favorite megalomaniac, drew this reaction from one bitter insider: 'He knew that her husband was threatening to kill her, but he refused to back off. Personally, I think the husband shot the wrong person.' "

Aside from the fierce intensity that he brought to the editing of *They All Laughed,* Bogdanovich developed another consuming need in the weeks after Stratten's death: to set the record straight. The articles that had seemed to circle the globe after her murder—"Playmate's Love For Film Boss," "Named—Film Boss Lover of the Playmate" and The *Village Voice*'s "Death Of A Playmate"—all emphasized Stratten's *Playboy* connections, as if they were all she had had to offer. Bogdanovich felt he was the only one who could tell the full truth and decided that this must be done in book form. In the fall of 1980, between weekend visits to Vancouver to comfort Mrs. Hoogstraten and Louise, he planned the book's structure.

Further spurs to the writing process came when MGM and NBC announced the production of *Death of a Centerfold*, a TV "docudrama" of Stratten's story, and, immediately afterward, director Bob Fosse bought the rights to Teresa Carpenter's *Voice* article, which he planned to film for the Ladd Company as *Star 80*. Later, Hugh Hefner weighed in with his own tribute to Stratten in *Playboy*. Indeed, hardly a month went by without additional reminders of the murder. "What's been published so far," Bogdanovich declared, "is full of contradictions, because so few people knew the facts. No one knew her, certainly not Hugh Hefner, and Bob Fosse never even met her. Her story has to be told properly, and there's no one else who knows it but me."

David Scott Milton believes that writing his book on Stratten provided necessary therapy for Bogdanovich. "He was at his lowest point before he started, not talking at all, which reminded me of Benny Gazzara before his divorce. That really scared me. Then I thought he was on the brink of a major breakdown when he started talking peculiarly—numerology, lights flashing, all that stuff. Peter *had* to write Dorothy's story. There was suddenly a kind of focus back in his life. He started to pour things out, he would be up all night writing. He became obsessed and possessed by it, but at least it gave him something to hang on to, a sense of purpose."

A sneak preview of *They All Laughed*, in Miami, proved a considerable disappointment. The picture worked for the first hour, comfortably holding the audience, but then seemed to lose their interest. Bogdanovich thought there were two reasons: it was the wrong audience, and the film wasn't properly finished. "I told them not to advertise it as an Audrey Hepburn movie and they did. I asked for a theater where college kids would come and instead got an older audience. They also got a movie that was thirteen minutes too long. More than the length, though, what bothered people was the construction of the movie. I realized it was cutting away too quickly for the average audience to get with it. Most movies tell one story, and here we were telling ten and going too fast."

Although Bogdanovich seemed unconcerned about the poor preview reaction, everybody else was worried. He knew that if he had been hot, coming off a success like *What's Up Doc?*, the studio would have backed him. But that was a long time ago . . . In any event, within a week he felt he had the problem licked. He took fifteen minutes from the running time, then restored a minute and a half on the advice of Frank Capra and smoothed the cuts.

Bogdanovich soon found himself caught in a squeeze play between Time-Life and 20th Century-Fox, the glow from the former's movie-making aspirations having already faded. Both *Fort Apache, The Bronx* and *Loving Couples,* which 20th Century-Fox had released, had failed at the box office. Fox feared that if they laid out the necessary dollars for a full-scale launch of *They All Laughed,* they would only be compounding their losses. In the end they agreed to no more than a few test bookings of the new cut in the Midwest: if these proved successful, they would consider expanding to the major markets of New York and the West Coast. Just two days before these crucial openings, in August 1981, *Variety* ran the first review of the film. It was a stunner. *"They All Laughed* is gorgeous fun," the review began. "Rarely does a film come along featuring such an extensive array of attractive characters, with whom it is simply a pleasure to spend two hours . . . It depicts a circle of friends the viewer would welcome being part of. There's a cornucopia of dazzling women on screen throughout, and they are just as varied and amorously aggressive as their male counterparts . . . Bogdanovich's direction is flawless, demonstrating that he's left the deadens of *At Long Last Love* and *Nickelodeon* far behind, and has continued even further in the fresh, open direction indicated by *Saint Jack.* "

Bogdanovich was understandably elated by the notice, although mindful of its caution about the movie's commercial prospects: "Sophistication and gentleness of the treatment unquestionably make for a formidable marketing challenge—but this is probably Peter Bogdanovich's best film to date, and thus deserves careful nurturing with critical support." The question now was whether Fox would rise to the occasion. In short order came the answer—'No', as company executives declared themselves unhappy with the Midwest test results. As far as they were concerned, any broadening of the release would represent good money thrown after bad.

Bogdanovich was shattered. His own assessment of the test results was far more positive, if obviously subjective. How could he allow Stratten's major screen appearance to be shunted into the sidings of TV and videoland and not have a proper theatrical release? "I'm not going to let Dorothy's film go down the drain because of a bunch of people arguing about money," he vowed. His solution to the problem was a bold one: he would buy the film from Time-Life, form a distribution company and re-release the movie.

After the test screenings, Time-Life had to compensate Fox to the tune of half a million dollars in order to get rights reverted and to remove Fox from the equation for good. Under the agreement Bogdanovich then made with Time-Life, his own company, Moon Pictures, would take over the picture, with the half-million reimbursement upfront to Fox. The balance of the film's entire negative cost, plus interest, was to be paid off by Bogdanovich from future box office receipts before the rights would be transferred to Moon Pictures, and even then Time-Life would retain a portion of the film.

Bogdanovich listened as the risk he was running was patiently, and graphically, explained by his business advisers. With the bulk of the box office take going to Time-Life, Bogdanovich could lose millions in print and advertising costs if the movie performed only moderately. He decided to press ahead anyway. If Stratten were to receive the recognition she deserved, what alternative did he have?

For Nelly the loss of her daughter was followed by an almost sadistically cruel legal battle. Word that Snider's family had filed a claim against the assets of Dorothy's estate left her shocked and incredulous. She put her case to Hugh Hefner: Was it *conceivable* that the Sniders could benefit financially from their son's murder of her daughter?

At this point, the full ghastly implications had to be spelled out to her. Since Dorothy's death had preceded Snider's, and she had died without making a will, her assets, it could be argued, had gone to him, if only for the brief period between her death and his. When he shot himself, all his inheritance was in turn passed along to his family.

Hefner moved quickly to appoint lawyers to fight the case for Nelly. The settlement that was eventually reached gave the Sniders a cash sum of $5,000 and possession of the now-infamous Mercedes, Star 80.

CHAPTER 22

During Bogdanovich's visits to Platt's house in the year following Stratten's death, it became clear to her that he and Louise had become extremely close. They were like two lost children: "Louise had got even quieter and was deeply fragile, tremendously fearful and deeply attached to Peter. I never could dislike her, even when her presence became such a problem for my own children, as her visits to Los Angeles became more frequent. They thought of her as a rival for their father's affections, like another daughter. She got away with things they didn't, because she was close to Peter in a way that they weren't. She wasn't his girlfriend, but she was privileged. There were just completely different rules for Louise."

Antonia felt as if she had grown by three years in the months after Stratten's death: "Louise and I watched each other grow up. At first I didn't get along with her at all. I was rebellious. I did everything. I was very independent, stayed out late, had boyfriends. For a while I wanted to be with my first boyfriend all the time—he was thirteen too. Now it's funny, but it wasn't then. I went through everything, bouts of drinking, all kinds of experiences. Louise was really *different*. I wasn't around much. I was living with my Mum and fighting with her a lot. When I left the house I would stay with my aunt Anna. At thirteen I went to stay with my Dad for nearly a year. On my fourteenth birthday we weren't talking. I was jealous of the whole situation."

Platt had married Tony Wade in 1980, both of them knowing that he had incurable cancer. Devastating amounts of medication were prescribed but they seemed to do little to prevent the ravages of the disease. In a desperate attempt to cope and to bring order to her life, Platt quit drinking for a while. It was to be a brief respite, for career success alone had failed to bring the fulfillment she sought. "My life had gotten completely and absolutely demoralized and unmanageable," she reflects. "Antonia was running away from home, which I thought was her way of trying to get her Peter's attention. It didn't occur to me that *I* wasn't providing a stable home for her. I felt Peter was neglecting our children. His reply was that I was irresponsible—but I was the one having trouble with them. Antonia and I were absolutely head-to-head, locked in a battle to the *death*. Dorothy's death, my struggles with Antonia, Sachy suffering because of it, my husband dying of an incurable disease, and his two children with me for most of the time—it was just too much. No wonder I went back to drinking! Peter pointing his finger at me *did not help*. He had no concept of the lives of real people, and I say this without judgment. He's an egotist in the complete sense of the word. He's not a sinful man, not a bad man, it's just that he can't see life from any other point of view except his own. It's not as though he thinks, if he does this, this will hurt Polly, or if he doesn't talk to his children it will hurt them. He's simply *incapable* of seeing things in any other way.

"When he didn't speak to Antonia for a year, because she was rebellious to him, he blamed *me*. And there were big money problems. It was then that I went into therapy, serious self-analysis. It was to be a great turning point for me. And Peter was embarking on his journey within as well. By now, though, we weren't speaking much."

In Bogdanovich's search for the truth about Stratten, he hired a detective to dig behind the scenes while he conducted interviews with various of her acquaintances. "These sessions were so ugly. The murder itself was beyond ugly but what happened afterwards was pretty ugly, too," he recalls. "People would come in here and I would interview them on tape. When I found one particularly ugly part of the story during those interviews, I went upstairs. I was so upset, but I didn't want to show it. I remember looking out the window and muttering to myself, 'It's so ugly, so ugly.' "

When Bogdanovich showed an early draft of his account to friends, they were taken aback by his *mea culpa* stance. He was critical of *Playboy*, of course, but harder still on himself. Bogdanovich admits that he was writing in a state of emotional turmoil. Even today he hardly knows how to describe that whole period. "I was numb at certain times, just dazed. The most terrible realization was that there was nowhere I could go to get away from it, this ever-present cloud and blackness . . . wherever I went it would be there. It was all inside my head. I wish I'd known more about Dorothy, that she'd told me more about her life, that we'd had more time. When you're making a picture, there's not that much time and we weren't together that long. And Dorothy was a secretive person. Her mother had taught her not to burden people with her problems. I blame myself quite a bit for what happened because I thought I was meant to be smart. And when someone dies in your family there's a guilt—survivor guilt—even when you've had nothing to do with it. How come I wasn't aware of what was going on, what the pressures in her life were, what her husband was really like? Other people said he was this, he was that, but *she* never said too much against him. There were certain events that were obviously wrong, like his stealing money from her, and she told me he was abusive as well, but she never told me he was violent. I just had no idea what we were dealing with."

Meetings with Patrick Curtis, Raquel Welch's ex-husband and manager, and one of "the few real gentlemen" Stratten had said she'd met at *Playboy*, prompted a dramatic change in emphasis in subsequent drafts of the book. It was Curtis who provided Bogdanovich with a less sanitized account of life at the Playboy Mansion than Stratten's. After his second marriage broke up, Curtis had joined in the behind-the-scenes activities with a vengeance. "The girls just end up lying there," was how he described the mansion's orgies to Bogdanovich. "Anyone who wants to get on is OK."

Stratten was scarcely through the mansion's portals on her very first night when, Curtis revealed, he had been the first of the circling hawks to pounce. He claimed to have ceased his advances after Stratten protested she had a boyfriend back in Vancouver. That same evening she had fended off the attentions of actor James Caan, then in the middle of a difficult divorce and living full-time at the mansion. (Bogdanovich had already heard from Stratten of his second seduction attempt.)

Curtis admitted he had later talked Stratten into taking a naked swim with him in the Jacuzzi grotto, in company with one of the regular Playmates. When the threesome had entered the mansion's game house after midnight, dressed in towelling robes, Hefner, apparently under the impression that his *droit du seigneur* had been usurped, had become furious. Stratten had no sooner gotten back to her room when Hefner's secretary called, around 1:30 A.M., suggesting that she join Hefner in the Jacuzzi. An hour later Stratten had called Curtis, sobbing bitterly and claiming that Hefner had "raped" her. "Is that part of the program?" she cried. "Is this what's expected of a Playmate?" After the "rape," Hefner had told Stratten he had assumed she'd already had sex with Curtis and that his "ego was hurt."

Bogdanovich had to steady himself as he listened to Curtis's sordid "truth." Stratten had mentioned Hefner's advances and how two other Playmates had been seduced by him, but had stopped short of further revelations. She had hinted at but clearly had been too ashamed to tell him the full story. For the first time Bogdanovich was confronted with more than a suggestion of the constant pressures and degradations Stratten had been forced to endure at Hefner's hands. His nausea was now followed by rage. No wonder she had been so upset in London at the rape scene in the theatre—now it all made sense! With Curtis's disclosures added to what Bogdanovich already knew of how *Playboy* had treated Stratten, an indictment against both the organization and Hefner personally was complete. To tell Stratten's story properly, Bogdanovich swore that he would leave nothing out—and, thanks to Curtis, he had the direction for which he had been searching.

Curtis went on to claim that he maintained a platonic relationship with Stratten even after she moved into his house, in the period before Snider's arrival in Los Angeles. Bogdanovich was so bruised and battered that he never paused to question whether an ulterior, self-serving motive might possibly lie behind Curtis's story, and when *The Killing of the Unicorn* was eventually published in 1984, Bogdanovich would gratefully acknowledge Curtis's "courageous stand" in coming forward.

Bogdanovich teamed up with Mark Damon's Producers Sales Organization (PSO) for the all-important rerelease of *They All Laughed*. The first PSO/Moon Pictures playdates were scheduled for November 1981, in New York, Nashville, Kansas, Scottsdale, Phoenix and Portland, to be followed in December by Seattle, Vancouver and Los Angeles. Bogdanovich's old buddy Dan Talbot provided the New Yorker theater as a favor, while Andrew Sarris, past differences with his ex-colleague apparently forgotten, weighed in with lyrical praise for the movie. "This is another supposedly unreleasable movie that turns out to be a minor masterpiece," he enthused in the *Village Voice*. "Part of my enchantment with *They All Laughed* is genuine surprise that Peter had it in him. ... What I admire most of all ... is his ability to be frankly confessional without overburdening his mercurial characters with his own sadness. The result is *La Ronde* and *Stolen Kisses* with an American accent, and I can think of no higher praise. See it, and curse me afterwards if you wish. After all, that is a reasonable risk for a critic to take in appreciation of a completely unexpected pleasure."

Time magazine felt differently. "Any film of practical consequence begins with a dream, an idea, at least an angle," its review observed, "but the intent of Peter Bogdanovich's new film remains one of the year's most dispiriting mysteries. Whatever the intent, the result is an aimless bust."

"Bogdanovich's best since The *Last Picture Show*," Bill Cosford countered in the *Philadelphia Enquirer*, before going on to rhapsodize over "the beautiful ensemble work, writing of genuine wit, careful construction and wonderful location filming. The participants seem to like each other, and in the movie they seem to love each other."

With reviews mixed, *They All Laughed* went on to make slight headway at the box office, and instead of the wider breakout Bogdanovich had hoped for, the best he got was a sporadic release pattern on a hit-or-miss basis. A major mistake was in disagreeing with Mark Damon over the terms they offered theaters. "I should have listened to him," Bogdanovich later admitted. "I didn't, and it cost me a fortune."

Later, in 1982, Bogdanovich almost clinched a deal with United Artists to take over theatrical distribution, but in the middle of negotiations it was revealed that Time-Life, which still controlled cable rights, intended to go for the fast buck and present the movie on its HBO network as the Christmas 1982 attraction. The deal with United Artists promptly fell through. In Miami and Dallas the film opened for the first time in the recut version in December 1982, a year after its initial release, winning rave reviews locally and capacity weekend business even though it was being shown concurrently on cable. A few months later Time-Life again ran the film on HBO, thus writing "finis" to its theatrical chances.

Mark Damon sold the movie in 40 foreign territories but overseas box office revenue followed the U.S. pattern. In Britain, where the film had only one theatrical showing, at the London Film Festival, Bogdanovich's ability to polarize the critics was never better demonstrated. "The trouble with Peter Bogdanovich is that he is forever trying to emulate people like Howard Hawks," Derek Malcolm complained (a little late?) in the *Guardian*. "*They All Laughed* is, I think, supposed to be a charming romantic comedy, but the progress is pretty painful. It's another case of Hollywood looking back at its better days and showing us just how much confidence it has lost."

Balancing that out, Richard Corliss in *Time* wrote, "Bogdanovich has been seriously out of form for years. Though other voices are already slapping him down for indulgence and waste I must demur: only the most curmudgeonly spirit would snipe at *They All Laughed*. It is a glorious pleasure. A cast full of starbright characters is superbly headed by Gazzara and—Bogdanovich's real coup—a still radiant Audrey Hepburn. And it's pleasing to see a New York picture that isn't festering on its mean streets. Bogdanovich's direction has a spring-heeled exhuberance that can't miss. And the music? Well, any soundtrack that has Ben Webster playing 'My One And Only Love' is alright with me." Barry Norman proved another enthusiast on his *Film '83* program for BBC TV, describing *They All Laughed* as "one of the best films of the year," and bemoaning the lack of a theatrical release.

For Bogdanovich it was now time to count the costs. Between the nonrefundable advances he had paid to Time-Life and his Moon Pictures overhead and PSO's expenses, the buy-out of Dorothy's picture had cost him over $5 million. And apart from residuals, he had very little money coming in from any other source between 1980 and 1983.

Many insiders in the business, who had stood by open-mouthed during the early seventies when Bogdanovich could do no wrong, were now equally amazed that commercially everything he touched seemed to collapse. Most considered *Saint Jack* and *They All Laughed* to be wonderfully accomplished pictures that had deserved to find large audiences; nevertheless, they had failed badly. Both had radiated a new warmth and involvement that marked a major change for Bogdanovich, and neither could be fairly traced back to any of his early idols. *They All Laughed* especially had come forth looking like an act of love and of sharing, not of selfishness. Even some previously hard-bitten antagonists marveled at its beautifully constructed plot and its charmingly effortless and witty dialogue.

When Dan Talbot, interviewed in New York, was asked if he thought Bogdanovich would bounce back, he was unequivocal: "I don't know what his specific plans are at this time, but the answer is yes, of course he will. The man is one of the most talented filmmakers in the world today." Critic Alexander Walker was asked the same question in London. "In my mind," he declared, "there's no question that he'll be back."

At this time, two new projects were bruited for production by Bogdanovich's Moon Pictures—*Twelve's a Crowd,* with Keith Carradine and Colleen Camp, and *I'll Remember April,* with Camp, John Cassavettes and Charles Aznavour, the first to be shot in Hollywood, the second in Paris. There was talk also of setting up a production base in Texas, with two remakes under consideration—director Edgar G. Ulmer's B-film classic, *Detour,* and George Barr McCutcheon's novel (previously filmed several times), *Brewster's Millions,* to star John Ritter. On a third film, *The Lady in the Moon,* Larry McMurtry was to share producer, writer and director credit. Why the move to Texas? "Because Los Angeles and New York have both succumbed to arrogance and complacency, a deadly combination," Bogdanovich explained.

In addition, at this time Bogdanovich took on financial responsibility for the completion of fledgling director Martha Coolidge's *The City Girl,* on which he became executive producer. Instead of bailing other people out and assuming additional risk by setting up his own productions, why wasn't he refilling his coffers by accepting outside directing assignments? "There's been no time," he claimed. "Dorothy's book has taken much longer than I anticipated, one reason being that until recently I haven't had the last couple of chapters, about the crime. Then I was asked to do *Private Lives* with Liz Taylor and Burton, which we were set to shoot in the Rivera until they decided just to film it on stage. I've been offered lots of pictures, but I'm pursuing my own properties. I think one can do films that are both artistically valid and commercial." In any event, the fact remains that none of the proposed Moon Pictures ever got off the ground.

Bogdanovich was thrown several lifelines during the desolate years of the early eighties. One was from fellow director Sydney Pollack. About to shoot *Tootsie* with Dustin Hoffman, he held out to Bogdanovich the chance to play the TV director, a role that eventually went to Dabney Coleman. Bogdanovich's responded that, while he appreciated the offer, he was simply in no shape to act. "It might have been fun," he reflects, "but it might have been sending myself up too much. Also it was eight weeks." If Bogdanovich had known that Sydney Pollack was sending himself up by playing the role of Hoffman's agent, he might well have reconsidered.

Another call came from John Cassavetes. "Peter, I'm depressed," his friend told him. "I'm just starting this movie, *Love Streams*. You gotta help me direct it."

"John, I don't know—"

"Don't argue. Just get your butt down here."

After getting involved in directing one scene, Bogdanovich could barely see an urgent need for him since everything on *Love Streams* seemed fairly well set up. But Cassavetes persisted and gradually drew Bogdanovich out of his isolation, helping him to feel that he could still function on a film set. When he saw the finished movie in late 1984, he was touched and surprised to note that Cassavetes had inserted a 'Special Thanks' credit at the end. "John, it's very sweet of you," he told him, "but you needn't have done it." Cassavetes laughed. "Nah, I wanted them to give you a codirecting credit, but the Guild wouldn't let me."

If some relationships were consolidated during this period, others suffered, like his friendships with Orson Welles and Norman Mailer. Bogdanovich had earlier been interested in filming Mailer's *The Executioner's Song* and had been upset when Mailer had seemed not to try hard enough to make it happen. After *They All Laughed* opened in New York, Mailer phoned with his detailed reaction to the picture, the last thing Bogdanovich wanted to hear: "I felt it was insensitive of him to assume I would react to a critique of this particular movie just as I would of any other. I . . . got furious and saw red. I let out all my irritation over the years with Norman, saying things I didn't . . . mean. I destroyed the friendship in one phone call."

Bogdanovich's relationship with Orson Welles took a distinct drop after his mentor made a highly cutting remark in a TV conversation with Burt Reynolds. Bogdanovich answered Welles immediately. "It's funny," he wrote, "I tuned in last night because I heard you were on the "Tonight Show" and I wanted to see what you were all thinking. I guess I found out. Love, Peter."

Welles sent two letters in reply, both in the same envelope. One was short and nasty, claiming his remark was thoroughly deserved. The other was extremely apologetic. "Choose the memo you want," a covering note suggested.

Welles called Bogdanovich a couple of times afterwards and one day steered the conversation to the interviews he and Bogdanovich had been preparing on and off over the past ten years. "I hope you're not just going to publish [them] after I'm dead," he said.

Bogdanovich, stung by this remark, proceeded to dig out everything that he had accumulated for the project over the years, five drawers full of tapes, transcriptions, memos and photographs. "He really didn't trust anybody," Bogdanovich laments. "He was just waiting to be betrayed. I sent the stuff back because I was . . . so irritated that he imagined I would betray him after his death."

CHAPTER 23

Aware that Stratten had put money aside regularly for Louise to "have her teeth fixed," Bogdanovich sent her to see Charles Pincus, "dentist to the stars," who examined her mouth, listened to her history of dental problems and announced that an operation would be necessary to correct her protruding lower jaw. She was referred to an orthodontist, Tom Ricketts, who learned that because Louise had been two months premature at birth, a breather had been inserted in her mouth, which had pulled her lower jaw forward. This, Ricketts explained, caused her bite to be in the wrong place, a condition that could be fixed by having Louise wear braces for a couple of years in preparation for an operation that would move her jaw "back to where it should have been in the first place." Ricketts concluded, "I know it sounds grisly, but it'll work. The hearing and throat problems Louise has been telling me about ought to disappear as well."

Bogdanovich agreed to the procedure and Louise required little coaxing. The operation proved a complete success and, as had been predicted, her hearing and breathing improved dramatically. Several years later, a headline on a supermarket tabloid would shriek, "Frankenstein Op for Slain Playmate's Sister," and Bogdanovich and Louise would be shocked, saddened and enraged by the implication that he had attempted to transform Louise into a replica of Stratten. When he found out that this story was to be used in a forthcoming TV series, *Scandal*, Bogdanovich had had enough: he asked his lawyers to threaten litigation and, as a result, the planned program was cancelled.

Litigation had already become for Bogdanovich and the Stratten Estate a well-traveled path leading in different directions. *Playboy*, accused of copyright infringement for its use of extracts from Stratten's journal, agreed to pay $15,000 for one-time retroactive rights. Blaine Novak and Douglas Dilge were faced with legal action for implying that a film they had produced, *Strangers Kiss*, was based on "observations" made during the Bogdanovich-Stratten affair. The suit was eventually dropped but not before the resultant publicity helped gain distribution for the movie. NBC and MGM were unsuccessfully sued for copyright violations in their TV film *Death of a Centerfold*, the judge in the case deciding that no infringement had in fact occurred.

When, late in 1983, an offer arrived from Universal to direct *Mask*, Bogdanovich was at first reluctant to accept, despite his precarious financial circumstances. "You'd better at least read the script" was the sage advice of business manager Bill Peiffer. Bogdanovich did, and was drawn to it mainly because it recalled Stratten's interest in the tragic case of John Merrick. Filming had just begun on *They All Laughed* when Stratten had gone alone to a matinee performance of *The Elephant Man* on Broadway. So fascinated was she by Merrick's story that she had sought out a book on him a few days later. Only after her death, when he went to see the play for the first time, did Bogdanovich understand the empathy Stratten had felt toward Merrick. Both their true selves had been masked by their outward appearances, his by grotesque ugliness, hers by dazzling beauty. "We all wear masks. We get the innocence beaten out of us until we put on a mask," was the subtext in both cases, Bogdanovich concluded.

Mask was the story of Rusty Dennis's son Rocky, a young boy afflicted with craniodiaphyseal dysplasia, a disfiguring congenital disease which deposits abnormal amounts of calcium in the skull, swelling it, in Rocky's case, to twice its normal size. Anna Hamilton Phelan, the first-time author of the script, had met Rocky while she was a visiting nurse at UCLA's Center for Genetic Research. She was struck by his positive attitude toward life, which she largely credited to the influence of his mother—belying his disfigurement. Bogdanovich agreed at least to discuss the project with producer Martin Starger. "It's got some potential," he conceded, "but the story construction needs to be tightened up. And I've no idea who could play the mother."

Starger read off a list of practically every actress in Hollywood between the ages of 35 and 40. Bogdanovich kept shaking his head—until they got to Cher. He had met her years before on an interview assignment during the brief period when Sonny and Cher had become a phenomenon. "Stop there," he told Starger. "She could be really interesting, because she could *be* that person, or people could make believe the character was her. It wouldn't be too much of a stretch—motorcycles, drugs, loud-mouthed, fast-talking." Starger picked up the phone and called Phelan. "What do you think of Cher for the role of the mother?" he asked. Phelan was astonished. "Why do you ask? What made you think of her?"

"Peter's with me now and thinks she'd be perfect. You seem surprised."

"I am, only because when I wrote the script, I had her in mind for the role all the time. I had a photo of her and a photo of Rusty in front of me on my desk while I was writing. I hadn't wanted to tell you that in case you said no."

When Bogdanovich and Starger put their casting idea to Universal, the studio was dead set against it. "Use Jane Fonda," Universal's motion picture head, Frank Price, proposed—a suggestion Bogdanovich immediately discounted ("Fonda as Motorcycle Mama? She'll be laughed out of the theaters.") Price then insisted that Bogdanovich test Cher. "Frank, that'll be real tough," Bogdanovich told him. "She's got a chip on her shoulder. She's really insecure. She doesn't believe anything a man says. She doesn't trust them, or anybody in authority, for that matter. She hated her father. When he was on his deathbed, she refused to go and see him. That's why she doesn't use her last name."

In spite of Bogdanovich's protestations and the fact that Cher had been nominated for an Oscar for *Silkwood* just before these discussions occurred, Price insisted that the actress do the screen test. Actually, Price seemed to have little time for *Mask,* being far more interested in his own project, the $30 million *Out of Africa.* If he could have put an end to the $12 million *Mask,* Bogdanovich felt that he would have.

To compensate for the implied slight to Cher's status, Bogdanovich did everything he could to make her test the most elaborate, comfortable and stylish ever. He had Laszlo Kovaks and his crew standing by for a whole day, ready to shoot a specially-written nine-page scene. He even agreed to use Cher's current boyfriend, Val Kilmer as Rocky, although he had to inform Kilmer he was too old to play the part in the movie itself. After taking one look at the completed test, the Universal brass dropped all their objections.

The casting of Rocky proved especially difficult, since the boy's eyes, the only feature anyone would see, had to be expressive but not too knowing. The actor had to be over eighteen but with a voice high enough to suggest a sixteen-year old, with freckles on his hands and with red hair. After many young actors had auditioned, each with a mask put over his head, slits cut for the eyes and mouth, Eric Stoltz finally turned up. He had been working at Universal for three months, and had kept asking if he could try out for this picture.

Bogdanovich noted at once the red hair, the high tenor voice. Could be, he thought. In the scene he was given to read, Stoltz, asked how he got the name "Rocky," explained that when he was in the cradle he liked to be rocked back and forth. Stoltz's reading was better than average, but when he got to the line "And so my mother called me Rocky," he said "Rock-y" in a sing-song way that made the hairs stand up on the back of Bogdanovich's neck. There was no hesitation. "That's the kid," he declared. In later talks with the young actor Bogdanovich liked Stoltz's personality more and more and was strongly confirmed in his choice for Rocky.

"What was funny," he wryly recalls, "is that when we got to shoot the scene he'd tested on, his real mother was there . . . He looked at her during the scene, but didn't say "Rock-y" the way he had in the reading. He'd forgotten!"

Bogdanovich met Rusty Dennis before shooting began. They shared a powerful bond in that she had lost her sixteen-year old son in 1978, two years before Bogdanovich had lost his Dorothy. Cher and Eric Stoltz talked to Rusty as well, and they shared Bogdanovich's view that she was one of the strongest and strangest women they had ever met.

Problems began to crop up during preproduction. Bogdanovich requested two weeks of rehearsal time, claiming that this would save Universal money on the back end. The studio argued the period down to no more than three days. Bogdanovich's choice of Sam Elliott to play Rusty's biker boyfriend—Cybill Shepherd had recommended him after appearing with him on *Yellow Rose,* a TV series—wasn't agreed upon until the film was a week into shooting. But once the shoot began, the main problem centered around Cher.

"She was lying on the couch for her first scene, and the doctor was to come in and say, 'Miss Dennis?' Her line was 'What?' " Bogdanovich recalls. "I wanted her to face away from the camera and say her line sharply, not sleepily. She wouldn't do it my way until around take nine, when I said, "Cut, print, that's terrific!" Then she looked at me and said, "You only like it because it's your idea." '

This reminded Bogdanovich of nothing so much as Lionel Barrymore's great line, "The best directors are the ones who make the actors think they did it all by themselves." He soon found that the quote summed up Cher throughout the movie. "Basically," he maintains, "she was an amateur, [but] she was used to being treated like a big rock 'n' roll star. She . . . has this enormous amount of resentment and acts as if she's being bullshitted all the time: Cher against the world. Her instincts weren't always wrong, it was just that she didn't know how to [use them]. I knew I was getting a good performance out of her, but it wasn't easy."

Cher sees the situation rather differently. "I felt Peter wanted to be doing my job, but had to hire me. I never really understood him. I never listened to his direction, because I never liked it. I didn't feel he knew what Rusty was about as well as I did." She has characterized her relationship with Bogdanovich during filming as "like being in a blender with an alligator." Perhaps for Cher the strain of being the star had a telling effect: after previously tackling only supporting roles, she was now being paid $500,000, and 5 percent of the profits, to carry the film. With *Mask* her career was on the line.

Bogdanovich felt that, in stark contrast to his star, Eric Stoltz was one of the most accomplished and professional actors he had ever worked with, especially since Rocky was one of the toughest roles he'd ever asked anyone to attempt. The makeup took four hours to apply every day. On one occasion, as Stoltz waited patiently for the next set-up, Bogdanovich turned to him and asked, "Eric, what's it like under all that makeup?"

"Well," Stoltz replied, "if you can imagine wearing ten wool ski masks, one on top of the other, you're getting close."

Bogdanovich saw and appreciated the great emotional change Stoltz had to experience during the movie, a change that continued to echo Stratten's reaction to Merrick's plight. "He would walk around on location made up every day as Rocky—he had only a single day off in our 62-day shoot—and people would react to him in the way they did to the real Rocky: they'd yell at him and make horrible jokes. He saw what it was like to be judged by your looks."

For Stoltz an unfortunate occurrence followed in the wake of *Mask*. Having been cast for the lead in Steven Spielberg's *Back to the Future*—Universal's Sid Sheinberg had seen the *Mask* dailies and had recommended him—the young actor was having trouble in the role. The first Bogdanovich heard of it was when Stoltz called and confided in him. "Peter, I just don't know how to work their way."

"He's an actor who needs to be handled. He's a little bit shy and he has to be helped," says Bogdanovich. "Next thing I knew he'd been fired from *Back To The Future* halfway through the movie. I phoned Spielberg. 'It just didn't work out,' he told me. It was a shame, a real setback for Eric, because of course [then] everyone wondered what on earth was the matter with him. Basically, everybody else in *Back To The Future* was giving a TV kind of performance. Eric's deeper than that. He wanted to give it more."

At an early stage of *Mask* Bogdanovich agreed to use Bruce Springsteen music tracks after being assured by Rusty Dennis that Springsteen was her son's recording idol. He then went further, playing Springsteen's music on the set between takes to create an authentic atmosphere. Only later would this reverberate with a vengeance.

While *Mask* was still shooting, the movie *Irreconcilable Differences* was released. Starring Ryan O'Neal and Shelley Long, it portrayed the meeting and stormy marriage of a male director and a female writer. When the former's career takes off, he ditches his wife for the star of his first big movie and then, after a period of success, runs aground with a musical remake of *Gone with the Wind* (not entitled *At Long Last Love*, but close: *Atlanta*). After this extravaganza fails, his estranged wife recovers from her erstwhile decline and overtakes him in the career race.

In more than one particular the movie was an obvious send-up of Bogdanovich and Platt. Spotting the Bogdanovich allusions that were dotted throughout the picture became all the rage in the Hollywood community during the few weeks of the film's run. Platt was perhaps less discomforted, since, for a change, her side of the story was being told, although she was not pleased with the way her character developed. "She became such an awful person!" she protests, chuckling. "But what really bothered me was that the Peter's character was so much more sympathetic and funny! She was a *bust* when she became a success! Peter told me once that he had this nightmare after we split up, that he did a play in New York that was a flop and I was on the cover of *Time* magazine. His nightmare—my fantasy!"

CHAPTER 24

Bogdanovich had broken off diplomatic exchanges with *Playboy* back in 1981, when he refused to cooperate on the magazine's tribute to Stratten. Hefner was therefore naturally curious—and anxious—about the slant Bogdanovich's book would take. Anxious if only because his organization had been continually rocked by a barrage of adverse publicity throughout the seventies and early eighties. The shockers had included the 1973 death from a drug overdose of Wilhemina ("Willy") Ray, a Playboy model and mansion regular; the suicide of Hefner's secretary, Bobbie Arnstein, after her cocaine "connection" had been established; and all sorts of prurient revelations about Hefner and porn star Linda Lovelace *(Deep Throat),* as detailed in Mike McGrady's 1980 book, *Ordeal.*

And in 1984 Hefner could still feel the scars from Teresa Carpenter's *Village Voice* article, "Death of a Playmate," which had won her a Pulitzer Prize. It was Carpenter's contention that Stratten "was not destroyed by random particulars but by a germ breeding within the ethic." Snider, Carpenter maintained, had "bought the [*Playboy*] dream without qualification . . . Instead of fondling himself in the dark, instead of wreaking abstract vengeance on a centerfold, he had ravaged a Playmate in the flesh." The article had been written from a strongly feminist perspective and throughout this period the women's movement had raised an ever-increasing din in *Playboy's* ears.

Hefner, who insists that his organization has always been in the vanguard of the battle for civil liberties and the First Amendment, managed to obtain an advance proof of Bogdanovich's *The Killing of the Unicorn: D. R. Stratten 1960–1980*, one that had been purloined from the Manhattan offices of its publisher, William Morrow. An early jolt was provided by Bogdanovich's claim that on his first visit to the Playboy Mansion with Cybill Shepherd, Hefner had hinted they should "join" him sometime in the Jacuzzi. Hefner's hopefully raised eyebrows and his sidelong smile "did it for Cybill," Bogdanovich reported: she had told him later she had felt nauseated. If that was the case, Hefner fumed in response, why had Shepherd brought her new husband, David Ford, to tour the premises?

Far more appalling, however, was the book's accusatory tone, its unrelenting attack on the whole philosophy behind Hefner's empire and its contention that *Playboy* seduced and ridiculed women. Bogdanovich went further than even Carpenter had dared. The Playboy Mansion was described as "a temple of sexual promiscuity," presided over by the sinister, hedonistic and dictatorial figure of Hefner himself.

As if this weren't outrageous enough, Hefner was convulsed with fury by Bogdanovich's disclosure (from Patrick Curtis) that he had "raped" Stratten on her first night at the mansion, and that this and its subsequent "trauma" had caused Stratten to marry Snider. Bogdanovich concluded that when the marriage collapsed and Hefner barred Snider from the mansion, he ignited the spark that produced Snider's murderous explosion of violence. Bogdanovich also charged that apart from exploiting Stratten while she was alive, the organization continued its nasty work after her death, merchandising nude photos and videocassettes of her that, Bogdanovich maintained, were nothing more than specimens of necrophilia.

In the end Hefner's reaction was tinged with relief. "This is so crazy," he confided, "it will never be published. The basic theme is a lie . . . Poor Bogdanovich is going nuts, any publisher can see that. All we have to do is talk to representatives of Morrow. When they know what is going on here, they aren't going to touch this with a ten-foot pole. Bogdanovich is a pathological liar."

The 42-page list of objections Hefner's law firm prepared had an effect opposite to the one intended since it enabled Morrow to make

The Killing of the Unicorn virtually libel-proof. There was, indeed, at least one significant change in the book when it was published in the fall of 1984: the accusation of "rape" was softened to "seduced." Publication of the book was followed by a disclaimer from *Playboy:* "Peter Bogdanovich's pathological obsession with the life and death of Dorothy Stratten has resulted in an outrageous work of fiction which does a terrible injustice to Hugh Hefner and others at *Playboy* who knew and loved her . . . Hefner played no part in the romantic triangle that led to the murder and suicide of Ms. Stratten and her husband. In an attempt to purge his own feelings of guilt, Bogdanovich has invented an entire scenario, complete with fictionalized incidents, conversations and motivations, in which others are blamed for his own culpabilities."

In his various television and press interviews to promote his book, Bogdanovich skillfully dealt with the fairly probing questions put to him:

* How did he account for Hefner's shrill reaction?

When Hugh Hefner says I'm lying, that I'm a pathological liar, I say that I'd like to hear *him* tell the story. What does Hefner *do* up there? Why doesn't he come out and tell us what he *does* do? Is he Father Christmas or what? I might not have told everything, but I'm sure telling a lot more of the truth than he's ever told in his career. . . . He's just trying to defend himself and a lifestyle that fosters promiscuity. Snider saw *Playboy* as his Utopia and Dorothy as his entrée. It isn't just Hefner who shares culpability, but his whole antifeminist philosophy. Dorothy told me cleaned up versions of things—the constant passes made by guys and the demands of the photographers. Dorothy wasn't the kind of person who went around crying on people's shoulders. She kept things to herself. I didn't realize the extent to which she was being pressured at *Playboy.*

* Why had he written the book in the first place?

Everyone else concentrated on Snider, a pimp and drug dealer. No one had told Dorothy's story. . . . I wanted people to realize that Dorothy was a marvelous human being, not just a Playmate, and that she was a victim of *Playboy* and Hugh Hefner. I didn't write the book to make money—90 percent of the royalties go to Dorothy's family, 10 percent to me for tax purposes—I did it to clarify Dorothy's life. And I found out certain things I hadn't known. . . . I came to a different place about the whole sexual revolution, the whole battle of the sexes, as a result of Dorothy's death. I had always sympathized with the woman's role, but I'd never made it a conscious thing. . . . The Playboy Mansion is a prison where Hefner keeps his Playmates under tight control—not to keep them safe from exploiters, but so he can exploit them.

* What about the numerous times Bogdanovich himself had used the same facilities at the mansion he now excoriated?

There is a public Playboy Mansion and a private one. The private part, the upstairs, secret part, was something I had nothing to do with—I describe in the book this one exception when I got caught in a situation and felt horrible about it—but mainly I didn't *do* anything up at the mansion. Am I supposed to confess to something I didn't do? What most people assume is that I'm the kind of man who makes passes at women. I'm not like that. I never have been.

* How could he hold anyone else responsible for Stratten's death, other than the man who pulled the trigger?

Hefner knew what kind of person Snider was. I had never met him. I certainly had no idea he was a lunatic.

* Didn't he feel *any* responsibility for the tragedy?

I do feel guilty, of course I feel guilty, I wish I'd done more, I wish I could have saved her. It was Dorothy's tendency to keep things to herself—that was her tragic flaw. She didn't feel Snider was my responsibility or my worry. My only wish is that she had.

* Why had he chosen to divulge intimate details of his lovemaking with Stratten, right down to her favorite position, "seated missionary"?

There are specific reasons. . . . it's not titillation or showing off. I felt that in each case it revealed something about Dorothy that was quite surprising or important. For example, the scene in the Jacuzzi, where we make love and she felt uncomfortable, that was revealing because it obviously harped [*sic*] back to the incident with Hefner. To me, it's fairly obvious why I put in that instance about who's on top, so to speak. I wanted to show the strength of her character as a woman in a situation like the one she was undergoing at the time—a woman who had just been called frigid by her husband, who had managed to go beyond her problem, who'd grown up enough that she was able to be strong in a sexual situation. I think it shows something about the kind of woman she was and I hope it encourages other women to be strong in that area.

Almost to a man reviewers slammed Bogdanovich's book. *Unicorn* was described as "creepy . . . no doubt deeply felt, but rather deranged too—a mix of brutality, romanticism, self-righteousness, mythomania and prurience," and "a shabby little shocker" that goes "from the tragic to the embarrassing to the goofy" with "a wince on every page."

"Dorothy's still being exploited as a commodity," one reviewer claimed. "It ends up being about the death of Bogdanovich's own sense and sensibility," another concluded. "The gauche indiscretions are a sign of how desperately Bogdanovich has lost his way." The book was condemned as "doodle," "bitter, condemning and crusadingly righteous," "unintentionally repellent," "shrill," and "overwrought." Bogdanovich was "a man out of control, blinded by anger, thrashing out madly. In apportioning blame for the tragedy, he points a trembling finger at everyone involved except himself." One of the kinder comments had the writer conceding he could understand why Bogdanovich had felt the need to *write* the book, "but I wish he hadn't *published* it."

The reviewers weren't alone in being dissatisfied. In spite of Bogdanovich's smooth answers to interviewers, he left many observers with questions: How could he blame Hefner for Stratten's death—surely it was *Bogdanovich*, not Hefner, who had spent four months wooing and six months sleeping with Snider's wife? Why hadn't he confronted Snider face to face himself, instead of leaving it all to Stratten? Hadn't Stratten been used no less by Bogdanovich and Hefner than she had by Snider—Bogdanovich in his constant search for that perfect blonde ingenue to replace Cybill Shepherd and to mold into his very own screen goddess, Hefner in his search for a woman of such youth and beauty that even Hollywood would be impressed? And how could Bogdanovich attack Hefner for his centerfolds when he himself had stripped Cybill Shepherd bare in *The Last Picture Show?*

One of the questions the *Voice's* Teresa Carpenter had addressed to Bogdanovich (that he chose not to answer)—"When was the first time you learned you were being followed?"—produced his later observation: "Ironically, the question was *the first time I had heard of it."* Had he known sooner, Bogdanovich claimed, even as late as August 14, "subsequent events might have been different." But, according to his own account, "Dorothy became certain [during the filming of *They All Laughed*] that *she* was being observed and followed." Surely, that should have been enough to arouse his suspicions and take action. Or did he assume Carpenter's use of the word "you" applied only to himself and excluded the woman he was living with? The statement in *Playboy*'s 1981 tribute to Stratten had been unequivocal: "Bogdanovich had found out that (Snider's private detective) was following Dorothy. It infuriated him."

Regardless of the outcome of the dispute between Bogdanovich and Hefner, reviewers noted that the two of them were at least totally united in their condemnation of Paul Leslie Snider. "There is still a great tendency," Hefner had earlier pontificated, "for this thing to fall into the classic cliché of "small-town girl comes to *Playboy*, comes to Hollywood, life in the fast lane," and that somehow related to her death. That is not what really happened. A very sick guy saw his mealticket and his connection to power slipping away. And it was that that made him kill her."

As if to compensate for his failure to confront Stratten's husband alive, Bogdanovich went to extraordinary lengths in *The Killing of the Unicorn* to portray Snider posthumously him as "a dimestore pimp," "a sleazy pimp from Canada," "a petty racketeer" who had "for several years dealt in drugs and prostitution." With his "vulgarity and strutting machismo," his "sleazy taste and braggadocio," Snider was "just this side of a bum." By the time Bogdanovich's opinion of Snider had been filtered through the columns of *Vanity Fair*, he had become nothing less than a "crawling-the-walls psycho." Was this the man Stratten had married eighteen months after their first meeting, and nine months after her arrival at *Playboy*?

And did Bogdanovich's claim that Snider was a petty racketeer who had dealt for several years in drugs and prostitution really hold up? Prostitution yes, but his old gang, the Rounders, had long denied the drugs myth. "He used them, but wouldn't peddle," they had testified. "He was scared to death of them." And, as Hefner had discovered, Snider had no record of drug convictions. A subsequent report published in *Cosmopolitan* maintained that Snider "was clever enough to steer clear of drug traffic in his business, even though drugs went hand in hand with prostitution. He successfully evaded underworld pressure to push hard drugs, which was no easy chore, because he was paying certain crime figures for protection against arrest."

James David Hinton shook his head when asked, a decade later, if Snider's actions had ever appeared inevitable. "Of course not," he replied. "I don't know anybody who is homicidal, so I didn't know if what I was seeing in Paul was homicidal. I only saw the side of Paul that told Dorothy she was to be home at a certain time, not to smoke, all that stuff. And later, that awful remark about her photographs. When I saw Paul being erratic I just thought he was doing things I wouldn't do. I think this is where Paul is the real story: He knew he was never again going to have the chance he had with Dorothy. People who commit suicide are saying, 'Look at me.' Well, nobody cared about Paul, so if he just killed himself nobody would have bothered. *But if he could bring the walls down with him . . .!* That's where his selfishness took him. I felt that his identity was entwined with hers. I'm not sure he even loved her—he may have done, but mostly she was his identity, and a strong one for a guy who was scrambling. I've softened a little on him in the last ten years, I think I've changed. I really did think he was evil, but now I think he was just pitiable."

Teresa Carpenter had taken upon herself the task of providing an element of balance for Snider, stressing in her *Voice* article some of the benefits Stratten had gained from his tutelage in the crucial early stages of her career. He had frowned upon her smoking, had insisted that her drinking be kept moderate and if, since Stratten was not drawn to cocaine or marijuana, he had judged Librium to be OK, Snider, like many others, had no conception of the depressive, unpredictable side effects the ostensibly helpful tranquilizer could produce. Moreover, he had warned her in advance of what to expect at the mansion, had taught her how to duck and swerve to avoid the passes that would be made.

Finally, although Snider had asked his and Dorothy's Canadian lawyer, Ted Ewachniuk, to mount a case against Bogdanovich for "enticement to break [their] management contract," he had privately acknowledged that there was no way he could fight the wealth and power of the establishment arrayed against him. "Maybe this thing is too big for me," he confided, deeply depressed, to friends. He couldn't reach Stratten, cocooned as she was by the lawyers and advisers Bogdanovich had obtained for her. "This is really hard," he sobbed to his roommate. He wrote notes for Stratten that he never finished, confessing his inability to "make it without you." How could he go back to Vancouver alone, dragging his dead dreams behind him, defeated and humiliated?

TV writer-producer Gary Allison's introduction to the Stratten-Snider drama was made in the spring of 1980 by none other than the ubiquitous Patrick Curtis, Bogdanovich's star informant. Snider, Curtis told Allison, was "being shoved aside by someone richer and more powerful." Allison was astonished at the lack of concern this seemed to engender: "It's very hard for people like Bogdanovich and Hefner to relate to Snider," he points out. "You have to accept certain brutalities, and both of them are very well protected. To do what they were doing was like throwing a match in a bowl of gasoline. They weren't aware of the consequences. Snider was *not* a total loser. He was backed into a wall. The gates at Hefner's mansion are no higher than the ones at Bogdanovich's, and Snider couldn't get past either."

The inescapable implication in the views of both Carpenter and Allison is that, *left to their own devices,* Stratten and Snider might have survived as a couple—at least until a civilized, mutually satisfactory settlement did them part. (In its report on the deaths, the *Los Angeles Times* had quoted an unidentified source, "close to the couple" as saying the pair had recently been seeing a marriage counsellor.) (This claim Bogdanovich has studiously refused to acknowledge.)

Certainly Stratten would not have been the first star to emerge with an uncouth husband trailing behind her. After all, weren't coarse, sleazy and shady beginnings just below many of the smoothest surfaces of today's Hollywood establishment? Perhaps with the kind of tutelage that Stratten had enjoyed, Snider's rough edges, too, could have been chipped away. Richard Brander, whose acting classes Stratten had attended, was surprised to discover that Snider had talent of his own. "I'm not interested," Snider retorted when Brander pointed this out to him. "I only come here to watch over Dorothy." To friends he described his biggest dream, the one he looked to Stratten to help him achieve, as not a chain of brothels or discos but as ownership of his very own horse ranch. Perhaps casting that first stone at Snider from behind electrified gates and fences was just too easy.

Gary Allison also shares Blaine Novak's earlier sentiments regarding

Stratten: "Everyone who saw her said she had 'Star' written all over her. Peter was a *vehicle* [to] the *next step*. According to his book . . . they were practically engaged, but all that is after the fact." As for Patrick Curtis, Allison sees him as a "charming sociopath" who had "shot Bogdanovich off on a trajectory from which he isn't about to come back."

Many reviewers were skeptical also about Bogdanovich's characterization of Stratten as an almost pathologically shy youngster forced by Snider, completely against her will, into being test-photographed in Canada. While no one suggested that Stratten was enthralled with the idea, hadn't Bogdanovich overstated the case in his attempt to place her on a pedestal of impossible purity? In Bogdanovich's airbrushed account, Stratten had to be coaxed by Snider before she finally agreed, in tears, to the sessions. Snider stripped to his shorts first; then he and photographer Ewe Meyer persuaded Stratten to disrobe. When she cried, Snider pleaded with her: "Do it for me, baby." Not so, according to Meyer, who reported that he found Stratten, after showing initial signs of nervousness, to be perfectly pliant. "She was eager to please," Meyer was to testify. "I hesitated to arrange her breasts, thinking it might upset her, but she said, 'Do whatever you like.' "

On a related incident, Bogdanovich's book seems to imply that Snider was present at a subsequent photo session set up with Ken Honey, a Vancouver photographer familiar with *Playboy*'s requirements. Although the shoot was indeed held at Snider's apartment, he was in fact at one of his auto shows at the time and unable to attend, let alone coax Stratten into doing anything. Again, her first *Playboy* session with Mario Casilli was without the benefit of Snider's presence, a glass or two of wine serving to relax Stratten on this signal occasion.

Perhaps Stratten herself gave the definitive answer to the nude photo question, with no help from anyone, when she spoke over the phone to Betty Goodwin of the *Los Angeles Herald/Examiner* during the shooting of *They All Laughed*. She declined to name the hotel she was phoning from ("A girl has to be careful, you know," Stratten cooed), but readily addressed the query, "What was it like posing nude for *Playboy* the first time?" "I was a little bit shy about it," she told Goodwin, "but not shy about my body. Obviously, if *Playboy* wants to shoot your body they're saying, be proud of it. I was shy about standing in front of this strange man, the photographer. And I didn't know how to pose. It took three days of learning to be natural. After a while you don't feel nude. Your mind is concentrating on the camera. It's very hard work. The Miss August pictures took six weeks of posing for ten hours or more a day. The Playmate of the Year pictures took a period of five months. They get right down to perfection. A good picture isn't good enough. They chose twelve pictures out of a possible 15,000." Obviously, this was Stratten in her emergent PR role, but playing it with professional aplomb, a modicum of pride in herself and a considerable degree of style that belied the blushing flower Bogdanovich portrays.

The harshest judgment of *The Killing of the Unicorn* was that it didn't represent a book at all but an alibi, and that it should have been entitled *I Didn't Kill Dorothy Stratten*. While this accusation undoubtedly contains a strong element of truth, only a handful of commentators paused long enough to make the humanitarian concession the whole sorry episode cried out for: that Bogdanovich, a man confounded by grief, was dubiously advised while researching the book—and, even more to the point, that it had been written not with a pen, but with a naked nerve-end.

There was one deeply disturbing aspect of Bogdanovich's book that no one elected to challenge: What price investigative reporting? Back in 1980, several months after the coroner's report had been issued, Teresa Carpenter's *Voice* article was still able to note only tentatively that "Dorothy had, apparently, been sodomized, although whether this occurred before or after her death is not clear." Bogdanovich's book was much more graphic and emphatic. There was, he declared, "enough evidence to prove without doubt that Snider used the bondage machine to strap down his estranged wife and rape her, and that he also sodomized her so forcibly and with such brutality that it literally tore her body apart . . . After freeing her, he fired a shotgun point-blank at the left side of her face . . . During the next hour Snider apparently moved the body a number of times, holding her head up by the hair. He had rear-entry intercourse to orgasm with the corpse . . . then he turned the shotgun on himself and blew his face away."

Bogdanovich's version of events was regarded as definitive after *The Killing of the Unicorn* was published, the subsequent U.S. pick-ups from the book encircled the globe and echoed a hundred times over. "[Snider] tied his wife into a bondage device he invented," the *Philadel-*

phia Enquirer declared, "raped her, killed her, raped her dead body and then committed suicide." In the same paper, another reporter slightly rearranged the wording: "Snider, who tortured, raped and blew Stratten away with a shotgun, then sodomized the corpse." *Vanity Fair* put it this way: "[Dorothy's] estranged husband, a former pimp and crawling-the-walls psycho, tortured and executed her on a bondage apparatus." *California* magazine reported: "[Snider] tied her up and brually sodomized her. Then, after shooting her in the head with a shotgun, he had intercourse with the corpse."

In his "definitive" account Bogdanovich chose to totally disregard both LAPD Lt. Glenn Ackerman's statement that there was "no sign of a struggle" between Stratten and Snider and the report filed by Michael Shepherd, the investigator from the coroner's office who, like Ackerman, had actually visited the murder scene.

According to Thomas T. Noguchi, the ex-Chief Medical Officer of L.A. County, forensic science had provided the *officially definitive* answer to the question of rape: "Alert to the possibility," he reported, "the investigator at the scene took fingernail scrapings and hair samples for analysis, and a sexual assault test was performed. There were *no laboratory findings of sexual abuse* [Italics added]—only of 'possible sexual activity.' " Michael Shepherd, Noguchi added, had filed a "particularly excellent report."

What he failed to add, however—perhaps because he thought it was irrelevant—was that the sexual assault test had been specifically requested by the LAPD. Nor did he choose to elaborate on the strips of tape, "used and unused," that Shepherd had reported as having been found in the murder bedroom and that, clearly, were part of the bondage apparatus—although whether "used or unused" on the day of the murder, or earlier, went unrecorded.

Shepherd's report noted, "Near [Stratten's] head, but at an angle away from her, a 'Love Seat' sexual appliance was on the floor. It was set into a position for possible rear-entry intercourse." From this it is easy to see how Bogdanovich had reached his conclusions. But it is also possible that the "Love Seat" had been set for a previous encounter, and that its presence in the room on the day of the murder had no more relevance than the presence of a television set or any other piece of furniture.

The autopsy report itself makes for grim, if revealing, reading, but

it definitively states that "there was no injury or tissue damage whatsoever that could be attributed to overzealous sexual intercourse."

In the face of this, what is to be made of Bogdanovich's claim that
Snider had "sodomized [Stratten] so forcibly and with such brutality
that it literally tore her body apart?" An official at the coroner's office
turned stoney-faced when presented with this statement. "People are
entitled to form any conclusions they want," he told me. "Even so, this
is pure fantasy. There is no evidence to support the use of force of any
kind. Dorothy would have suffered contusions had she been restrained
around her wrists and ankles. There were no contusions. And there
wasn't even conclusive evidence of intercourse, let alone of *violent* intercourse and sodomy."

But surely Bogdanovich must have had *some* evidence to support his
rape and violent sodomy contention? "Not from the coroner's office,"
I was assured. I was shown Michael Shepherd's original, hand-written
six-page report, together with fifteen pages of subsequent analysis—
including the results of the sexual assault test—all of which seemed to
support the conclusion of the autopsy report.

There was just one more source to check out—the LAPD files. In Los
Angeles County, an average of 200 deaths are reported each day. Of
these the coroner's office handles 50, and on the average conducts 20
autopsies among them. From time to time the LAPD "takes over" from
the coroner's office and is given full access to its files. I had reason to
believe this had happened in Stratten's case and that the LAPD had
carried out further tests long after the coroner's work had been completed.

The first reply from the LAPD Press Office to my inquiry was that
only a coroner's report existed on Stratten's case, and no other. When
I persisted, pointing out that I had heard that the LAPD had carried out
further tests on its own, I was told that by then the case was closed and
that nothing was to be gained by a reopening of the files. Dissatisfied
with this, I determined that I had to see the results of the separate LAPD
tests—if indeed they existed, and after weeks of trying, and with the help
of a source within the office of the Chief Coroner, I was finally handed
copies of the documents.

They revealed that, on October 3, 1980, nearly three months after
Stratten's murder, L.A. Police Detective Richard DeAnda had re-

quested that test slides taken from the coroner's office be referred to an analyst at the LAPD. The first "Analyzed Evidence Report" indicates that two vaginal slides were examined, two anal slides, two oral slides, one "body surface" slide and one "external genital area" slide. The report, prefaced by the legend "DO NOT FILE. DESTROY AFTER USE," concluded, "Spermatazoa are present on each of the vaginal slides. All other slides test negative for seminal fluid; no spermatazoa were found." The report was completed on November 5, 1980, and signed by the analyst and his supervisor. (In *The Killing of the Unicorn*, Bogdanovich mistakenly claimed the coroner found semen in her vagina and rectum.)

On the same day, the suppressed documents revealed, DeAnda was back at the LAPD laboratories with a request for a further analysis, this time of the sperm found on the vaginal slides, presumably to discover whether the semen had come from Snider or another source. (The coroner's office had confirmed to me that it would have been perfectly possible for the sperm to have been secreted the night before the murder.) The results of the second test were inconclusive: "Slides did not exhibit any antigenic activity," the report, of November 20, ran, "[nor any] identifiable enzymatic activity." Since Stratten had been cremated three days after her death, leaving behind only these LAPD reports and the coroner's findings, my search for further evidence now had to be considered over.

What were DeAnda's motives in requesting the additional tests? Were they carried out on behalf of a private citizen? Certainly private citizen Peter Bogdanovich, who was to write in *The Killing of the Unicorn* that he and Stratten had made love the night before her murder, and who in his foreword to the book was to acknowledge DeAnda's "compassion and grace in dealing with me on the horrible details of the crime," can be seen as someone with an interest in the test results.

The unavoidable conclusion, despite what has been repeated endlessly in print and portrayed on the screen, is that the speculation on violence, sodomy, torture and necrophilia that surrounds Stratten's death is ill-founded and, indeed, flies in the face of all save the most circumstantial evidence. Thomas T. Noguchi's verdict that there were *no* laboratory findings of sexual abuse, only of "*possible* sexual activity" bears repetition. It therefore remains a distinct possibility that Stratten *surrendered* to Snider in a last, mistakenly conciliatory gesture before he turned on her and ended her life.

Nothing can bring Dorothy Stratten back from the dead, but her family and loved ones are entitled to have the record set straight—to know that her end, when it came, was mercifully quick.

CHAPTER 25

Hugh Hefner drew some comfort from the withering reviews of Bogdanovich's book and stuck to a single line of defense against the accusations leveled at him: that Stratten had died because of her affair with Bogdanovich, not because of *Playboy*. At the same time he swore he wouldn't rest until every damaging point had been refuted. And if a little mud-slinging could also be arranged, so much the better.

He soon turned his attention to Patrick Curtis, the chief source of the slant Bogdanovich's book had taken after its first drafts. Curtis had first visited the mansion in the early seventies, becoming a regular soon afterwards. In April 1981, eight months after Stratten's death, and a year before he told Bogdanovich of Hefner's encounter with her in the Jacuzzi, Curtis had been summoned to the mansion and informed that it would be more "comfortable" if he stopped visiting. "This followed a series of incidents that involved his character," Hefner maintains. (According to Bogdanovich, Curtis told him he was "chagrined that he had participated in [*Playboy*'s] orgies and decided he would just as soon not go back.")

When Hefner later contacted Curtis and questioned him about the account of events he had given to Bogdanovich, Curtis's astonishing reply was that his story had been "quoted out of context." Hefner said that if that was the case, no doubt he would agree to sign an affidavit setting forth such a position. Curtis agreed at first, according to Hefner, but then became "incensed and huffy" about the *Playboy* tribute to Stratten that had suggested, however accurately, that he had made a pass at her himself. After this he—temporarily, at least—backed out of signing the affidavit.

On November 12, 1984, Curtis attended a gala fund-raiser at the Century Plaza Hotel, given by a Vietnam veterans group and honored by the presence of such luminaries as Bob Hope, Charlton Heston and James Stewart. As the organization's president, Curtis was resplendent in the uniform of a Marine lieutenant colonel, and was photographed in his officer's formal mess jacket, complete with gold pilot's wings and the Navy Cross, Bronze Star, Distinguished Flying Cross, Air Medal and Purple Heart. His only previous claim to fame had been as Raquel Welch's manager and ex-husband; now it seemed he was Captain America as well!

Intrigued and curious, Hefner decided to check out Curtis's hitherto unsung military career. Oddly enough, in files dating back to the turn of the century, the Marine Corps had no record of a Patrick Curtis ever holding a commission in the U.S. Marines.

Informed of Hefner's discovery, Curtis changed his mind yet again and made his way to the Playboy Mansion in January 1985—his first visit since being shown the door four years earlier. He brought with him the signed affidavit that Hefner had requested, stating he had "never said," nor "did he believe," that Hefner had either "forced his attentions on" or "pursued" Stratten. Nor was Hefner "responsible" for her death. In fact, Curtis felt that Stratten "genuinely admired and appreciated" Hefner. Since handing over the affidavit, Curtis has refused all interviews.

Bogdanovich reacted angrily to this new "testimony" and the doubts now thrown on his published account. "Curtis's affidavit isn't a retraction at all," he asserted. "He's not denying Dorothy's call to him after the Jacuzzi incident, because he knows it happened. All we are interested in is the phone call." As for Hefner's juicy discovery that Curtis was masquerading as an officer if not a gentleman, this mattered not to Bogdanovich: "Whether he is President of the United States or Lieutenant Colonel of the Army, Navy and Marine Corps doesn't make any difference," he maintained.

As far as Hefner was concerned, the only accurate portion of Curtis's allegation was that he and Stratten had spent some time in the Jacuzzi—but two weeks *after* she arrived at the mansion, *not* on the first night. And it was more like 8 P.M., not the early hours of the morning: "We hugged. We were naked," he blithely admitted, "but there was conversation very early on that she was engaged to be engaged, and that was that." Stratten had made no come on; he had made no pass. "But even if I *had* slept with Dorothy," Hefner protested, his delivery now worthy of Jack Benny at his peak, *"what was wrong with that?* At that point in time, she wasn't married to anybody. Besides, why is sleeping with me that traumatizing, while sleeping with Bogdanovich brings you three steps nearer to heaven?!"

Hefner's chief of security spent several months in 1984 digging for dirt on Bogdanovich and finally discovered what at first seemed like a fairly innocuous legal action for back pay filed against him by Bill Jordan, a private detective who had been in charge of security at Bogdanovich's home in 1981. But further probing resulted in a memo, prepared for Hefner by Lisa Loving of *Playboy*, allegedly based on conversations with Jordan. It stated that Jordan had first learned of an affair Bogdanovich was having with thirteen-year-old Louise from his employees, who had cited instances of the two meeting surreptitiously, once in Bogdanovich's bedroom. Then, on a trip to Venice, Italy, the memo continued, Jordan himself had walked into Bogdanovich's bedroom and discovered the director and Louise sleeping together—just sleeping—whereupon Jordan had left the room, went back outside and knocked on the door to give Bogdanovich some warning. Jordan's people had later informed him that they were quitting because of Bogdanovich's "child molestation." The next day Bogdanovich told Jordan the staff were sleeping on the job and he was firing them.

Following a lead they claimed Jordan gave them, *Playboy* staffers contacted Burl Eldridge, now Nelly's ex-husband, who recalled that Bogdanovich had begun flying to Vancouver every few weeks at the end of 1980 to spend weekends with her and Louise. At dinner parties, Bogdanovich would "arrange it so he could sit next to Louise." Then they would "embrace and kiss all through the meal."

Eldridge maintained that his protests about this behavior were drowned out by Nelly, who would tell him that Bogdanovich was just "a millionaire showing his gratitude." When he brought the subject up with Louise, she would say, "You're trying to interfere. You don't want me to have anything." She would lock herself in her room and phone Bogdanovich, who would phone Nelly, who would then scold Eldridge. And soon Nelly and Louise began visiting Bogdanovich in Los Angeles.

Eldridge had "felt like punching" Bogdanovich, he told *Playboy*. He saw himself as "a poor man" being "pushed away" by "this millionaire." And Bogdanovich was buying items like a $10,000 necklace and a $2,000 piano for Nelly and her daughter.

Their visits to Los Angeles became more frequent—Christmas, Easter and school holidays were bad enough, Eldridge felt, but the last straw came when Nelly chose to be absent on their first wedding anniversary, in 1981. When he called Bogdanovich's home to complain, Bogdanovich's reply was that Louise was being given a birthday party, and if her mother chose to be there instead of remaining with her husband, that was Eldridge's problem. "You're the lowest thing on God's green earth," Eldridge shouted at Bogdanovich.

Most damaging of all, Eldridge alleged finding an entry in Louise's diary that indicated she and Bogdanovich had made love. And he was convinced Nelly was involved as well.

In 1984 a national gossip columnist leaked part of the story: "I know you know that Dorothy Stratten was the 1980 Playmate, and that her lover was Peter Bogdanovich. What you might not know is that Dorothy had a sister, Louise, and what you *for sure* don't know is that Louise's new beau is Peter Bogdanovich . . . *Louise is a teenager.*"

CHAPTER 26

With Universal planning a spring 1985 release for *Mask,* Bogdanovich handed over the completed film, Springsteen music and all, in the fall of 1984. But when he returned from a European trip in December, he was stunned to discover that the studio had breached the "final cut" clause of his contract in the most savage manner imaginable. Gone were the Springsteen tracks that Rocky had loved, together with eight minutes of what Bogdanovich regarded as key scenes in the movie. Universal explained that Springsteen had wanted too much money for his tracks, obliging them to use Bob Seger instead, and that the cuts reduced the film's running time to a "more acceptable" 120 minutes.

Bogdanovich was in no shape to deal with this. The flak resulting from publication of *The Killing Of The Unicorn* refused to dissipate. He was on a Valium course that was supposed to calm his nerves but seemed to be producing the opposite effect, forcing him to resort to sleeping pills to get some rest.

Faced with Universal's adamant refusal to reinstate either the Springsteen music or the cut scenes, Bogdanovich pondered his course of action long and hard—and as rationally as he was able. A sequence of a biker's funeral was gone, as was a happy campfire episode that had Rocky and Rusty singing a touching and hilarious duet of "Little Egypt," and thus providing what he saw as necessary leavening to the otherwise unrelenting seriousness of the film.

Bogdanovich grimly reflected on the likely consequences to his career of standing up to the studio. Few ever dared take on the mighty giants like Universal and its parent company MCA, but he felt that if he allowed himself to be steamrollered in this situation, he would be surrendering not only for himself but for Rusty and Rocky as well. And maybe even betraying the memory of Stratten. To the astonishment of the Hollywood community, Bogdanovich went ahead and filed an $11 million lawsuit jointly against Universal and producer Martin Starger.

Between Curtis's retraction and Jordan's and Eldridge's assertions, Hefner felt he had enough "solid" material to refute the bulk of Bogdanovich's most damaging accusations against him and splash considerable mud around at the same time. Then, without warning, while pondering how to make his "revelations" public, Hefner suffered a stroke, at 2A.M. on March 7, 1985, coincidentally just a few hours before *Mask* was due to open in moviehouses across America. He was in his bathroom, reading a newspaper, when suddenly he found himself unable to understand a word. Feeling thoroughly disorientated, he went straight to bed. The next morning he was unable to talk in complete sentences and came within a hairsbreadth of being hospitalized. His full recovery a week later he attributed to a positive mental attitude and the drug Decadron. Hefner blamed his condition on "stress developed over the last year in reaction to the pathological book written by Peter Bogdanovich." Although his staff had advised him to forget it, he was unable to do this. "They came out with this whole macho thing, that you've got to be tough," he railed. "Well, it's lies, it's lies. You pay for it and you pay for it in the middle of the night."

When Universal's version of *Mask* opened as scheduled on March 8, it was a sad irony that Bogdanovich garnered some of the best reviews of his career. "Powerful drama from Peter Bogdanovich," *Variety* trumpeted. ". . . the movie taps human feelings with a depth rarely felt in films." *Newsweek* found it "genuinely moving; *US,* spellbinding . . . unforgettable;" *People* raved that *"Mask* touches the heart and conscience. Cher is astonishing and Eric Stoltz is near miraculous." In the *New York Times* Vincent Canby again separated himself from his fellow critics, this time on the negative side of the fence. Perhaps he regretted the solitary praise he had lavished on *Daisy Miller* over a decade ago. "To be fair about it," he now conceded, "Mr. Bogdanovich didn't originate this project. However it came about, *Mask* is one of those movies that tries so hard to get their supposedly universal message across (don't we all hide behind some mask or other?) that they are likely to put your teeth on edge more often than they bring one little, lonely teardrop to the eye. . . . *Mask* is a movie whose ugly exterior hides not a beautiful world, but a sentimental one. For all its four-letter words, *Mask* milks the emotions as shamelessly, and as clumsily, as *Pollyanna*. It's the kind of story that would work better on television."

"*Mask* is superb, a beautiful film," Gene Siskel insisted. *USA Today*, although objecting to the "phony" presentation of bikers, declared *Mask* to be "Bogdanovich's best film since *Paper Moon*."

What, most observers asked, was Bogdanovich's beef? Four days after the movie's opening, and with box office tills already signaling a major hit, Bogdanovich called a press conference in Hollywood to clarify his position on the lawsuit. He began by listing the alterations that Universal had made in his "final cut" and charging that they had been made by the studio behind his back. "This is not just about a movie," he declared, "but about a real mother and a real son." He admitted that he had not actually talked to anyone at Universal for over six weeks, but had been led to believe that "the boat had sailed" as far as restoring the film to his version was concerned. (That it had. The movie was due on 800 screens within days of the conference.)

"In my original cut," he explained, "the movie opens with Springsteen's "Badlands" and closes with "Promised Lands." I've offered Universal to make up the extra $100,000 for this music. Rusty Dennis saw the film and asked, 'What happened?' Her son loved Bruce Springsteen, but didn't even know Bob Seger. She also told me that the cutting of the biker's funeral robbed movie audiences of finding out what Rocky felt about death—that it was a beginning, not an end."

Springsteen, it was disclosed, had offered to give half his film money to Rocky's mother and the other half to her favorite charity, although Bogdanovich conceded that Universal had known nothing of this until just a few days before. Sensibly, in view of the glowing reviews, Bogdanovich took the opportunity to emphasize that he was not totally unhappy with Universal's cut of *Mask*. "It's now a three instead of a five—make that four," he quipped.

A frosty response came in short order from Frank Price and Martin

Starger. "We do not feel," their statement ran, "that it would serve the best interest of the film to engage in a point-by-point public refutation of the many false or misleading statements attributed to Bogdanovich."

When Marilyn Beck of the *New York Daily News* contacted Bogdanovich he was defiance itself. "Universal," he told her, "will never pull anything like this again on anyone when I get through with them. I ain't scared of these people." Her subsequent article sounded the clearest warning yet: "Peter Bogdanovich is starting to sound like a man determined to sabotage his own career. I'm not taking sides in the war he's waging with Universal. However, his zeal in making the battle so public is not only harming the potential of a truly excellent film, it's damaging his reputation in the industry. He had better believe his name now spells trouble within many executive suites."

As the movie's release expanded across the country, Bogdanovich revealed that Bruce Springsteen and CBS Records had agreed to free use of their music for two screenings, to prove its value. "I don't want to be quoted with the word 'ludicrous,' " Frank Price responded, "but the picture is already playing nationally . . . The fact remains we don't have the rights to the Springsteen music and we never did have. I raised the red flag with Bogdanovich the first time the singer's name was mentioned in preproduction meetings. Though it was fine for us to use him, I mentioned that we'd failed previously to strike a deal on using his music for a film, and that it might be a problem."

Nine or ten minutes of Springsteen music would have cost more than $1 million, according to Price, while Bogdanovich had agreed to a $226,000 music budget. Universal had tried to reach a deal with CBS Records, but negotiations had broken down over the company's insistence on 25 percent of the movie's subsequent video receipts. Unwilling to set such an industry precedent, Price refused.

Martin Starger stated that Bogdanovich was "always aware" of the Springsteen problem, but "refused to ever consider alternatives." He added that Bogdanovich had departed in December 1984, for a three-week trip abroad, taking his final director's payment and leaving behind a 124-minute version of the film that included four Springsteen numbers on which the problem was unresolved. And both Price and Starger strenuously maintained that *Bogdanovich himself* had cut the biker's funeral scene that he now complained was missing from the movie. "The very first cut Bogdanovich showed me was 142 minutes," Starger asserted. "It was clearly too long and he knew it. Sometime after that, he removed the biker scene himself and that was the last I saw of it."

Price conceded that the studio had deleted the Little Egypt scene after Bogdanovich's final cut had been handed over: "It was an artistic difference which we felt improved the film and eliminated another four minutes. We still released the film at 120 minutes, despite Bogdanovich's contract for a 115-minute movie. This is a very peculiar kind of controversy and we are frankly baffled by it. Here we have a very successful picture that has received good critical reviews and is doing excellent business. And it may be the best film that Bogdanovich has ever done."

In making such responses, the studio was at least taking several steps back from its initially aloof stance. The mighty Universal had bowed to the considerable pressure raised not only by Bogdanovich but also by a letter of support from the Directors' Guild. Further backing came in an open letter to the Universal brass carried by *Variety*'s International Edition in its March 20, 1985 issue, which said, in part:

Dear Messrs Price and Starger,

We are writing to protest your censorship of Peter Bogdanovich's *Mask* in clear violation of the director's artistic and expressive intentions, and probably his contractual rights as well.

In reversing the film's message behind the director's back, you have made it necessary to carry this controversy into the public arena. While we deplore the need for this fight, we support the director's rights, in the words of Gilbert Cates, "to get his vision on the screen,"

Sincerely,

Woody Allen	Francis Coppola	Jerry Paris
Hal Ashby	Milos Forman	Ivan Passer
Budd Boetticher	Samuel Fuller	Martin Scorsese
Martin Brest	John Huston	Don Siegel
Mel Brooks	Henry Jaglom	Robert Towne
Frank Capra	Gene Kelly	Billy Wilder
John Cassavetes	John Landis	Fred Zinnemann
	Jack Nicholson	

Yes, even the impish Billy Wilder, who had joined the anti-Bogdanovich brigade in the wake of *At Long Last Love,* was now rallying behind him, his *schadenfreude* apparently abandoned, along with those other Hollywood legends, foot soldiers and newcomers.

Regardless of this support, two separate strands of responsibility clearly emerged in the dispute. Universal contended and Bogdanovich admitted that he had left them with a "finished" film, complete with Bruce Springsteen's music on the soundtrack, though a financial agreement for its use had not been finally established. In turn, Universal, while a question remained over who had cut the biker's funeral scene, blithely acknowledged chopping four minutes of running time from the film on the basis of "artistic differences," with themselves apparently the sole arbiters.

Price and Starger asked for a full airing of the disagreement before the new Professional Standards Committee of the Directors Guild, set up by their 1984 contract to deal with problems caused by what they considered unprofessional practices. "Bogdanovich's complaints are without foundation and clearly defamatory to us," Price stated. "Marty and I both value our reputation in the industry, and when we received the letter from the group of directors, we decided to respond before the DGA rather than try to deal with each individual director."

During the *Mask* uproar, Neil Canton and Frank Marshall, working on Steven Spielberg's Amblin lot at Universal, were delighted to have Bogdanovich as a lunch guest while *Back to the Future* was being edited. They all regretted that so much time had passed since their last meeting and joked together, somewhat ruefully, about the conflict with Universal. Bogdanovich's attitude came across as at least semi-penitent: "I guess I've done it this time, folks."

He was seriously concerned about the impact the bitter dispute was having in the industry and among the public. "All I did was tell people it wasn't my picture," he claims. "They thought, 'It's moving, charming, touching. Hey, maybe he didn't really direct it at all.' Nobody could *know* unless they'd seen my version, which was thirty to forty percent better. Frank Price was the culprit, he was the one who screwed it up. I think it had something to do with *Out of Africa* being a more expensive picture and very much his baby. Really *Mask* was Sid Sheinberg's, and there was tremendous conflict between these two guys. In the end it boiled down to ego between me and Frank and Sid and also ego between CBS Records and Universal. *Mask* got caught in the middle and was the loser."

CHAPTER 27

Fully recovered from his stroke, Hefner decided to attack Bogdanovich with every weapon in his armory and called a press conference at Playboy Mansion West on April 1, 1985. With over 100 newspaper and TV reporters in eager attendance, Hefner chose to begin the proceedings with a less than riveting dissertation on how the change of lifestyle occasional by his "stroke"—exercise; a biofeedback regimen; the elimination of tobacco, salt, butter, Dexedrine and regular Pepsi from his diet; earlier nights and "dropping the baggage of a lifetime"—had transformed him. He followed this with the showing of a documentary his company had put together on Stratten. There she was, joyously dancing and talking to Hefner, laughing delightedly during her photographic sessions and, during the Playmate-of-the-Year-award ceremony, profusely thanking Playboy's boss for his support.

As soon as the screening, was over, Hefner got down to the dirt on Bogdanovich. "We learned that there was pursuit of Dorothy's entire family in the months and years after her death," he declared, his tone suddenly grave. "Pursuit of the mother, and the breaking up of her marriage, with the husband claiming adultery, followed by the seduction of her thirteen-year-old sister, Louise, and the establishment of a romantic relationship as a pathological replacement of Dorothy that has continued from that time until the present." He went on to say that he had heard that Bogdanovich planned to marry Louise. "I've known of this for six months," he claimed, "but I couldn't deal with it until three and a half weeks ago. The stroke gave me permission."

It was put to Hefner that sex with a minor under the age of sixteen was a felony in Los Angeles. "Are you saying Mr. Bogdanovich is guilty of a felony?"

"Absolutely, without question," Hefner replied. "We know of it from a number of sources."

"What will you do if Bogdanovich sues?" a reporter asked.

"I assume we'll countersue," Hefner answered as he proceeded to deliver his coup de grace. He introduced Nelly's ex-husband, Burl Eldridge, who then repeated what he had already told Hefner—that he was convinced Bogdanovich had had sexual relations with Louise, and had "no doubt Bogdanovich had been sleeping with both his step-daughter and his wife in the same bed in Vancouver."

How had he stumbled on this? reporters asked. Eldridge replied that he had walked into Nelly's bedroom on one occasion "and found Louise's nightclothes on one side of the bed, her mother's on the other side, and Bogdanovich's flightbag at the bottom of the bed."

In the face of a rather subdued response to his astonishing trump card, Eldridge seemed a little deflated and mumbled something about how he didn't really know how Nelly "figured in this charade." He swiftly changed tack, accusing Bogdanovich of trying to remake Louise into Stratten through plastic surgery. "Peter has had her jaw shortened," he charged. "He's done quite a facelift number on the girl."

The next day's headlines brought an immediate outraged reaction from Bogdanovich. "Hefner sells sexual lies every month," he angrily declared to the press. "This one about Dorothy's surviving family is just the latest. When he said Dorothy enjoyed sex Playboy-style, it was a lie. When he said he had no responsibility for her pornographic murder, it was a lie. Now he shows naked pictures to prove she loved it, when all it proves is how much he exploited her. And he tells sexual lies about her mother and sister and me to prove that I exploit them. All of this is a smokescreen to distract everyone from his mass exploitation of women, Dorothy and her family in particular. The truth is Dorothy's estate is moving against Hefner and all pornographers by supporting the women's civil rights antipornography law currently pending in L.A. County. This is the *real* story."

Neither of Hefner's two chief witnesses were reliable, he asserted, describing private detective Bill Jordan, with whom he was still in litigation over back pay, as a "charlatan," and pointing out that Eldridge had quit his job "to live off Nelly" when she inherited Stratten's estate. As soon as he heard Bogdanovich was writing a book about Stratten, he wanted to write one as well, and sat around the kitchen table "pumping her for information."

Bogdanovich tried to have the last word on the "expensive presents" issue: "Money at that time became meaningless to me and to spend it on Dorothy's family was a small way of putting a bandage on a wound. What people don't understand is that if Dorothy hadn't been killed, she would have been divorced from Snider and she and I would have eventually married. In that case, Louise would be my sister-in-law and Nelly would be my mother-in-law. And nobody would feel that that was odd."

Paul Caruso, Bogdanovich's council, volunteered that in 1983 the Los Angeles Police Department had conducted an investigation into possible sexual misconduct by his client, and that the case had been closed without the filing of charges after the police concluded that the incidents said to have been witnessed by a bodyguard on Bill Jordan's staff could not have been observed from where he stood. West LAPD spokesman Lt. Dan Cook confirmed Caruso's statement: the department's Juvenile Division had "conducted a most thorough investigation last year. We could find no evidence that any crime had been committed in the city of Los Angeles and we even sent detectives to Canada to talk to Ms. Stratten and her mother personally. We could find absolutely no evidence and there was nothing said [at Hefner's press conference] that I'm aware of that sheds any additional light on the investigation."

Lisa Loving at *Playboy* maintained that their sources within the LAPD still regarded Bogdanovich as "dirty," but because Nelly and Louise had denied sexual misconduct and most of the alleged acts had taken place outside Los Angeles, the District Attorney had been unable to proceed with the case. Capt. John White of the LAPD Juvenile Division declined to comment specifically on Playboy's allegations, other than to assert his department's position—"that it's detrimental to [Hoogstraten] to discuss these things"—and to confirm Lt. Cook's assertion that the case was closed—"unless someone comes forward with new information."

Hefner's applecart was further upset by a statement from Bill Jordan.

He had met Lisa Loving, he admitted, but claimed he had made none of the statements attributed to him in Loving's memo to Hefner. "And if asked," he added, "I will deny them."

When Platt and Bogdanovich had lunch together a few days after Hefner's press conference, she was shocked at his appearance. "He was very, very ill," she recalls. "He wasn't sleeping, and he was paranoid about his phone conversations being taped, the mess with Universal and Hefner having his children followed. He was on the brink of having a nervous breakdown. I pleaded with him to seek help, I told him he would die from it if he didn't, for I knew the pain he was going through. He could see that I had made a recovery—of sorts—and agreed to get help."

The very next day Gloria Allred, an indefatigable attorney for feminist causes, entered the fray from her Wilshire Boulevard office. On behalf of Louise, she announced, she was filing a $5 million lawsuit in Los Angeles Superior Court against Hugh Hefner and Burl Eldridge, charging libel and slander. Louise, she said, had made up her mind to sue while in Los Angeles visiting Bogdanovich. Friends had told her, on the phone from Vancouver, that her boyfriend had been asked, "Did you know that your girlfriend was seduced ever since she was thirteen-years old?"

With Louise and her mother at her side, Allred spelled out her client's anguish: "Louise hopes that this lawsuit will send a clear message to Hugh Hefner that he must stop making false statements about her, damaging her reputation and causing her immeasurable grief. Is it not enough that Louise has lost her only sister? Must she now be faced with losing her reputation and credibility as well? All that Louise has ever wanted is to lead the life of a normal teenager. Hugh Hefner is making that impossible."

Nelly probably betrayed only a part of her own anguish as she declared, "Louise has done nothing wrong. Nor myself. Mr. Bogdanovich has been a friend to our family. He has not been sexually involved with me or my daughter Louise at any time. Spare Louise more hurt, that's all I'm asking." As for Bogdanovich, Nelly said he would "testify in LB's case and support her to prove that what Hefner said about us is totally false."

When Louise was asked about the allegations of plastic surgery, she explained that Stratten had set aside money for braces and that orthodontists had recommended that she also undergo surgery—but for medical not cosmetic reasons. Why did Louise think Hefner had leveled all his accusations in the first place? "I've no idea," Louise replied. "Maybe he's unhappy with his own life and wants to get back at somebody else. I don't know."

In answer to the question of whether Bogdanovich had ever "fondled" her client in Vancouver restaurants, Allred exclaimed, "That's false!"

"That's very false," Louise agreed.

A reporter asked why she had decided to sue. Again Allred answered. "She wanted to do something and I advised her what her options were."

"I wanted to end it," Louise added. "Everybody listens to everybody else talk and I haven't been able to say anything."

"And it's about you," Allred interjected.

"It's about me."

Did Louise intend to marry Bogdanovich? "No, there's no plan for that," Louise replied.

"You don't understand why Hefner would say such a thing," Allred added. "How could he know? You don't even talk to him."

"I don't even know him."

So far the conference had gone well. Now it changed abruptly. How about Eldridge's claim that he found an entry in her diary indicating that she and Bogdanovich had made love?

"Oh, *God!*" Louise burst out.

"Stop!" Allred ordered. "Just wait a second. I don't think you should respond to anything in an alleged diary."

Had Bogdanovich bought a $10,000 necklace for Mrs. Hoogstraten and a $2,000 piano for her? "I don't know the prices for the stuff," Louise replied.

The press became more aggressive: Wasn't it true that she and Bogdanovich had kissed in public? Hadn't they been seen in the same bed in Venice? At this Louise began to shake her head and weep. All too aware that the whole sorry event was being filmed, Allred again interrupted. "I just want the record to show that she is shaking her head 'no' to the allegations that she did those things. And the reason she isn't saying anything is because she's crying."

Hefner's brief statement after Louise's press conference—"It appears that finally the truth will be known"—masked his considerable disappointment that Louise had been the one to bring the suit. *Playboy* has a tradition of not initiating lawsuits; if Bogdanovich had brought this suit, Hefner might have countersued. Now this option was denied him. On the positive side, he would now be able to subpoena witnesses to whom he was denied access before. But most observers thought that Hefner would find it tough to beat Louise's suit, since so far his allegations were unsupported by any concrete evidence. Moreover, because Louise was not a public figure, it would be easier for her counsel to argue that her privacy had been invaded and her reputation damaged. Finally, what jury in the world would take the "Great Seducer's" side in his attack on a young woman's virtue?

When at this time Bogdanovich misguidedly tried to talk Cher out of promoting *Mask*, she took the opportunity to get back at him over their differences during shooting. "One of the scenes he keeps talking about is my scene," she told a reporter. "If I can live without it, he should be able to live without it. He was just amazed that the studio people were screwing with his work. Basically, what I said [to him] was, 'You know *you* screwed with my work, now *they're* screwing with my work, and I don't really give a damn.' They really didn't hurt it as much as Peter hurt it in the beginning . . . Some of my best work isn't on the screen, but do you trash the movie because you didn't get one hundred per cent? Do you say you're taking your marbles and going home? *Not me!*"

Platt for one was saddened that the Universal suit detracted from the film's critical reception, box office success and—far more important—Bogdanovich's comeback. Her own view of the film, shared with *USA Today* critics Jack Mathews and Mike Clark, is very much based on the first-hand experience she and her husband had had during shooting of *The Wild Angels*. "Having made that way back in the sixties, we knew what these guys were like. There's a laughable scene in *Mask* where Cher and her husband have a big party, then afterwards, like some sort of Hollywood social couple, they walk their friends out to the front yard to say goodbye. *Please!* It was Peter trying to glorify these bikers, which was not keyed in with the point of the movie—that these outcasts, rude and unsocial, were accepting of the monsters. I wish Peter hadn't been so ill when he made *Mask*, it would have been even better."

While Cher and Martin Starger traveled to the 1985 Cannes Film Festival to promote the movie for Universal, Bogdanovich got there under his own aegis, thereby setting up two opposing camps immediately. "It's like he has to fail in such magnitude that he destroys everything," Cher railed, "Springsteen's music was all that Rocky played and it was all we played on the set. It's the music I heard when I saw a rough cut of the film. But I'm also a Bob Seger fan, and when I heard his music with the film I didn't go home and jump in the bathtub and open up my wrists."

Bogdanovich's weary reply came from a man nearing the end of his tether. "A director must fight to maintain the honesty and integrity of what he's doing. I'm not trying to destroy anything. I'm trying to build something called Truth."

Soon after *Mask* had turned into Universal's biggest hit in a long time—and having contributed, together with Anna Hamilton Phelan, one percent or a fifth of their points to Rusty Dennis to augment the modest $15,000 she had received from the studio—Bogdanovich took the advice of the Professional Standards Committee and decided to drop his lawsuit. In an obvious reference to his efforts to dissuade Cher from promoting the movie, the Committee's judgment was that "It was not ethically acceptable for one artist to induce another artist to withdraw such artist's support from a project with which the artist is associated." The committee also recommended that communications between parties should always be maintained, even during apparently unresolvable differences.

Bogdanovich later tried to rationalize the events that had led to the morass. "What I wanted to do in the first place was threaten a lawsuit, and then meet with the studio," he claims, "but my agent handled things badly and the message wasn't communicated. Then everybody got macho. Suing the studio was the single worst thing I ever did in this business. The whole town really got scared of me. Everybody thought I had to be crazy to sue them when I had such a good picture. What would stop me suing anybody else? It wasn't the wisest thing I ever did, but I didn't know what else to do. I was just so frustrated that this picture—that I knew could be a smash-hit—was being reduced to half what it could have been."

Bogdanovich went straight from Cannes to Majorca and checked into a hotel. He lay on the bed, staring at the fan on the ceiling as it slowly turned in the breeze from the lattice window. He knew he was in the deepest trouble of his life. The battle with Universal was lost, he had two depositions to face in a suit being brought against him over *The Killing Of The Unicorn,* Louise's suit against Hefner was going ahead, he was virtually bankrupt—and physically and mentally he was exhausted, in no shape to even think about finding his way back. Five years after losing Stratten, he was certain now the grief would never leave him.

"I've fucked up," he thought to himself. "I've fucked everything up. I'm a complete fuck-up."

CHAPTER 28

When Bogdanovich returned to the States, his staff and family were shocked at his appearance. He had lost a considerable amount of weight, which had the effect of exaggerating the already deeply-etched lines in his face. His eyes had sunk into their sockets, his pallor had deepened and his nerves were shot; he was incredibly jittery, jumping every time the phone rang.

Bogdanovich had read somewhere that the fifth year after the death of a loved one was the worst time of all. For him this would prove heartbreakingly true. He visited Stratten's grave on the night of August 13, 1985, and as he knelt there with his floral tribute, a terrible sense of panic and desolation began sweeping over him. Soon he was shaking uncontrollably. It was as if Stratten was going to be murdered the next day and there was absolutely nothing he could do to stop it. The rest of the month was like a nightmare.

On the 29th, five months after instituting the suit against Hefner and Eldridge, Louise and Nelly dropped all charges. The anti-climatic end to the affair took place as attorneys for both Hefner and the Hoogstratens signed releases. Louise's original attorney, Gloria Allred, had been replaced two weeks earlier by Bogdanovich's attorney, Paul Caruso, with Allred choosing to make no comment on the reasons for her withdrawal. According to Hefner, Caruso had been the one to advise his clients to drop the case, after initial depositions had been taken. No money, or other consideration, had changed hands, and Hefner had agreed to relinquish his right to countersue for malicious prosecution. With Bogdanovich said to be "out of the country," it was left to Nelly to explain the about-face: "We never understood what a burden would be caused by filing and prosecuting a lawsuit," she told the press. "Louise's grades in school have suffered. Her health has suffered. And the preoccupation with the responsibilities of prosecuting a lawsuit has prevented her from pursuing her life and kept her trapped in memories of the past and of her sister's murder. Winning this lawsuit, which might have taken five more years, was not worth even one more day of the pain and suffering involved."

Hefner was unable to hide his elation: "This feels like the dawn of a new day!" he crowed. "I've only been trying to defend myself and my reputation . . . It was Bogdanovich who made it appear as if I was attacking a teenage girl." He threw in at least a smidgen of magnanimity. "I feel sorry for him and everyone involved."

Anna Bogdanovich believed that her brother had put himself in a toxic state by the amount of Valium and sleeping pills he had been consuming. If he got his body cleaned out, she reasoned, his mind would follow. She found a clinic and convinced him to check in for a detoxification program. "It was a kind of fasting place," Bogdanovich recalls. "I didn't eat for nine days, just drank water. The first few days were hell, then I was able to come down. I spent two weeks there in a private room. It wasn't fancy, but it did the job. I started sleeping again and all the toxins came out. Then after nine days I slowly started taking food."

Bogdanovich continued his convalescence in Canada, staying with the Hoogstratens for several weeks before bracing himself for the return to Los Angeles in late 1985. Again at Anna's insistence, Bogdanovich started seeing a therapist.

With a monthly income of $75,000, expenses of $200,000 and debts amounting to $6 million, Bogdanovich had no alternative but to file for bankruptcy in November 1985. It was the dreadful ending to a dreadful year. He made an arrangement with his creditors whereby he would continue living in the Bel Air mansion he had purchased for $375,000 in 1973; its worth was now estimated at $3 million, and if all else failed it would provide each of his creditors with some compensation. So he still had a roof over his head, and a splendid one at that. Long gone, however, were the cook and butler Bogdanovich had retained in the heady days of Cybill Shepherd and the seventies. A housekeeper was kept on but she no longer lived in.

Any hopes Platt may have entertained of collecting child maintenance arrears from Bogdanovich seemed to be gone. (His reported largesse to Mrs. Hoogstraten and Louise had made this a particularly bitter pill for her.) Bogdanovich had reached the stage where going back to work and making a movie was no longer a matter of choice but of absolute, unrelenting necessity. Over the years he had had many discussions about doing a movie for Dino De Laurentiis. As far back as the post-*Nickelodeon* period, he had been offered *Hurricane* by the producer and turned it down: "I didn't fancy standing there in Pago Pago shouting 'More wind,' " he had joked at the time. After *Saint Jack* discussions had taken place regarding an adaptation of Peter Maas's *King of the Gypsies*, but the project had been constantly stymied by the difficulty of casting the title role. De Laurentiis had summoned Bogdanovich to his home one day after a dozen different stars had been considered and discarded.

"I have a *brilliant* idea," he had declared, ushering Bogdanovich into his lavish den. "And don't tell me no this time. Listen first! Listen! *Think!*" Only when both of them had been seated comfortably did De Laurentiis lean forward over his massive desk and, looking to either side of him, as if to ensure no one was listening, had whispered, in magisterial tones, "Robert Redford." It had been all Bogdanovich could do to keep a straight face. "Dino!" he had protested, *"Robert Redford* for *King of the Gypsies?"*

"Don't tell me no! I know what you're going to say, but we'll curl his hair and dye it black. Don't tell me no, *think* about it!"

After that there was *Paradise Road,* to be adapted from a book by David Scott Milton, with Bogdanovich and Milton working on the screenplay together. De Laurentiis expressed interest, especially if they could get the cast they wanted—Frank Sinatra, Dean Martin, Sammy Davis Jr.—the Rat Pack reassembled, with the addition of Jerry

Lewis—in a tale of over-the-hill gamblers breaking the bank in Las Vegas. When the project was in its earliest stages, one day Milton listened, astonished, as Bogdanovich called Sinatra and described, at great length, a scene they had only just started kicking around. He put the phone down fifteen minutes later. "Sinatra likes it," he said. "Jesus, can you remember what I just said? Quick, get it down on paper!"

After De Laurentiis cooled to this project, Bogdanovich worked on another development for TriStar that eventually fell through. De Laurentiis then reemerged. "Forget *Paradise Road*," he told Bogdanovich. "I've now got a wonderful project called *Illegally Yours*. With just a little fixing, it'll be perfect for you."

At first glance, *Illegally Yours* looked like an attractive proposition, a return to a *What's Up, Doc?*-type screwball comedy. But even with Rob Lowe and Colleen Camp heading the cast, there was a kind of pall over the picture from the beginning. "It wasn't much of a script," Bogdanovich recalls, "but I needed the money desperately, I was absolutely broke, and this was definitely going ahead. I took it." Louise, now known personally and professionally as "L.B. Straten," was given a small part in the movie, as a gum-chewing teenager, and Mrs. Hoogstraten made a brief appearance as a flustered juror.

David Scott Milton quickly detected the warning signs. "My feeling from the beginning was that *Illegally Yours* wasn't going to work. Peter always gives me his scripts to read before he starts any projects. He never showed me this one."

At the last minute, only days before shooting was due to start in late 1986, De Laurentiis decided in his wisdom that he wanted the script changed. "It's gotten too black," he declared. For Bogdanovich, it was either rewrite or forget the whole thing: in view of his financial condition, he rewrote. The situation rapidly slid from bad to worse as shooting began, in Florida. "Rob Lowe was difficult," Bogdanovich claims, "despite the fact he was getting more money than he'd ever been paid before. His mind just seemed to be on other things all the time. Colleen's father was dying and the weather in Florida was unbelievably bad; it was like the Arctic. Inside it would look like a beautiful day, while outside it was freezing. We had to change the location halfway through the picture. Then we didn't have enough time to finish it properly when the money began to run out. We never shot a chase that was supposed to take place at the end, so we were left with no finale. And some scenes we shot were so badly acted we couldn't use them. In the end Dino just lost all faith in it and said 'OK, finish it.' When we started cutting it we realized how many problems we had, so it was like rewriting during cutting. Since we didn't have an ending, we had to make something out of nothing. *Illegally Yours* was without question the worst experience of my career from beginning to end. There wasn't one good thing I can say about it."

Milton observed his friend during the cutting stage as he tried to make sense of the fractured footage: "He worked, worked, recut, worked and recut, and knew it was going no place. It just refused to [come] together."

At least *something* in Bogdanovich's life began to come together at this time—his relationship with L.B., who had moved to Los Angeles to stay when she turned eighteen. After a while, says Bogdanovich, it became clear to both of them that there was more between them than friendship. He soon recognized that he didn't want to be with anybody else. Nor did L.B.

De Laurentiis's notorious financial woes held up the release of *Illegally Yours* until May, 1988, when MGM opened, and closed, the movie in a one-week engagement in San Francisco and San Jose. Then it was mercifully shunted off to videoland, the great movie factory outlet in the sky. *Variety* described the picture as "an embarrassingly unfunny attempt at screwball comedy, marking a career nadir for Peter Bogdanovich and his miscast star, Rob Lowe." If Bogdanovich had been the hottest director in town in the first half of the seventies, his temperature had to be considered sub-zero as the eighties drew to a close.

CHAPTER 29

Bogdanovich can look back now on the time after Stratten's death when he and L.B. were thrown together like two shipwreck victims. "She couldn't talk to her mother or brother after the tragedy; she couldn't talk to anybody but me. I could talk to other people, but nobody knew Dorothy as well as L.B. did, so we had grief in common and love in common, because we both loved her. I don't think that anyone understood the relationship between L.B. and Dorothy. I didn't see it myself until after she was gone. It was much closer than sisters. Dorothy taught her about her teeth, her shoelaces, how to get rid of her lisp—everything. She took her places, worked on her homework with her, she was like a second mother to her. So the loss was incalculable. It's just as real and fresh to her as if it happened last week and not ten years ago. Unless people have been through the kind of tragedy when you lose somebody in a shocking way—whether it's in a plane crash, or a murder, or an accident when somebody's young life is cut short, there's a tremendous amount of love left that doesn't end after a year of mourning. It doesn't end at all—it's there, and it's something you live with every day. You live with it by ignoring it, or by dealing with it in some way. Nelly ignores it, pretends it's not there. She won't talk about it, that's her way of dealing with it. In L.B.'s case it's as though an atomic bomb exploded at her feet and she didn't die—but she's reverberating forever. We were both at the epicenter and survived."

Bogdanovich's marriage to L.B. took place in Vancouver on December 30, 1988. The couple visited Nelly after the ceremony, but had decided in advance against telling her their news at that time. Instead, it was broken to her the following day—by the same CBC-TV reporter who had informed her of Stratten's murder. Had Bogdanovich's insensitivity in personal relationships been demonstrated yet again? Or had he, possibly with good reason, already given up hope of obtaining Nelly's blessing?

He certainly miscalculated the media reaction to the wedding. Although he had assured L.B. this would be modest and, hopefully, delayed, the news was flashed on TV before they even crossed the Canadian border. And it was on front pages everywhere the following day, as was Nelly's stunned reaction. "Now I've lost two daughters to Hollywood," she grieved, her distress heartbreakingly clear for all to see. "This happened to my other daughter, who got her head shot off, and it's gonna happen to this one . . . I feel he wants her because of a guilt trip . . . He didn't do it, but he was involved . . . If he is in love with one daughter, how can he be in love with the other daughter? I've cried before, and I cry now because I've lost another daughter."

For David Scott Milton, the marriage came "out of a clear blue sky. I met Peter one afternoon in December and he was worried because L.B. was up in Vancouver and was having trouble getting back into the country. Then he said, almost in an offhand way, "I guess the only thing for me to do is marry her." I thought he was making a joke and we laughed. The next I heard they were married. I have a feeling it happened very precipitously. I don't think it was planned, but I think he should have talked to Nelly first."

Few would disagree, probably Bogdanovich included, although there had clearly been a severe breakdown in his communication with Nelly before the wedding. "She'd been through hell," he admits. "Then she only spoke to one person from the press, who confronted her on her doorstep. Boom! There was a mike and a camera and it was like she was back five years. What she said horrified her later. Then CBC sold that tape to everybody and it looked like she'd said the same thing over and over again. John Cassavetes told me he was very upset with Nelly for going off the deep end, he felt it was an unnecessary low blow. John had a line which I thought was very profound. 'How do you start balancing people's suffering?' he asked me. 'How do you know she suffered more than you did? Maybe what you suffered would kill other people—how do you *weigh* suffering?' I don't hold it against her, she was sick at the time."

Several months later Nelly revealed her continuing inability to come to terms with the event. "I still haven't dealt with it," she admitted, "but I've made friends with Louise and I'm not mad at her any more. I'm still upset, though, that she didn't tell me. Young people don't know at the age of 20 what they want from life and I feel she was robbed of something too soon and too fast. But I still love her and wish her well." Even this conciliatory statement omitted any reference to Bogdanovich himself, indicating that the breach between them remained far from mended.

Platt sees Nelly as a tragic victim. "She comes from a long line of broken women, like a character out of a book. I have a lot of compassion for her losing two girls, but we have to face facts. She participated in it until it didn't go her way. I thought she was irresponsible. She allowed whatever happened to happen between Peter and Louise. Whether it was sexual, we'll never know, but whatever it was developed into a very strong relationship. And because she encouraged it and *then* opposed it, she's once more fulfilling prophecies. She's the one who's lost her child and it's no good blaming Peter for taking her away from her."

Platt, who had begun to worry about the girl's future, was happy to see L. B. married and rallied to her ex-husband's defense when the sniping began. "I told Peter he should marry Louise a long time ago. I think Peter was embarrassed by his attachment to Louise . . . I don't think he wanted people to know . . . I think he was afraid they would accuse him of the things they've accused him of. I used to say 'Who cares? . . . What's wrong with it?' In other cultures people fall in love with sisters of the deceased and marry younger women. Everyone was saying it was a shameful thing, maybe including Peter. I think his hiding of his feelings for her was stupid. It's *wrong* for people to judge others. If Peter wished to marry Louise, and if she was able to judge whether she should be married to him—which is another question—then I think it's their affair. Louise is a very kind and loving girl and has been very sweet to my children, who love her now. What happens to her is of importance to them and therefore to me. Louise is an unhateable person. My children are happy with the marriage, because she's no longer involved in their sibling rivalry. She was his girlfriend, now she's his wife. I'm just thankful that my children want to be self-sufficient, because Anna and Louise are both completely dependent on Peter. In a sense he's their whole life.

"Because Louise has had absolutely no real exposure to the world outside for years, she's kind of fascinating! She doesn't act like other people. She worships the ground Peter walks on, so in that she's no different from other women who fall in love with charismatic men. I used to be like that! She looks at Peter the way, I guess, that men dream of being looked at. The problem with Peter is he doesn't associate with the world as we know it. He doesn't want to go out there. Keep inside that pumpkin shell—Peter, Peter, Pumpkin Eater! And yet Louise *must* . . .

"She has an opportunity to grow now as Mrs. Peter Bogdanovich. She's no longer this vague, shadowy presence. She knows a lot about films and can go about her own life. I think she'll make it, no matter what happens. I don't think she'll find out who Louise is, though, for many years."

David Scott Milton looks at his friend's marriage from a historical perspective: "In the old days it was very common that if a brother got killed, the wife would then marry the other brother. A lot of times it was a sense of family responsibility, but in Peter's case I think the emotional sense of family was transferred to these people. First, you have to accept that he was desperately in love with Dorothy in a tremendously romantic way. When that was broken, to emotionally transfer to the sister seemed natural. Now they're married, I see such a change in Louise. She's no longer a child, she's suddenly a woman."

If Platt has one wish, it would be for Bogdanovich to move out of the house in Bel Air and stop burying himself in the past. The practicality of this is another matter, for none of his creditors wish to take over his home, preferring instead to have him continue to make movies and pay off the money he owes. "He owes me a lot too," Platt points out, "but I don't need it. I just worry that [if] he fails utterly . . . my children will be trapped taking care of this sad man in his big old decaying house, spending the rest of their lives looking after him. I would have to help him to protect my children.

"There's a theory that men like Peter remind us of helpless children and those of us who are grownups feel it incumbent upon ourselves to take care of them. Peter knoweth not what he does, he's not of this world. He never has any idea what anybody else in life has gone through. He's never been able to put himself in anybody else's shoes. 'The only time you care about anybody,' I told him once, 'is when it's on celluloid!"

"Peter and I are both following what our parents taught us to do. He's living from hand to mouth and I'm living in a motorhome. We seek what we know! My family moved every year and I can't stay in the same place more than two years. I hate possessions, I like to buy nice things but I can't stand being hindered, being weighed down by them. Just as Borislav and Herma used to sit penniless in their apartment in New York, Peter's locked inside his poor millionaire's mansion in Bel Air. If he wants to spend $50, he has to ask his accountant. So we all go back to our roots, our upbringing—after 20 years in Hollywood! Wouldn't it be wonderful to break that pattern? Maybe we will, all of us!"

CHAPTER 30

The filming of *Texasville*, Larry McMurtry's sequel to *The Last Picture Show*, began as an intriguing yet unlikely possibility. Several studios, Columbia included, turned down the idea. In the absence of their backing there were enormous problems to overcome in raising funds for the project, not least of which was the credibility gap surrounding Peter Bogdanovich. And the movie would only work if most of the leading members of *The Last Picture Show* cast—Cybill Shepherd, Jeff Bridges, Randy Quaid, Cloris Leachman, Eileen Brennan, Timothy Bottoms—could be reassembled.

Bogdanovich had years before dropped Sue Mengers as his agent and signed with the Harry Ufland Agency. Then he had left Ufland and turned to Jeff Berg at International Creative Management. It was the kind of musical chairs, Bogdanovich wryly admits, that usually denotes a troubled career. And by early 1988, still retaining a warm relationship with Jeff Berg, he decided that it was time for a further change.

Following a visit to Washington in March, to press home to the U.S. Congress his aversion to the colorization of old movies, on the plane back to Los Angeles he found himself sitting next to Mike Ovitz of Creative Artists. It soon became apparent that Ovitz was interested in representing him. "If you didn't have this reputation for being so difficult," the agency head told him frankly, "there'd be no trouble at all with you. After all, there are only a handful of people around who really can direct. And you're one of them."

Bogdanovich duly signed with CAA and was introduced to his key contacts, Martin Baum and Rick Nicita. "They really pushed *Texasville,*" Bogdanovich now gratefully acknowledges. "I'm so fortunate to be with those guys." Backing for *Texasville* was finally obtained from Nelson Entertainment, a company that—ironically—releases its movies through Columbia Pictures. In a roundabout way, therefore, the studio "inherited" *Texasville* despite its earlier refusal to back the picture.

Polly Platt had agreed to come on board James L Brooks' *Terms of Endearment,* adapted from the Larry McMurtry novel, as "a friend of the project," in the process copping an Oscar nomination for her production design. After Tony Wade's death from cancer in 1986, an assignment on *The Witches of Eastwick* provided an opportunity to bury her grief in work, and by 1987 she was at last able to shake off what had become an addiction to alcohol. A request from Jim Brooks to executive produce *Broadcast News* followed. Ahead lay further production credits, on the well-received comedy *Say Anything,* then on 1989's smash hit *War of the Roses.*

Cybill Shepherd had a daughter, Clementine, named after John Ford's *My Darling Clementine,* one year after her marriage to David Ford. By 1982, with a divorce on the horizon, Shepherd decided to relaunch her career from the bottom. A season in summer stock, at Orson Welles' instigation, rekindled the desire to act. After Dorothy Stratten's murder Shepherd saw a tremendous change in Bogdanovich, "like a light had gone out somewhere."

A series of TV movies led to one of the most astonishing comebacks in Hollywood history—as the costar, opposite Bruce Willis, of *Moonlighting.* In 1987 Shepherd married chiropractor Bruce Oppenheimer. One set of twins and less than two years later the couple had filed for divorce.

In the Spring of 1989 Shepherd met Polly Platt for the first time in a long while. The motorhome on the 20th Century-Fox lot that represented her pied à terre was close to Platt's office. Since Platt was considering the purchase of a new motorhome, Larry McMurtry suggested there was no one better equipped to give advice than Shepherd.

Platt hesitated, but not for long. She had often passed Shepherd's trailer and had regretted not stopping by. "Peter's asked me to do *Texasville,*" Shepherd told her, "and I'd love to do it, it's such a great idea. But frankly, I'm scared after *Illegally Yours.* What happened?"

"It's one of those things we'd all like to draw a veil over," Platt replied. "He had to do *something* to keep the money rolling in and that's what came up. It was a compromised movie."

"I've got a great idea," said Shepherd. "Why don't *you* work on *Texasville?*"

"I haven't been asked," Platt replied, perfectly matter of fact. "And even if I had, I couldn't go back to working with Peter." Although it hurt her to admit it, Platt knew that she and Bogdanovich could never recapture what they had together.

"So what do you think, Polly?" Shepherd persisted. "Should I do *Texasville?*"

"Yes, you should. It's historically significant, Cybill—a 'sequel' made in 1989 to a movie made in 1970."

Platt found Shepherd enchanting—and uproariously funny, as the subject turned from *Texasville* to her split from her husband and her search for a new man. As they spoke, and long after the meeting was over, Platt found proof of her theory that men fall for the same woman over and over, for she could see a lot of herself in Shepherd. Repeatedly she asked the same "what if" questions of herself: *What if* she and Peter had stayed together? What if they'd never seen Cybill on the front cover of *Glamour* magazine that day in the supermarket? What if Sal Mineo had never handed her *The Last Picture Show* to read? What if they'd never left New York in the first place? Platt knew that such a line of thought could be taken too far—and could echo endlessly. She also knew the price Cybill had paid for her relationship with Bogdanovich, shouldering the blame for the failure of his work. Tough as it was to be a successful woman in Hollywood, it was tougher still to be unsuccessful after you've been successful.

After her meeting with Polly Platt, Shepherd agreed to sign up. Jeff Bridges was next to be approached. Bogdanovich had originally called him while he was on holiday with his family in Hawaii in 1987, when *Texasville* was first published, and alerted him to the possibility of filming the sequel. In *Texasville,* set in 1984 during the oil slump, Bridges' character, Duane, has become an overweight, ageing "oil millionaire" $12 million in debt, with a wife, Karla, steadfastly refusing to acknowledge the problem. Into their lives comes Shepherd's Jacy, back from an Italian B-movie career and the tragic death of her son. The interplay between the three chooses not to follow a conventional pattern. Bridges read the book and was knocked out by it, despite the prospect of having to gain thirty pounds to reprise his role. "Come on, let's go, I'm game," he confirmed in 1989.

When Bogdanovich's script was dispatched to the other original actors, Cloris Leachman fretted that her role was too small. "Sure it is," Bogdanovich agreed, "but it's crucial. Ruth Popper represents continuity in the community." Eileen Brennan, back to full health and strength after a near-fatal car accident in the early eighties, readily agreed to return as Genevieve Morgan. Timothy Bottoms accepted what amounted to a cameo as Sonny, mainly because of a side deal with Bogdanovich allowing him to shoot a documentary on the movie's progress that was to be shown on cable television. Randy Quaid, whose career was kick-started by Bogdanovich, jumped at the chance of coming back as Lester, now president of the troubled local bank.

With rising young actor William McNamara signed for the role of Duane's philandering son Dickie, busy playing around with both his father's current and ex-girlfriends, only the key role of Duane's wife Karla remained to be cast. After several actresses had been considered, vivacious brunette Annie Potts was asked to read with Shepherd and Bridges at Bogdanovich's Beverly Hills home. The session went like a dream. After a decade of notable appearances, both on television in the hit series *Designing Women* and in no fewer than thirteen movies, culminating in the part of the droll secretary Jeanine in *Ghostbusters I* and *II*, Potts had her first major big-screen role. Bogdanovich's lead casting was complete.

The Last Picture Show had brought enormous changes to several lives. For Bogdanovich the return to Texas produced a welter of emotions and poignant memories of moments that could never be recaptured. "Going back to Archer City was just amazing," he told me on location. "Walking down that same street where I'd been 20 years before I suddenly remembered what I was like at 30! I felt so old then—because I was so young! If only I knew then what I know now. Nobody had ever heard of any of us until *Picture Show* burst on the scene. Now people have heard too much about some of us and are probably sick of us—but there's expectation for *Texasville*. We're doing this one in the spotlight.

I'll just have to try to make the picture and not worry too much about expectations."

Cybill Shepherd found her return to Archer City both frightening and strange. She buried her face in her hands and laughed when she was shown a clip from *The Last Picture Show* in which Jacy has Duane slide his hand along her thigh. "I'm embarrassed," she declared. "It's funny, as actors we're used to making fools of ourselves for a living, particularly me. I saw the whole movie again recently and was very moved by it. I hope so much that we can make a great movie this time too."

Jeff Bridges was equally affected by a sense of deja vu when he returned to Texas. "I was in my hotel room the other day—maybe it was in the air, I don't know, but all of a sudden it was 20 years ago. This is like picking up where you left off. Now we're older and have more experience, and it's more fun. The chemistry on this movie's good, real good."

While memories were all around, so much had changed. Bogdanovich's idea of booking *The Last Picture Show* into the local multiplex during filming added a distinctly surreal dimension to the experience. Watching the cast on screen in black and white in the evening, in the setting of the mid-fifties, and then strolling on to the *Texasville* set in the morning, with the same participants acting the same roles in the mid-eighties, was strange indeed. (With Jeff Bridges' *The Fabulous Baker Boys* showing next door, the Wichita Falls movie house enjoyed a record three-week run.)

Twenty years earlier the cast and crew had stayed at the Days Inn in Wichita Falls, thirty miles from the site of the main location in Archer City. Now Jeff Bridges had his own suite at the Sheraton and Cybill was installed in an upscale summer-lease residence, complete with three kids, maid and cook. Where *The Last Picture Show* had been made for just over $1 million, Jeff Bridges alone was picking up $1.75 million for his contribution to *Texasville* and Cybill Shepherd, $1.5 million (as a favor to Bogdanovich). The facade of the original Archer City picture show, the Royal, was still standing, but a water tower now inelegantly loomed over it.

I stood and watched the set up of a long and complicated scene between Duane and Karla in their bedroom, with the former despondent after flicking through an old photo album. "Are you happy?"

Karla drawls at one point. "I guess," Duane replies, shrugging and looking the picture of resigned misery. Because it was shot on a cramped set—the bedroom of an actual Texas house rented for the occasion—the scene required several takes before it was satisfactorily in the can. The interplay between Bridges and Bogdanovich was fascinating, with the actor suggesting a nuance to be added here, a gesture there, and listening intently as Bogdanovich agreed or made counter-suggestions. Bogdanovich had, after all, suffered through the rigors of the midlife crisis that besets Bridges' character, making him superbly qualified to advise on Duane's mood shifts. "Jeff's an artist, pure and simple," Bogdanovich would gratefully acknowledge.

After a few days of filming, with the temperature outside fluctuating between 105 degrees at midday and below freezing at night, the buzz was unmistakable. Even among this galaxy of remarkable performances, that of Kansas-born Annie Potts was a standout. "An actor's job is to support the director's vision," she told me as I drove her back to our Wichita Falls hotel one evening. "The only hitch with this movie is maybe Peter doesn't know me as well as I know me! The manner in which Peter shoots is always for the edit. In parts of the script we play tiny bits and I always wanted to play out the whole scene. It took me a while to get used to that, but I feel I've begun to understand his methods. Sometimes there's a freedom within surrender!"

A near disaster followed a few days later when Bogdanovich, perched high on a crane close to the swimming pool at the back of the rented house, fell heavily to the tile below and badly bruised his shoulder. Although clearly in agony, he insisted on resuming the shoot within minutes. "He's a son of a gun," Eileen Brennan chuckled. "And I still love him."

Editor Rick Fields gave an intriguing insight into Bogdanovich's often divisive on-set persona. "There isn't a member of a crew anywhere that doesn't think he can direct any shot better at any given moment," he told me. "This crew is one of the best I've seen. They really work hard in difficult circumstances—they have to light the whole of Archer City for a nighttime scene with a five-mile cable. Peter can't think about that, he has to concentrate on what's going to be on screen. He's out there 24 hours a day trying to get this as good as it can be. Sure, there's natural resentment in the crew and Peter has this arrogant air about him, he's sophisticated. The crew still likes working for him, but feel they've been asked to do too much for too little, because the production facilities are not there to support them. This unit is working to a tight budget and there's no overtime, they're not getting the best food, there's no snacks laid on between meals—it's thin on that end, and Peter gets blasted for that too. It's like being in the army, they've got to have somebody to hate. Peter always devotes a lot of time to the actors and the crew may resent that as well. The good news is that the real Peter—the one who stunned audiences with his stylish, racy story-telling capabilities—is back."

Barry Spikings, president and chief operating officer of Nelson Entertainment, has links with Bogdanovich that stretch back to the rescue of *Nickelodeon* during his spell at EMI. As he hovered benignly over the proceedings, he took time out to explain his philosophy of moviemaking. "I try to take a long term view of people," he told me. "If they have talent it very rarely goes away. It's a matter of creating an environment in which they can use that talent. When Peter first gave me McMurtry's book I really thought it would be better suited to a mini-series. His script persuaded me otherwise. I couldn't be more impressed watching him now. All of the actors involved have been working over and above the call of duty out of loyalty to Peter. I think the mood in America is right for this picture; the people who are going to the movies are reexamining their lives.'

On a few days' leave from her production duties on *War of the Roses*, Platt arrived to watch the shooting of *Texasville*. She hugged Antonia, there to take stills for a book on the making of her father's new movie. (Sachy was left behind to run the Santa Monica apartment Platt had bought for her two daughters.) Platt recognized her long-time friend Larry McMurtry standing on the sidelines. He looked at her with a sly expression on his face. "What are *you* doing here?" he asked, smiling.

"Healing old wounds," Platt replied.

"Nice trick if you can do it,' McMurtry drawled.

As Platt viewed some of the dailies, she saw how consistently Bogdanovich was addressing himself to the scene in hand, his touch never surer. Strange that he had had to come back to Texas to find himself again, she thought, a place he knew little about, with which he had no obvious rapport and where, in a sense, their saga had really begun.

Antonia watched as her mother and father, temporarily reunited, talked happily together on the set and warmly embraced Shepherd when she appeared. The three of them chatted away like lifelong friends. Later, Antonia, a bemused expression on her face, said to Platt, "Watching the three of you this afternoon really taught me something." 'What's that, Toni?' Platt asked.

Antonia put her arms around her mother and held her tight. "That *anything,*" she replied, "absolutely *anything,* can be healed."

The most difficult person for me to catch up with on the *Texasville* shoot wasn't Bogdanovich or his daughter Antonia. It wasn't Shepherd, Jeff Bridges, Eileen Brennan, Tim Bottoms or Annie Potts. It wasn't cinematographer Nicholas Von Sternberg (son of Josef), it wasn't editor Rick Fields (son of Verna), it wasn't producer Barry Spikings of Nelson Entertainment. It was Bogdanovich's young bride, Louise—L. B.

She had been all set to assist Bogdanovich on *Texasville* but then, in July, had dislocated her knee while dancing at his birthday party. She accompanied her husband to Wichita Falls nonetheless and was helping to edit his weekly CBS spot, in which he focused on many of the screen's most luminous stars and directors.

"We haven't given many interviews," Bogdanovich told me when I first asked asked if I might talk to L. B. "You mean you haven't given any," I replied. "That's—about right," he conceded, eyeing me lugubriously over his spectacles.

When we finally did meet, at the end of my six-day visit to Wichita Falls, L. B. was still walking with a limp, and stooping a little as if to deemphasize her height. Her blue eyes looked troubled as she sat down opposite me, and she kept nervously brushing back her shoulder-length blonde hair. Although not the glamorous beauty her sister was, she has an air of sweetness and charm, of little-girl helplessness, that is totally disarming and instantly appealing.

The ice between us was broken by comparing notes on our favorite movies. I had made up my mind that I would not mention Stratten unless she did, and I soon discovered she wanted to talk of little else.

"Was Peter a good teacher?" I asked her first.

"Definitely," she replied.

"You were a blank page?"

"Yes. I've learned so much from him. He thought I might be interested in old movies, but he wasn't doing it to teach me. I love them and

. . . the more I've seen the more I've learned. Peter gave me the cutting of his CBS show to do; he would tell me what clips he wanted and I would go and do it."

"Are you at the stage where you might make up your own mind about which clips to use?"

"Yes. I pick my own clips now. And edit them. Watching Peter edit, I compared notes with him and now I'm into that side as well. Basically I've learned through watching and listening to Peter. I love editing. I've seen *The Last Picture Show* three times in the past few weeks and each time I see something different in the editing. It's amazing, a great movie. I love it."

"Do you ever feel you are reading about someone else when you see your husband's name in the paper?"

"Yes, it does feel like that. It's the same going out somewhere with him and people coming up to say they love this, they love that, because I don't think of who he is. When you're doing a picture like this, that's when it hits you."

"He's this big director?"

"Exactly. It's amazing what responsibility he has. I've only been in two pictures with him, although we don't count *Illegally Yours!* As far as we're concerned, his last picture was *Mask*. But this feeling of being with someone famous—I had the same feeling with my sister, she had a lot of fans, so I was used to it already with Dorothy. Since childhood I've felt it was a strange kind of feeling, having someone close to you who's famous."

"I know you and Dorothy were very close."

"We were very, *very* close. She was like my mother, my friend, my sister—everything she could be."

"Have the years since 1980 flown past?"

"Usually it feels like 1980 was yesterday. It depends on how I feel, I change every day."

"Will you be glad to see the back of this decade?"

"It's been tough. Truthfully, the eighties have really been the start of my life in a way. I was twelve when Dorothy was murdered and [as] I went into my teens; it was a big part of my life. It was the most difficult thing I've had to go through and I feel as if I'm still going through it."

"Do you think, like Peter, that leaving the eighties is going to make such a difference?"

"No. I don't know if the nineties are going to make a real big difference to me—like starting a new life or something. It doesn't work that way. It's only a number, after all, and you try to deal with the next year as best you can. Things happen to you and I'm glad that we're going forward. The eighties weren't great, no."

"Do you write poetry like Dorothy did?"

"Things are in my head and I write them down. I have to do that to understand what I'm doing. Yes, I write poems like Dorothy's, and a lot of different kinds of things. My brother writes poems as well."

"I bumped into him the other day and we talked for a while."

"He told us. I'm very happy he's here, but I don't know him as well as I'd like to. We've grown in . . . separate directions . . . I was in his room when he was writing poetry and he wanted me to hear some of it. I didn't know he could write like that!"

"You all seem to have that ability."

"It's strange. We don't really share that with other people."

"How are relations with your mother now?"

"All I know is that my mother is not the same woman as I remember . . . and that's why I like to think of 1980 as yesterday. I want that relationship with my mother back. But we can't go back, nobody can. She's so different now that I'm trying to find out who this woman is . . . I feel—like, *who is she?* It's very difficult . . . really hard to deal with. She's not doing that well, but better than she did a year ago. She's very happy my brother's here right now and I think she's slowly trying to [find] her way back again. I think she's accepting my life. She just has a lot of fear."

"Understandably, I guess."

"My mother's funny. She tries to tell me things, but doesn't go into detail. She's trying to say she loves me, and wants what's best for me, and she's trying to get back to me. 'Tell Peter hello,' she'll say and 'I hope the movie's going well'—but what does that *mean?* She doesn't come to the point and tell me what all that *means.* I have to piece it together for myself and help it along."

"She doesn't communicate directly with Peter?"

"No."

"Wouldn't you have been better off telling her you'd got married— or telling her before that you intended to?"

"It wasn't *possible* to tell her, there were a number of reasons. I ended up staying [in Vancouver] about two months more than I should have stayed because of her. She did a lot of damage, but I don't hold it against her because I understand. Yet I want her to understand me. There's no bitterness between us now."

"It would be good to see her reconciled with Peter."

"Of course. She knows that. She knows it would be good and it will come. Time is a healer. I think by this Christmas we'll all be together again. I'm going to Europe with Peter for a week, then Canada, after we've finished *Texasville*, and I'm going to try to get her to come to L.A. for Christmas. She's going through another bad time right now—her mother is dying back in Holland.'

By now we'd been talking for twenty minutes or so. I suspected that L.B. wanted to say a lot more, but two of Bogdanovich's assistants had appeared saying that he wanted to see her before he lined up his next shot. As L. B. looked across the table at me, her eyes were anxious. "Time to go, honey," one of the minions insisted. "We're not through yet," L. B. told her calmly but displaying an unexpected mettle. "Tell Peter we're *almost* done."

As soon as the assistants withdrew, I asked L. B. if she missed having her family around all the time. "Yes I do," she replied, "because there's nobody around who shares the same memories. My mother and my brother are all that I have."

"The memories are all locked away in Canada?"

"Yes. I can talk to Peter, but [his] memories of my sister are not the same as what I have. I can tell him something I've remembered and he'll say, 'Oh, how wonderful,' but it's not the same as feeling it and saying, 'God, yes, I remember,' and adding to it. I'm at the point where I can do that, but with my mother it's as though she's only had me and my brother; it's as though there never was another child. That's really *hard* on me and Johnnie, but we're beginning to talk about it a little bit . . . We've all dealt with what happened in a different way. John's in the middle—between my mother, who won't talk about it at all, and me. Johnnie's closed in, but he can open up once in a while, it depends. He wouldn't go to see *They All Laughed* when they showed it here last week. He couldn't—yet I could."

L. B.'s way of dealing with the memory of her late sister is to constantly return to their happy times together in her dreams. This often makes for painful awakenings, with the tragic events of 1980 brought eerily close over and over again.

Our interview was brought to an end by a the return of Bogdanovich's assistants to remind L. B. that he was waiting to see her. As I said goodbye (she was still talking as she was virtually led away), I felt a tremendous wave of compassion for her. She had been at the epicenter of it all and she clearly was still reverberating. Something she had revealed at the very start of our meeting had nagged at me all through the interview.

In Alfred Hitchcock's *Notorious*, the heroine, played by Ingrid Bergman, is held captive and slowly poisoned by her husband, Claude Rains. Her rescue by Cary Grant seems an impossible dream. From L. B.'s disclosure that *Notorious* is her favorite movie, I'm convinced that, at least subconsciously, she identifies with the character played by Bergman. In John Ford's *The Searchers*, Natalie Wood is kidnapped as a child and raised by Indians until, years later, as a teenager, she's finally tracked down and rescued by John Wayne. *The Searchers* is L. B.'s second-favorite movie.

Of course, Bogdanovich was being protective of L. B., by allowing our interview only at the last minute and then restricting her opportunity to talk, an opportunity she had seized eagerly. But does he appreciate the difference between protecting and stifling? I wondered. Is he still Peter, Peter, Pumpkin Eater?

In *The Killing of the Unicorn* Bogdanovich quotes Stratten saying she felt "manipulated, controlled and smothered" by Paul Snider. "If you love something, set it free," he recalls her writing to her husband. "If it comes back to you, it's yours—if it doesn't, it never was in the first place." While there is no easy parallel to be drawn between Snider and Bogdanovich, the latter should at least heed the words Stratten addressed to her husband on another occasion: "Let the bird fly."

If a death can tear families apart, it can also bring them back together. Nelly's mother died in Holland in mid-November 1989, just two weeks after *Texasville* finished shooting. Bogdanovich, by then on holiday in Europe with L. B., was reunited with her at the funeral.

CHAPTER 31

With L. B.'s words still echoing in my head when I returned to Los Angeles from Wichita Falls, it came to me that Stratten's story will not end as long as she lives in the memories—and the dreams—of those who loved her. As I lunched with Polly Platt next day, the thought reemerged—but with an unexpected and shocking difference. I was totally unprepared for Platt's revelation.

"I've never talked about this to anyone in the ten years since it happened," she began, "but Paul Snider telephoned me the afternoon he murdered Dorothy. I didn't know who he was at the time, there was just this guy on the phone, being absolutely hysterical and demanding to speak to Peter. I told him he had the wrong number. He *screamed* at me to give him the correct number. It was very disturbing, but I eventually got him off the line. I thought it must have been an actor or someone Peter had crossed.

"Two days later a couple of plain-clothes policemen came to my door, wanting to know why Paul Snider had phoned me. It was only then I made the connection. Apparently they'd traced the number he'd dialed through the telephone company and it was, naturally, something they had to check out. Maybe they thought I was the hit lady, the embittered wife who'd put Snider up to it, . . . They were very nice, but I just had to listen as they talked about how normal Dorothy had looked, until they turned the body over and saw half her face had been blasted away, how the walls had been spattered with blood, the ants . . . I was just . . . petrified . . . I couldn't talk about it to anyone, either then or since, not even Peter—*especially* not Peter. The police figured out that Snider had gotten my number, which Dorothy would have had to phone Toni and Sashy, from her handbag."

One possible implication here seems particularly horrifying: that Snider had desperately tried to contact Bogdanovich in order to lure him to the death scene—and then murder him, too. "I was so destroyed in any case," Platt continued, "and filled with horror to be in any way associated with the tragedy, that I suppose the visit and the revelation of the phone call were just pushed to the back of my mind . . . I was enraged with Peter that I'd even been dragged on to the edge of the affair . . . all sorts of things were going round in my head. *My children had been to Snider's house!* After the police had gone, I just sat down and cried. The thought of Snider talking to me on the phone as he stood over Dorothy's corpse was just too much. I felt so sorry for that poor girl. And I felt as if the chilly breath of death had been allowed into my home."

Perhaps the liaison between the LAPD and the coroner's office broke down over this point, for until now the official time frame of the murder and suicide has never been contradicted. Yet to the best of Platt's recollection, the call came *late* in the afternoon, perhaps as late as 4P.M.—two hours after Snider was supposed to have killed himself. For him to linger not just for one but for several hours after killing Stratten makes the whole affair even more macabre.

Years earlier Bogdanovich was quoted by a normally reliable source as saying, "I've never told the truth about myself before and I won't do it now." When I asked him about this, in his Bel Air home in June 1989, Bogdanovich took a deep breath and pushed his horn-rimmed spectacles further up his nose. "What *is* the truth?" he asked, an earnest, owlish expression on his face. "It's relative. If you'd asked me the truth about something ten years ago and asked me now, you'd get a different answer, because the truth has changed, or my perception has changed and what I thought was the truth turns out not to be the truth. I went through some therapy in the last four years and found out certain things

I'd been doing in my life and why I'd been doing them. I've learned a lot." ′

When asked if he would change anything if he had *The Killing of the Unicorn* to write over again, Bogdanovich replied that he would. "I'd be a little harder on myself," he conceded, "for not knowing more, for not realizing the consequences of my own actions, for not realizing that my presence in someone's house is an endorsement. And I'd be a little less hard on Hefner."

An aspect of Bogdanovich's book that will never be subject to revision, however, is its idealization of Stratten. Bogdanovich grants that people are entitled to disagree with the portrait he presents. "But *how can they know?*" he asks. *'I* knew her. *They* didn't." On that issue—and on the subject of his star witness, Patrick Curtis—the normally loquacious Bogdanovich will brook no further discussion.

He agrees that he had used the media in the past, especially at the beginning of his career, when it suited him, and has been used and abused in return: "A terrible thing happens in the media in Hollywood. Show business is like the comic strip in newspapers. *We're* the thing people read for entertainment. Basically, most people have too many problems to *really* care about which movie star is doing it to whom. It's just diversion. *However,* somebody has to actually live those lives. . . ."

In another mood, and on another occasion, Bogdanovich was more conciliatory. "What's the point in saying the media is this or that?" he asked. "They're doing a job. It's a story. You can't accept the good part and then complain about the bad part. . . . People sometimes know about me for the wrong reason, but it translates into interest in my films."

Without sacrificing an iota of respect for the directors he is known to revere, Bogdanovich can today coolly reflect on how his adulation for them backfired. "Truth to tell, it started because of me," he says, "although for years I never wanted to discuss it, because I couldn't figure out why I'd been so anxious to give away credit. When people asked me about *Targets,* I said it was my homage to Hitchcock, then I said *The Last Picture Show* was influenced by *The Magnificent Ambersons.* In *What's Up, Doc?* I called Ryan 'Howard' in a tip-of-the-hat to Hawks. I got myself into that hole simply because I felt bad working when all those old directors I knew were judged virtually unemployable. Just about everybody I met was at the end of their careers and I felt tremendously in debt to all of them—particularly the ones who'd taken the time to talk to me. And I wanted to return the favor. It got to be so ridiculous that even a good critic like Vincent Canby said in his review of *Paper Moon* that it was my homage to Shirley Temple! I'd never liked Shirley Temple and regarded *Paper Moon* as a direct, diametric answer to Shirley Temple. When people asked me why I shot *The Last Picture Show* in black and white and I said Orson Welles told me to, they really thought I meant that! Orson certainly encouraged the idea, but I can't say I did it because he *told* me to. Even with *Saint Jack*, Canby saw it as an imitation of an Alan Ladd-Far East movie, which was pretty weird. He didn't even mention it as a period piece. Canby was very nice to me several times, but that whole way of looking at my stuff was confused by my genuine admiration for the older directors. And why shouldn't I say so? They'd created the art form and the industry, after all. I've always felt that art is a kind of relay race where you're given the baton to carry for a certain length of time and then it's your duty to pass it on. That's what I felt I was doing until Dorothy was killed, then I wanted to pass it on. Only help from my friends got me over that.

"There are two kinds of sons, I'm led to believe through psychology, the kind that want to kill their fathers and the kind that don't want to embarrass their fathers. I'm one of the latter, so when my own father died I took on a lot of surrogate fathers, whether it was Hawks, Ford or Welles. My mother used to argue with me that these people really weren't like my father at all. Borislav was generous to other artists to a fault in a way that never helped him. I followed my instincts, I guess, and looking back now—yes, I see that I set myself up."

Bogdanovich sees himself as having changed over the last few years in his way of handling people. The direction in which he has moved, he is aware, would have pleased his mother. "We can all change, we can all improve," he says philosophically. "Possessive? I don't know about that. If I am, maybe it goes back to my being left alone quite a bit as a kid. My parents went places and often left me alone, which I didn't like. I wasn't *neglected*, that's something different entirely. Anyway, here I am now. At fifty. I still think I have some good movies left in me. For seven years it was one every year and now I'm hoping to make one after the other for the next three years, just to make up for the eighties. Robert Graves said there are necessary and unnecessary poems and that the ultimate question for a poet should be: Is this poem necessary?

So yes, I'm trying to make some *necessary* movies, as opposed to those that really aren't."

He still talks like a newlywed about his relationship with L. B., how it has grown, and how different it is from that with Stratten. "It's not a transference, as many people think. It's different altogether, just like L. B. and Dorothy's personalities are different. As different as a Taurus is from a Pisces. Our relationship just became inevitable at a certain point. She thinks I'm the same age as her! We've been through a lot of problems together in the last few years, helped each other tremendously through our grief and developed this pretty strong bond."

Bogdanovich's therapist had earlier summed up the couple's prospects for a happy, lasting marriage. "I don't know if it'll work out for the two of you," he told his patient, "but I'd sure as hell hate to be someone else who falls in love with L. B.!'

The "old wounds" that Polly Platt and Larry McMurtry joked about on the *Texasville* set are "as healed as they'll ever be," Platt maintains. "Louise's presence helped bring Peter back from the brink. Now he's in the best place I've ever seen him, mentally and emotionally. He's living a real life at last and can finally let me in as part of his early life. He'll never fall in love again, though—I'd stake my life on it—because he's still in love with Dorothy.

"I have great hopes for him. There's a lot riding on *Texasville*, certainly, but there's always a lot riding on your next movie. He's had his down-and-out time, he's paid for his arrogance. People in this town feel badly for him. The time is right for Peter to come back with a great movie.

"My feelings now for him are the strongest, most loyal and most affectionate that anybody could have. I love him *exactly as he is*. I feel tremendous affection for him. We still have our differences, in many ways we could not be further apart, but when I look at him I feel *sheer clean love*. It's amazing. It doesn't make me sad, nor does it make me go home and wish I were in his bed." Platt paused and reflected before continuing, "Maybe that's what we all need—to go through everything, the hate, the torment, all of it—and come out the other side!"

CHAPTER 32

If all had gone according to plan *Texasville* would have been both a critical and commercial hit. Bogdanovich had expressed the hope to me back on the Texas set that his movie would premiere at the 1990 Cannes Film Festival; ominously, that event went ahead without *Texasville*. A leaked report that audiences were walking out of sneak previews in June brought this laconic understatement from Columbia to *Variety:* "I guess you know that's not a good sign."

Although the reviews were mixed on *Texasville's* eventual release in September 1990, even some of the favorable notices had a regretful air. Roger Ebert's thumbs up was followed by the question: "Is *Texasville* as good as *The Last Picture Show?"* And the answer: "No, because the previous picture was complete, and this one seems to lack a genuine reason for existence."

Vincent Canby in the *New York Times* was another hesitant supporter. "There are times," he lamented, "when *Texasville*, like Larry McMurtry's novel on which it is based, seems top heavy with eccentrics. Yet also like the book, the movie becomes seriously involving . . . Miss Shepherd is exceptionally good. No less effective is Miss Potts, whose performance also grows richer as the film goes on."

The Village Voice's Georgia Brown found *Texasville* "frantic and talky, its characters thin" and was thoroughly turned off by its "cacophony of

Texas twangs." For *Variety*, the movie was "long on folksy humor and short on plot. Several fine performances can't hide its pointless nature."

UPI's Vernon Scott, on the other hand, was an unabashed enthusiast, declaring, *"Texasville* is a great movie. Jeff Bridges and Annie Potts give Academy Award winning performances in this witty and sexy sequel to the American classic." Chicago *Tribune* Syndicate's Marilyn Beck also singled out the cast: "Jeff Bridges and Cybill Shepherd give the best performances of their careers . . . Annie Potts is a superb addition to the cast of *The Last Picture Show*," while *Sixty Second Previews'* Jeff Craig described the movie itself as "poignant, fascinating and sexy."

On balance, it now seems that while *The Last Picture Show* was always going to be a hard act to follow, Bogdanovich made it even tougher by defying expectations and abandoning the elegaic tone of the original, introducing in its place a distinct element of nihilism. And if *Texasville* was intended to stand alone, as Bogdanovich claimed, why did he layer it with references that were meaningless unless *The Last Picture Show* was fresh in the mind?

Far too much time was spent on the supporting characters, notably Duane's son Dickie, who seemed not so much to have inherited his father's juice as to have drained it. Humor? Too often of the strained dinner-theater variety. Romance? A tantalizing hint that Duane and Jacey might rekindle the embers fizzled. Pathos? Sonny's predicament was affecting, but Jacy's loss of a child seemed merely to have left her cranky and prone to outbursts of petulance. What we were left with, while competently made, was too often uninvolving, almost as if Bogdanovich has experienced so much drama in his own life that he could no longer bring himself to portray deep emotion and pain on the screen. Surprisingly, for such a personal project, the quality most noticeable by its absence was warmth.

Despite what many felt was a first-class advertising campaign, *Texasville* bombed in its 354-cinema break across the U.S., garnering a meager $1.7 million in its first two weeks of release.

By this time Bogdanovich was already several weeks into shooting the latest Richard Pryor/Gene Wilder comedy, *Another You*, in New York City, for Columbia/TriStar. His response to *Texasville*'s failure was to blame Columbia for giving the movie too broad a release and for not priming the market with a timely rerelease of *The Last Picture Show*. "We're all pretty much agreed it's opened too broadly too soon," he told *Variety*. "And lots of critics felt it had been too long since they'd seen *The Last Picture Show*. It was always our feeling that they should be seen together." He confided that Columbia president Frank Price, late of Universal and his adversary in the *Mask* fracas, had advocated putting out both movies and playing them simultaneously at separate theaters, a suggestion with which Bogdanovich had fully concurred.

"There was a lack of agreement in the ranks," he continued, "and a lot of mistakes. I think we've seen the picture does work with thoughtful critics and thoughtful audiences." If only, *Texasville*'s backers must have pondered, there had been more of the latter. Even if "the ranks" had agreed with the idea of limited day and date and a simultaneous video release of *The Last Picture Show* to back *Texasville*, Bogdanovich admitted there would have been a problem: "Although it is only twenty years old, the negative of *The Last Picture Show* had to be completely restored. The sound was lost, and one shot of Cybill naked was stolen."

With the box-office take of *Texasville* topping out at just over $2 million, its theatrical run was soon history. So, for that matter, was Bogdanovich's direction of *Another You*. Following a visit by a Tri-Star accountant concerned that the film had fallen behind schedule and was well over budget, Bogdanovich was fired and replaced by Maurice Phillips. One report had the TriStar honchos looking over their shoulders at their new Japanese bosses, sweating over Sony's wrath if they failed to move to control and rectify the film's budget situation. Another had Gene Wilder and Richard Pryor putting up a "him or us" threat. Bogdanovich called a press conference to lay the rumors to rest and present his side of the story. When, at the last moment, this was abruptly canceled and the well-known "creative differences" wheeled out to explain his departure, it was clear that Bogdanovich, gagged by Tri-Star's pending fee arbitration, for once had decided that discretion was the better part of valor.

If bad news comes in threes, Bogdanovich's third blow was a relative powder puff. In the full knowledge that he was already bankrupt for millions, the ICM agency chose the week after Bogdanovich's dismissal from *Another You* to sue him for $113,780 plus 10 percent interest, a debt that dated back to September 1989. Bogdanovich had apparently consented to repay $133,780 plus interest in July of that year, under an

agreement which forgave certain other debts. Only two monthly pay-
ments had been received, ICM complained. Rocky as the eighties had
been for Bogdanovich, it was beginning to look, on the evidence of
1990's triple whammy, that the new decade was also going to prove
something other than a bed of roses. Except . . .

Steven Spielberg's firm conviction is that someone who has made
great movies in the past can make great movies again. For some time
he has held the film rights to Michael Frayn's London and New York
stage smash, *Noises Off*, just waiting for the opportunity to snare Bogdanovich, whom he considers the perfect director for the comedy.
Following the split from *Another You*, the opportunity arose.

In January 1991, Bogdanovich talked to me for the first time about
the *Another You* debacle: "It had nothing to do with Sony causing a panic
at TriStar," he averred. "And it had nothing to do with Gene or Richie;
they're sweet guys. It truly *was* 'creative differences'; I was making one
film, the studio wanted another. In many ways, though, it's the best
thing that could have happened, I was never really comfortable with the
project, I should never have taken it in the first place. Steven's offer,
which had been bubbling along for a while, couldn't have come at a
better time."

One month later he elatedly confided that Michael Caine, Carol
Burnett, John Ritter, Julie Hagerty, Christopher Reeve and Denholm
Elliott had been cast in *Noises Off*, with shooting set for May. Spielberg
had assigned Bogdanovich's old pal and apprentice Frank Marshall as
producer on the Amblin/Touchstone project, with executive producer
status being shared by Spielberg himself, Bogdanovich and Kathleen
Kennedy (Marshall and his wife, Kennedy, having produced all of
Spielberg's movies since *Indiana Jones and the Temple of Doom* and Marshall having made his own directorial debut with *Arachnophobia*).

More good news followed. Bogdanovich was already in talks with
Japanese investors interested in funding his own long-cherished project,
I'll Remember April, in which he envisages Michael Caine costarring with
Cybill Shepherd. And Columbia's lost opportunity to cross-promote
Texasville with *The Last Picture Show* in theaters was about to be rectified
on video. RCA/Columbia would release *The Last Picture Show* at the
beginning of April, with Nelson Entertainment's *Texasville* following a
few weeks later, each movie carrying a trailer for the other. The triple
whammy, it seemed, had just been neatly reversed.

Although Bogdanovich has emerged as a hardy survivor, he is undeniably at a career crossroads. While no one can take away his achievements to date, he now needs to consolidate them, retrieve the ground he has lost, and validate Spielberg's theory.

Speculation that Bogdanovich's marriage is built on guilt would be immediately discounted by anyone who has seen Beatrix and him together. (Louise, "LB Straten," became "Beatrix Stratten" during 1990.) Even if a trace of guilt does lurk somewhere in the complex mixture of his emotions, this very element could lead to the redemption Bogdanovich seeks. After Stratten's death he demonstrated the all-too-human trait of believing only what he wanted to believe, and the border between fact and fiction became as blurred as the sometimes vanishing boundary between his real life and the movies.

Regardless of what has happened in the past, Bogdanovich and Beatrix, Polly, Cybill, Nelly, Anna, Antonia and Sashy will perhaps build upon and maintain their relationships as the years pass. As for Dorothy, her memory will linger with all of them forever.

Today Bogdanovich exhibits charm, egocentricity, compassion, humor, arrogance and erudition in equal measure, all of them laced with a disarming hint of the unpredictable. The passions that have ruled his life might now change shape and reemerge as something finer. Larry McMurtry's theme in *Texasville*—that passions come and go while family bonds and true friendships endure—might make an excellent watchword for the nineties, for Bogdanovich and his women.

Come to that, for all of us.

FILMOGRAPHY

The Wild Angels (American-International: 1967)

DIRECTOR: Roger Corman
SCREENPLAY: Charles B. Griffith
PRODUCER: Roger Corman
CINEMATOGRAPHY: Richard Moore
EDITOR: Monte Hellman
MUSIC: Mike Curb
RUNNING TIME: 83 mins.
CAST: Peter Fonda, Nancy Sinatra, Bruce Dern, Lou Procopio, Coby Denton, Marc Cavell

(Peter Bogdanovich and Polly Platt rewrote much of the original material; Bogdanovich directed the second unit and credit title backgrounds and Polly Platt acted as unit production manager and Nancy Sinatra's double.)

Gill Women of Venus (American-International: 1967)
(Russian Title: *Storm Clouds of Venus*)

DIRECTOR: Russian: Unknown (U.S. scenes: Peter Bogdanovich)
SCREENPLAY: Russian: Unknown (U.S.: Peter Bogdanovich, Polly Platt)
RUNNING TIME: Unknown
CAST: Original Russian cast: Unknown (U.S.: Mamie Van Doren and "7 other girls)"

Targets (Paramount: 1968)

DIRECTOR, WRITTEN AND PRODUCED BY PETER BOGDANOVICH
BASED ON A STORY BY POLLY PLATT, PETER BOGDANOVICH
CINEMATOGRAPHY: Laszlo Kovacs
EDITOR: Peter Bogdanovich
MUSIC: Charles Greene, Brian Stone
RUNNING TIME: 92 mins.
CAST: Boris Karloff, Tim O'Kelly, Nancy Hseuth, James Brown, Sandy Barron, Peter Bogdanovich

The Last Picture Show (Columbia Pictures: 1971)

DIRECTOR: Peter Bogdanovich
SCREENPLAY: Peter Bogdanovich, Larry McMurtry
BASED ON THE NOVEL BY LARRY MCMURTRY
PRODUCER: Stephen J. Friedman
CINEMATOGRAPHY: Robert Surtees (monochrome)
EDITOR: Donn Cambern
RUNNING TIME: 118 mins.
CAST: Timothy Bottoms, Jeff Bridges, Ben Johnson, Cloris Leachman, Ellen Burstyn, Cybill Shepherd, Eileen Brennan, John Hillerman, Randy Quaid, Clu Culager, Sharon Taggart, Bill Thurman
ACADEMY AWARD NOMINATIONS: Best Picture, Director, Script, Actor (Jeff Bridges), Cinematographer (Robert Surtees), Supporting Actress (Cloris Leachman and Ellen Burstyn), Supporting Actor (Ben Johnson)
Best Supporting Actor Academy Awards for Ben Johnson and Cloris Leachman

Directed by John Ford (American Film Institute, 1971)

CONCEIVED AND DIRECTED BY Peter Bogdanovich
PRODUCERS: George Stevens Jr. and James R. Silke
CINEMATOGRAPHY: Laszlo Kovacs
NARRATOR: Orson Welles
RUNNING TIME: 95 mins.
FEATURING APPEARANCES BY: John Ford, Henry Fonda, James Stewart, John Wayne, Peter Bogdanovich

What's Up, Doc? (Warner Bros: 1972)

DIRECTOR: Peter Bogdanovich
SCREENPLAY: Buck Henry, David Newman, Robert Benton
BASED ON A STORY BY PETER BOGDANOVICH
PRODUCER: Peter Bogdanovich
CINEMATOGRAPHY: Laszlo Kovacs
EDITOR: Verna Fields
MUSIC: Artie Butler
RUNNING TIME: 94 mins.

CAST: Barbra Streisand, Ryan O'Neal, Kenneth Mars, Austin Pendleton, Madeline Kahn, Sorrell Brooke, Michael Murphy

Paper Moon (Paramount: 1973)

DIRECTOR: Peter Bogdanovich
SCREENPLAY: Alvin Sargent
BASED ON THE NOVEL *ADDIE PRAY* BY JOE DAVID BROWN
PRODUCER: Peter Bogdanovich
CINEMATOGRAPHY: Laszlo Kovacs (monochrome)
EDITOR: Verna Fields
RUNNING TIME: 102 mins.
CAST: Ryan O'Neal, Tatum O'Neal, Madeline Kahn, John Hillerman, P.J. Johnson
ACADEMY AWARD NOMINATIONS: Best Script, Best Actress (Tatum O'Neal), Best Supporting Actress (MADELINE KAHN)
Best Actress Award for Tatum O'Neal

Daisy Miller (Paramount: 1974)

DIRECTED: Peter Bogdanovich
SCREENPLAY: Frederick Raphael
BASED ON THE NOVELLA BY HENRY JAMES
PRODUCER: Peter Bogdanovich
CINEMATOGRAPHY: Albert Spagnoli
EDITOR: Verna Fields
MUSICAL CONSULTANT: Francesco Lavagnino
RUNNING TIME: 92 mins.
CAST: Cybill Shepherd, Barry Brown, Cloris Leachman, Mildred Natwick, Eileen Brennan, Duilio Del Prete

At Long Last Love (20th Century-Fox: 1975)

DIRECTED, WRITTEN AND PRODUCED BY PETER BOGDANOVICH
CINEMATOGRAPHY: Laszlo Kovacs
EDITOR: Douglas Robertson
MUSIC & LYRICS: Cole Porter (Music supervision: Artie Butler)
RUNNING TIME: 118 mins.
CAST: Burt Reynolds, Cybill Shepherd, Madeline Kahn, Duilio Del Prete, Eileen Brennan, John Hillerman, Mildred Natwick

Nickelodeon (Columbia: 1976)

DIRECTOR: Peter Bogdanovich
SCREENPLAY: Peter Bogdanovich, W.D. Richter
PRODUCERS: Irwin Winkler, Robert Chartoff
CINEMATOGRAPHY: Laszlo Kovacs

EDITOR: William Carruth
MUSIC: Richard Hazard
RUNNING TIME: 122 mins.
CAST: Ryan O'Neal, Burt Reynolds, Tatum O'Neal, Brian Keith, Stella Stevens, John
Ritter, Jane Hitchcock, Harry Carey Jr.

Saint Jack (New World: 1979)

DIRECTOR: Peter Bogdanovich
SCREENPLAY: Howard Sackler, Paul Theroux, Peter Bogdanovich
BASED ON THE NOVEL BY PAUL THEROUX
PRODUCER: Roger Corman
CINEMATOGRAPHY: Robby Muller
EDITOR: William Carruth
RUNNING TIME: 115 mins.
CAST: Ben Gazzara, Denholm Elliott, James Villiers, Joss Ackland, Rodney Bewes,
Mark Kingston, Lisa Lu, Monika Subramaniam, Judy Lim, George Lazenby
and Peter Bogdanovich as Eddie Schuman.

They All Laughed (Time-Life: 1981)

DIRECTOR: Peter Bogdanovich
SCREENPLAY: Peter Bogdanovich
PRODUCERS: George Morfogen, Blaine Novak
CINEMATOGRAPHY: Robby Muller
EDITOR: Scott Vickrey
MUSIC: Douglas Dilge
RUNNING TIME: 115 mins.
CAST: Audrey Hepburn, Ben Gazzara, John Ritter, Colleen Camp, Patti Hansen,
Dorothy Stratten, George Morfogen, Blaine Novak, Sean Ferrer, Linda
MacEwen

Mask (Universal: 1985)

DIRECTOR: Peter Bogdanovich
SCREENPLAY: Anna Hamilton Phelan, from her true story
PRODUCER: Martin Starger
CINEMATOGRAPHY: Laszlo Kovacs
EDITOR: Barbara Ford
MUSIC EDITOR: Denis Ricotta
RUNNING TIME: 120 mins.
CAST: Cher, Sam Elliott, Eric Stoltz, Estelle Getty, Richard Dysart, Laura Dern and
Harry Carey Jr.

Illegally Yours (MGM/UA: 1988)

DIRECTOR: Peter Bogdanovich
SCREENPLAY: M.A. Stewart, Max Dickens
PRODUCER: Peter Bogdanovich
CINEMATOGRAPHY: Dante Spinotti
EDITOR: Richard Fields, Ronald Krehel
MUSIC: Phil Marshall
RUNNING TIME: 102 mins.
CAST: Rob Lowe, Colleen Camp, Kenneth Mars, Harry Carey Jr, Kim Myers, Marshall Colt, Linda MacEwen, Rick Jason, Jessica James, Ira Heiden, George Morfogen and L.B. Straten as Sharon Woolrich

Texasville (Columbia: 1990)

DIRECTOR: Peter Bogdanovich
SCREENPLAY: Peter Bogdanovich
BASED ON THE NOVEL BY LARRY MCMURTRY
PRODUCERS: Barry Spikings, Peter Bogdanovich
CINEMATOGRAPHY: Nicholas von Sternberg
EDITOR: Richard Fields
MUSIC SUPERVISOR: Karyn Rachtman
MUSIC EDITOR: Kathleen Bennett
EXECUTIVE ASSISTANT TO PETER BOGDANOVICH: Beatrix Stratten
RUNNING TIME: 125 mins.
CAST: Jeff Bridges, Cybill Shepherd, Annie Potts, Cloris Leachman, Timothy Bottoms, Eileen Brennan, Randy Quaid, Harvey Christiansen, Pearl Jones, Loyd Catlett, Jimmy Howell, Romy Snyder

Noises Off (Amblin/Touchstone/Buena Vista, 1992)

DIRECTOR: Peter Bogdanovich
SCRIPT: Marty Kaplan
BASED ON THE PLAY BY MICHAEL FRAYN
PRODUCER: Frank Marshall, Steve Sharkey
EXECUTIVE PRODUCERS: Peter Bogdanovich, Kathleen Kennedy
CINEMATOGRAPHY: Timothy Subretedt
CAST: Michael Caine, Carol Burnett, Denholm Elliott, Julie Hagerty, Mark Linn-Baker, Marilu Henner, Christopher Reeve, John Ritter, Nicollette Sheridan.

INDEX